IMAGES
of America

SAN FRANCISCO'S FERRY BUILDING

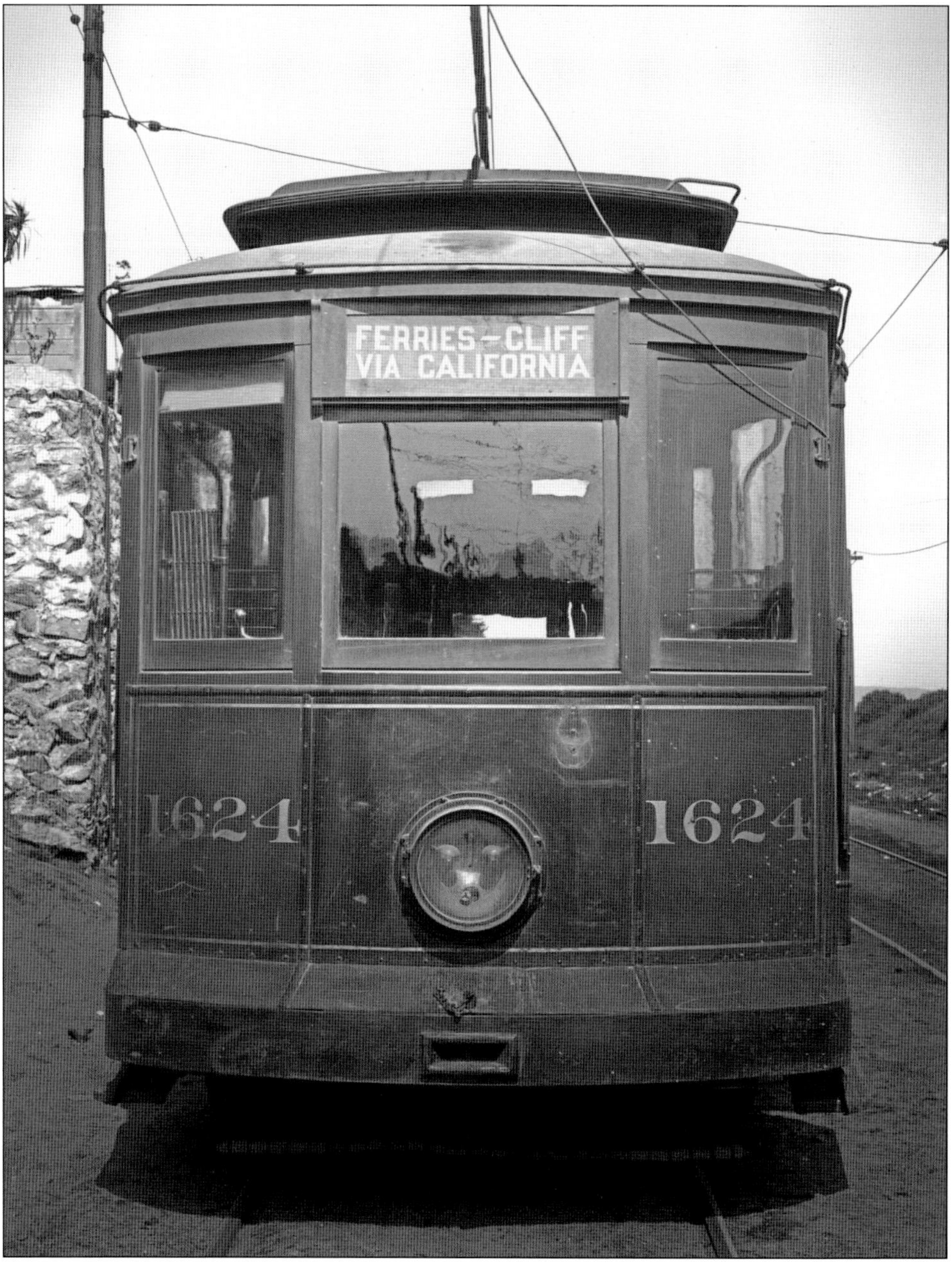

The No. 1 California streetcar, pictured here in 1908, left the Ferry Building a few times a day with sightseeing groups, stopping along the way for views. It went as far as the Cliff House at the western edge of the city, and then it looped back to the Ferry Building, all for 50¢. (Photograph by John Henry Mentz, San Francisco Municipal Transportation Agency Photography Department and Archive.)

On the Cover: The Ferry Building stands tall on the San Francisco skyline, welcoming the incoming ferry. The very visible "SP" sign sits atop Southern Pacific's building on the waterfront. There is lots to watch as the ferry approaches its slip, and the children do not want to miss any of the action. (San Francisco Maritime National Historical Park, B09.35767n.)

IMAGES
of America

SAN FRANCISCO'S FERRY BUILDING

Anne Evers Hitz

ARCADIA PUBLISHING

ISBN 978-1-4671-2626-7

Published by Arcadia Publishing
Charleston, South Carolina

Printed in the United States of America

Library of Congress Control Number: 2016961559

For all general information, please contact Arcadia Publishing:
Telephone 843-853-2070
Fax 843-853-0044
E-mail sales@arcadiapublishing.com
For customer service and orders:
Toll-Free 1-888-313-2665

Visit us on the Internet at www.arcadiapublishing.com

To Edwina and Bill. Thanks to you I had the good fortune to be born in San Francisco. Your "atta-girl" support helped me find my true north.

Contents

Acknowledgments		6
Introduction		7
1.	Early Days	9
2.	The Earthquake and Its Aftermath	19
3.	A Stunning Landmark	41
4.	Celebrations and Daily Life	51
5.	A Major Transportation Hub	71
6.	Ferries Cross the Bay	81
7.	Dark Days of Bridges and Freeways	101
8.	A Grand Restoration	117
Bibliography		127

Acknowledgments

So many people have helped me along the way. Kudos to my husband and kids, who listened to my endless tales of searching for Ferry Building photographs and historical documents. The patient librarians, historians, image archivists, and photographers who answered my many questions and helped me deserve a thanks as well: Christina Moretta, San Francisco History Center, San Francisco Public Library; Gina Bardi, San Francisco Maritime National Historical Park (SFMNHP); Katy Guyon, San Francisco Municipal Transportation Agency Photography Department and Archive (SFMTA Photo Archive); Allan Fisher, Western Railway Museum; Mark Paez and Renee Martin, Port of San Francisco; Kathleen Correia, California State Library; Tom Paiva Photography; Neil Malloch; Bonnie Fisher and Boris Dramov, ROMA Design Group; Cathy Cooke; and City Guides' Mary Miller and Charlton Schwartz.

I would also like to gratefully acknowledge the permission granted to reproduce the copyrighted material in this book. Every effort has been made to trace copyright holders and to obtain their permission for the use of copyrighted material. I apologize for any errors or omissions and would be grateful to be notified of any corrections that should be incorporated in future reprints or editions of this book.

Introduction

San Francisco, a city of fog, rolling hills, and cable cars, is perched on the north end of a peninsula, surrounded by the water of the San Francisco Bay and the Pacific Ocean. The Ferry Building, a bustling city landmark, sits grandly on the Embarcadero at the foot of Market Street, overlooking the bay, and welcomes thousands of locals and tourists daily. In its most recent incarnation, the Ferry Building's busy market/food hall features vendors selling locally sourced produce and artisan goods, and upstairs are the second-floor Grand Nave and two floors of prestigious office space, with a 660-foot skylight allowing light to shine down on all the floors. Above it all, the Ferry Building's tower stands tall on the waterfront, an iconic San Francisco view at the entrance to one of the world's best natural harbors.

But this building, so much a part of San Francisco's history and social fabric, has not always been so elegant and busy.

After San Francisco's explosive growth during the Gold Rush in the late 1840s, the once-sleepy town became a bustling port, and entrepreneurs abounded. San Francisco had been changed forever as the news of the discovery of gold in 1848 brought over 300,000 people to California from all over the world, and California became a state in 1850.

The port was chaotic, and the increase in ferry passengers required a fitting building. The original Ferry House, the first ferry depot, was completed in 1875, but it took a mere 10 years for the traffic to exceed the building's capacity. San Francisco decided to build something that befitted its new position as the gateway to the West.

A bond measure passed in 1892, and an aspiring young architect, A. Page Brown, was hired. The current building officially opened to great fanfare on July 13, 1898. As a reporter noted in the *San Francisco Chronicle* on January 11, 1895, "The design of this building is one combining simplicity with quiet elegance. Yet the ensemble is impressive. It is of the Italian Renaissance period and certainly compares more favorably with the great structures of similar character in the eastern states and Europe. Too much praise cannot be accorded to the architect, A. Page Brown, for the originality, the cleverness and the skill he has shown in his work."

For the next three-plus decades—before the Oakland-San Francisco Bay Bridge and the Golden Gate Bridge opened—commuters and tourists relied on ferries. After taking a ferry from San Francisco, a traveler could catch a train in Oakland to faraway places, or a commuter might board an electric train in Alameda or Sausalito to get home. In the early 1930s, about 50 million commuters and visitors passed through the Ferry Building annually. Riding the ferry was a way of life; an efficient, relaxed, and congenial way to pass the time. Compare that to automobile commuters today, frustrated when trying to get home and stuck in their cars on a bridge on-ramp in rush-hour traffic.

In the late 1930s, with the ushering in of the era of the automobile and the opening of the two bridges, the Ferry Building lost its purpose. At the lowest point, in the late 1950s, it was cut off from the rest of downtown by the controversial double-decker Embarcadero Freeway. Inside the building, the soaring expansiveness of the nave was cut in half when an extra floor was added to increase office space. It was forlorn and forgotten, cut off by the freeway from the financial and downtown district it used to serve. Many plans were proposed to revitalize the waterfront, including tearing down the Ferry Building and just leaving its tower between two enormous high rises. As local reporter Carl Nolte noted in the *San Francisco Chronicle* on June 9, 2000, "For a landmark, the Ferry Building has been treated pretty shabbily. In fact, it's been nearly all downhill since that great day when the Bay Bridge opened." Although San Franciscans loved the building, it had lost its usefulness.

"I can't think of any landmark I'd fight harder to save," *San Francisco Chronicle* columnist Herb Caen wrote December 30, 1962. "When it's aglow at night, its warm light shines all the way back to the (1906) earthquake . . . and to its days of glory as the gateway to the enchanted city. . . . The bay without ferries is like a lake without swans. And the waterfront without the Ferry Tower would be like a birthday cake without a candle."

However, in 1989, when the Loma Prieta earthquake struck, Mother Nature delivered an unexpected benefit—despite the widespread destruction and loss of life—by damaging the freeway and giving the city the opportunity to reimagine the waterfront and the purpose of the iconic building. After much political wrangling, the freeway removal began in 1991 and plans were put in place for a new waterfront and a revitalized Ferry Building.

Fast forward to 2003—despite an economic downturn in the early 2000s and after a meticulous, extensive four-year $100 million renovation, the beautifully renovated Ferry Building reopened. It has become a major destination for locals and tourists and reclaimed the stature lost during its dark days. It is now designated a San Francisco City Landmark and California State Landmark, is listed in the National Register of Historic Places, and is a US Civil Engineering Landmark. The entire waterfront has had a rebirth, and ferry ridership is increasing rapidly.

In the following pages, you will learn more about the building's intricate history and its central role as the main terminus for San Francisco. It has played an important part in the life of the city throughout its existence. For example, since the building withstood the 1906 earthquake and fire, residents poured through its doors with their possessions so they could take ferries to flee the city. When the Pan-Pacific International Exposition opened in 1915, over 18 million people visited the fair, many of them arriving on ferries and passing through the Ferry Building, which had a banner to greet them and extra trains and cabs outside to get them to the fair. From parades welcoming returning soldiers and US presidents to labor protests, fairs, and expositions—all began at the Ferry Building.

One

Early Days

San Francisco's harbor, with its attractive location and protected anchorage, was once a sleepy waterfront. All that changed when gold was discovered in 1848, and the California Gold Rush brought a flood of treasure-seekers. With the great migration west, the population grew from 1,000 in 1848 to 25,000 by December 1849. San Francisco became the focus of oceangoing and river traffic for California and was the center of extensive traffic on the bay. In 1863, Gov. Leland Stanford signed legislation that created a Board of State Harbor Commissioners (BSHC) for San Francisco, a group charged with construction and upkeep of the wharves, seawalls, and piers. One of the BSHC's first tasks was to construct a massive seawall to stabilize the shore, and by 1880, there were over two-and-a-half miles of seawall completed, with more than 800 acres of land created behind the seawall.

A proper port needs a ferry house, and in 1875, the BSHC built a wooden structure with arcades, at the foot of Clay and Market Streets. By the late 1880s, however, the BSHC decided to replace the Ferry House with something more grand and fitting to serve as San Francisco's transportation terminal. The commissioners wanted a building that was not only efficient, but something that would have symbolic importance as visitors arrived and departed the city. Voters passed a bond issue to build a new Ferry Building in 1892, and a young architect named Arthur Page Brown (known as A. Page Brown) got the commission. His idea was for a large, steel-framed building with a 245-foot clock tower to serve as a welcoming beacon. Construction began in 1896, and the Ferry Building (officially the Union Depot and Ferry House) began receiving passengers in July 1898. Arriving passengers entered through an elegant two-story public area with repeating interior arches and overhead skylights. The building helped transform a working area that had many forlorn wooden buildings in a state of deterioration. It showed that the city had ambitions for itself and its port.

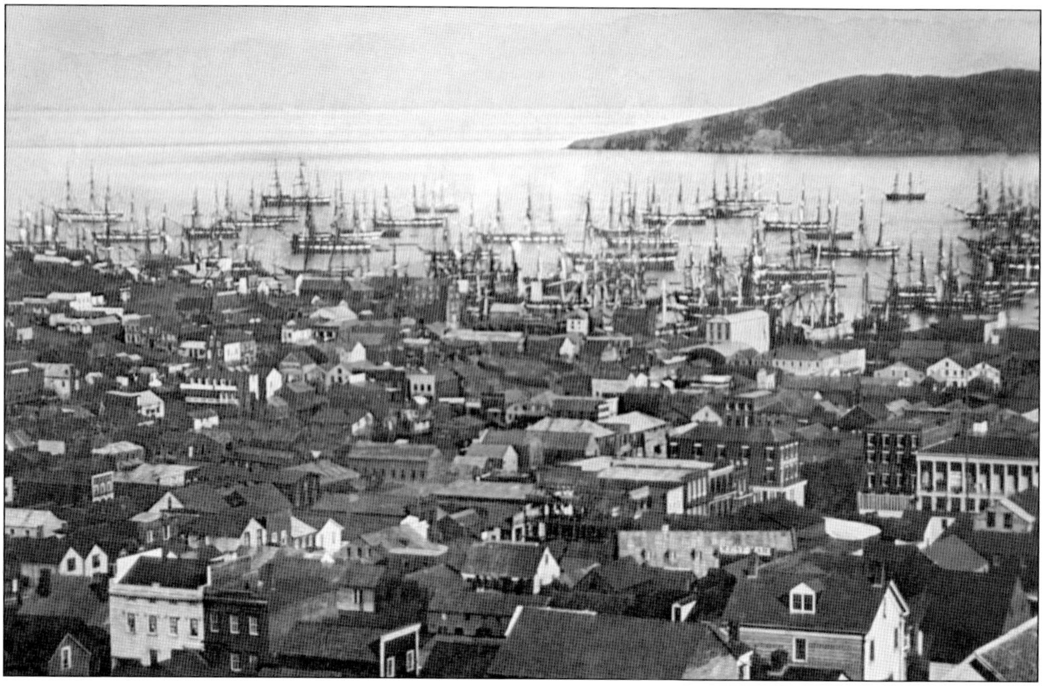

The first recorded ship to enter San Francisco Bay was the Spanish supply ship *San Carlos* in 1775. Between April 1847 and April 1848, only 11 ships dropped anchor in the bay: one barque, one brigantine, and nine whalers. The discovery of gold at Sutter's Mill in 1848 changed everything, and in 1849, over 90,000 passengers arrived in San Francisco Bay aboard some 650 American and foreign vessels. The c. 1850 photograph of San Francisco harbor at Yerba Buena Cove (above) shows Yerba Buena Island and the Berkeley hills in the background. The illustration of the harbor (below) is from *The Pacific Tourist*, Adams & Bishop's illustrated transcontinental guide of travel (published in 1881). (Above, Library of Congress; below, Internet Archive Book Images.)

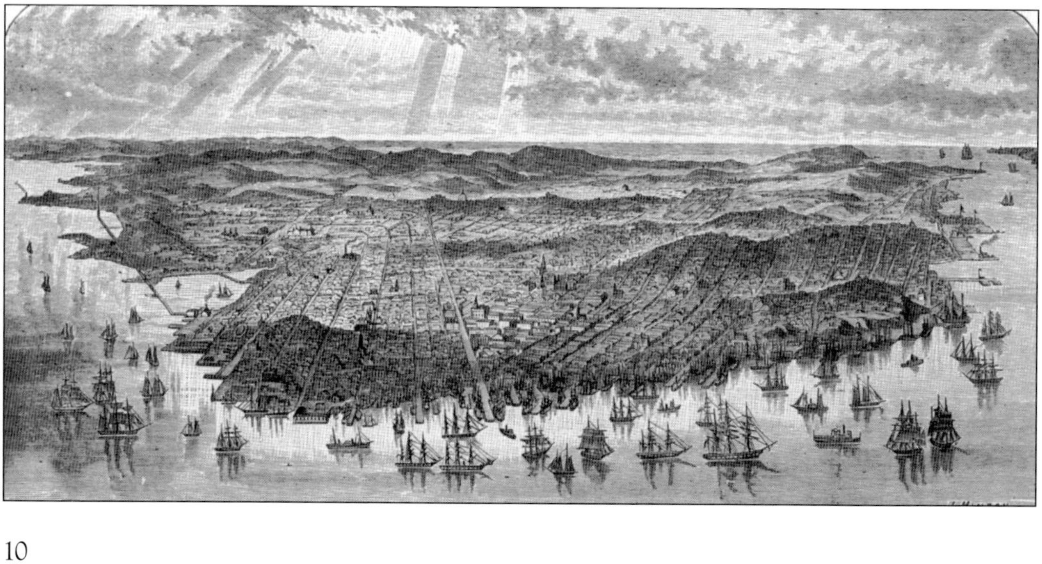

In this 1892 photograph, carts line busy Market Street, San Francisco's main thoroughfare, the widest street—120 feet—in town at the time. Three miles long, it cut across the city from the waterfront up to the hills of Twin Peaks. The grand boulevard connected the Ferry House and, subsequently, the Ferry Building to growing neighborhoods via horse-drawn streetcar and, later, via clattering cable cars. (Library of Congress.)

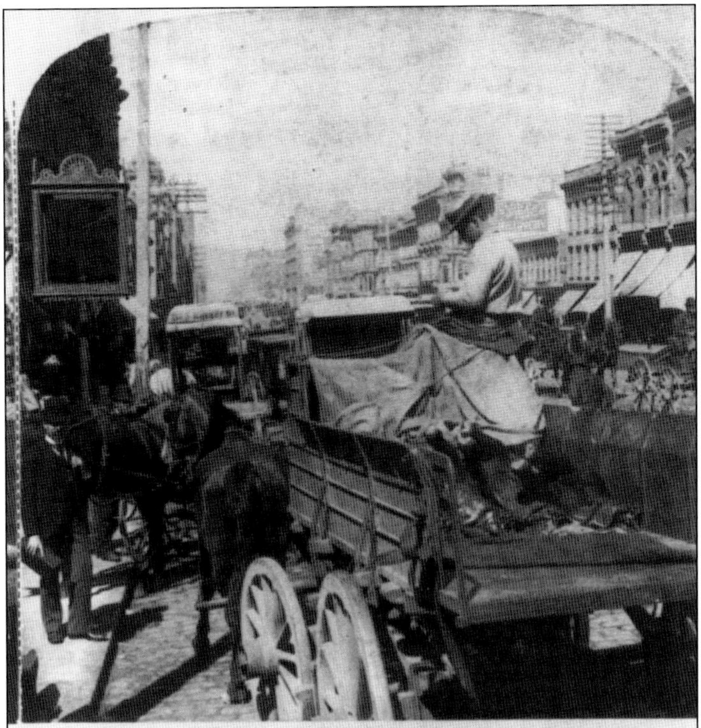

Market Street, toward the Ferries, San Francisco, U. S. A.
Markt-Straße, gegen die Fährboote, San Franzisco, Ver. St. N.-A.

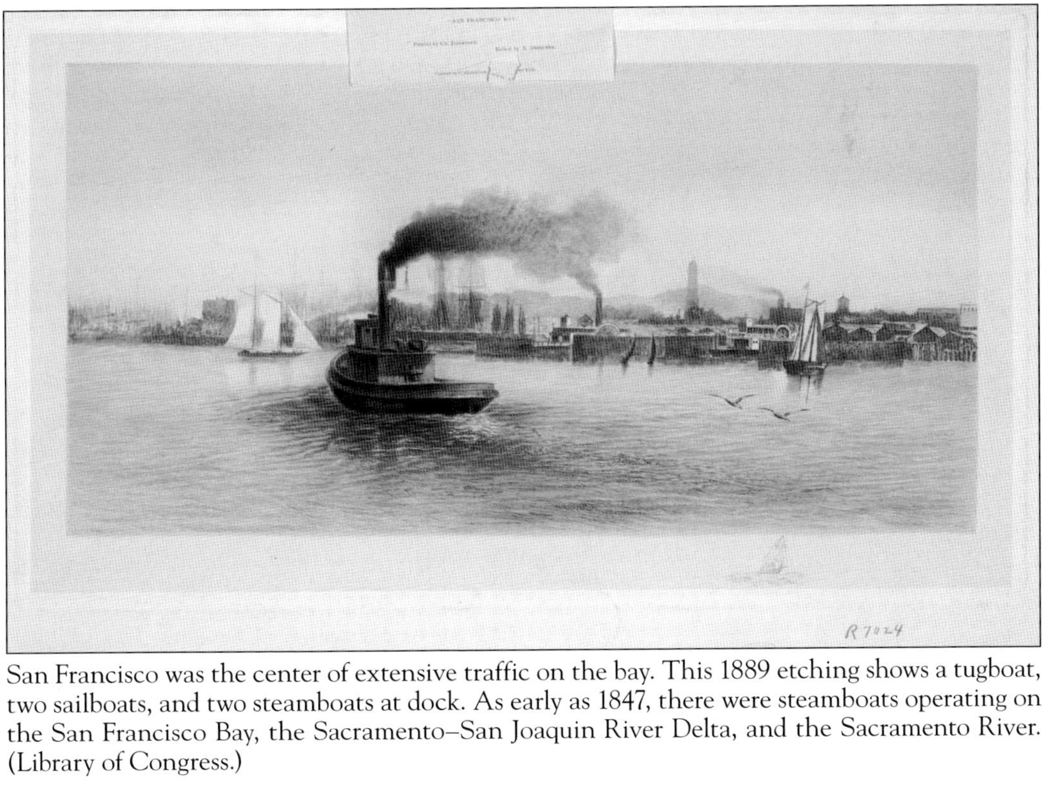

San Francisco was the center of extensive traffic on the bay. This 1889 etching shows a tugboat, two sailboats, and two steamboats at dock. As early as 1847, there were steamboats operating on the San Francisco Bay, the Sacramento–San Joaquin River Delta, and the Sacramento River. (Library of Congress.)

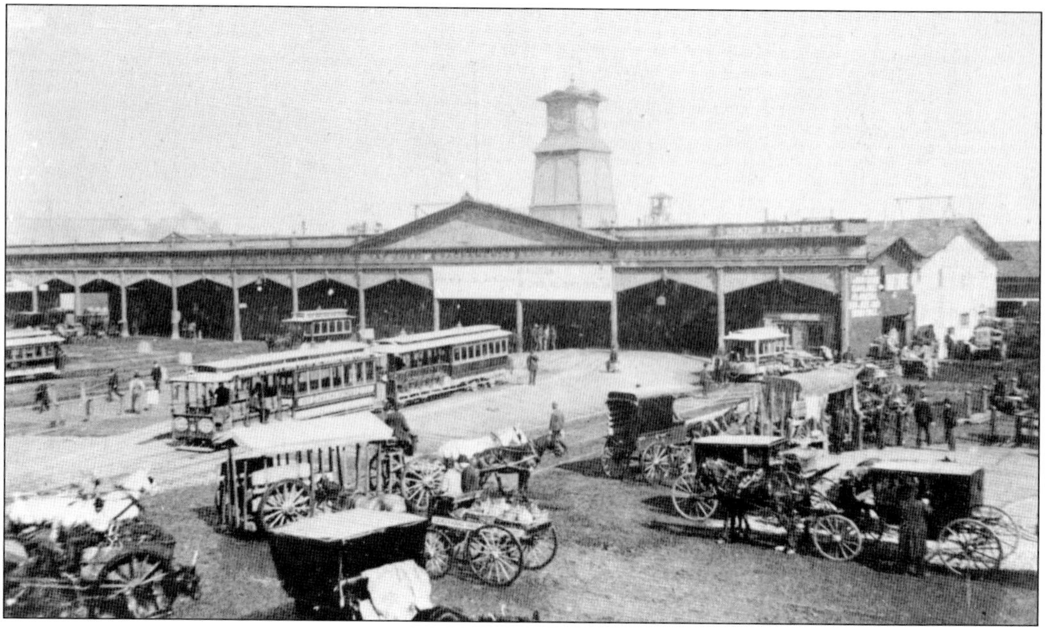

In 1875, the Port Commissioners, who saw revenues increasing from East Bay ferry traffic, decided the new Ferry House should be more elegant for those passengers who arrived in San Francisco and encountered carts, wagons, horses, sailors, miners, and merchants crowding the wharves. Completed at a cost of $93,000, the Ferry House was located near the foot of Clay and Market Streets. The wooden-arcaded shed attached to warehouse buildings included four slips, and became too small within 10 years of its construction, even with additional slips added by 1889. Central Pacific Railroad was the prime source of ferryboat revenue. (Above, SFMNHP, Proctor Collection, A12.8101n; below, Library of Congress.)

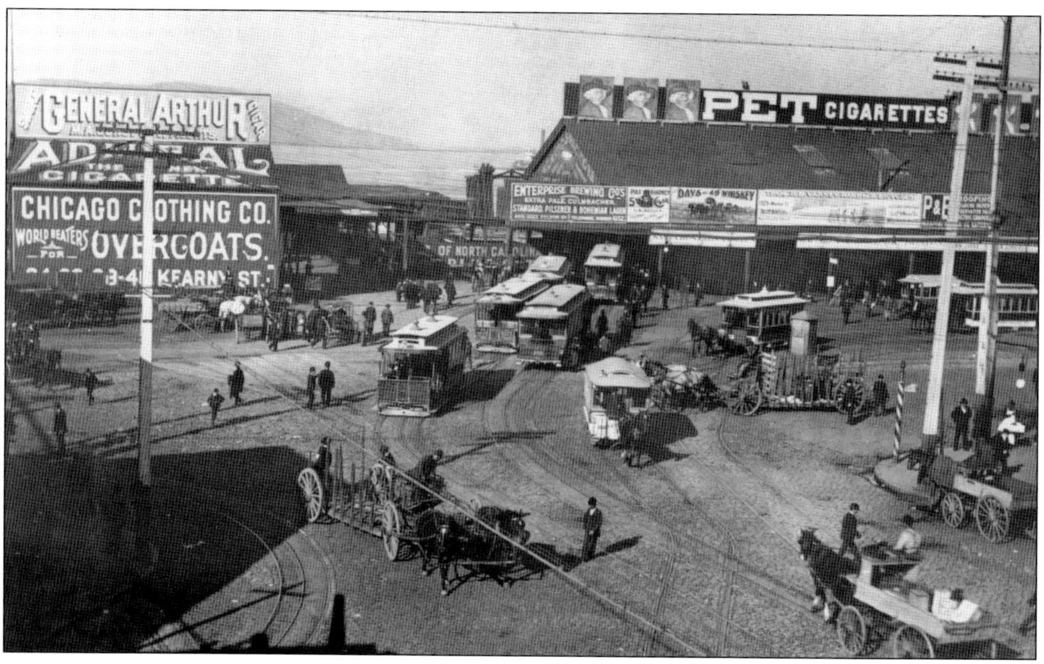

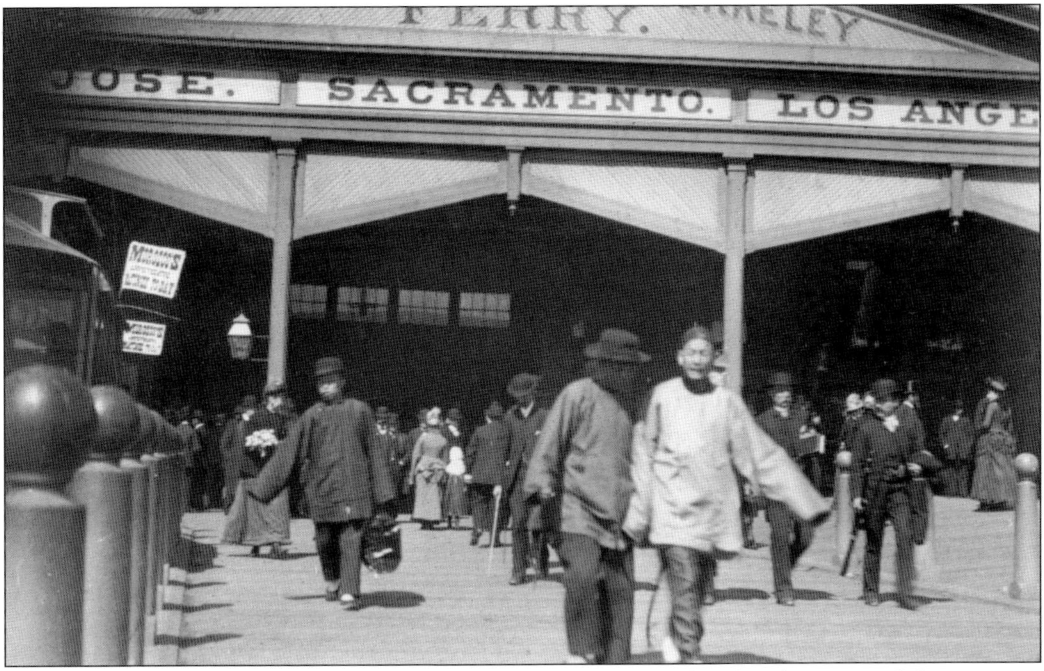

Commuters exit and enter the old Ferry House, with signs overhead indicating rail destinations such as Los Angeles, Sacramento, Chicago, New York, and San Antonio. Chinese passengers arrive in the city, perhaps traveling by train from Sacramento or somewhere in the Sacramento–San Joaquin Bay Delta. In the photograph below, Market Street cable cars wait at the terminal. In 1882, Leland Stanford, one of the "Big Four" (the group of influential businessmen who built the Central Pacific Railroad), and some of his associates bought the Market Street Railroad Company and converted its lines to cable haulage and changed the company's name to the Market Street Cable Railway Company. At its peak, the company operated five lines, all of which converged into Market Street to a common terminus at the Ferry Building. (Above, California Historical Society, CHS2013.1264; below, Western Railway Museum Archives.)

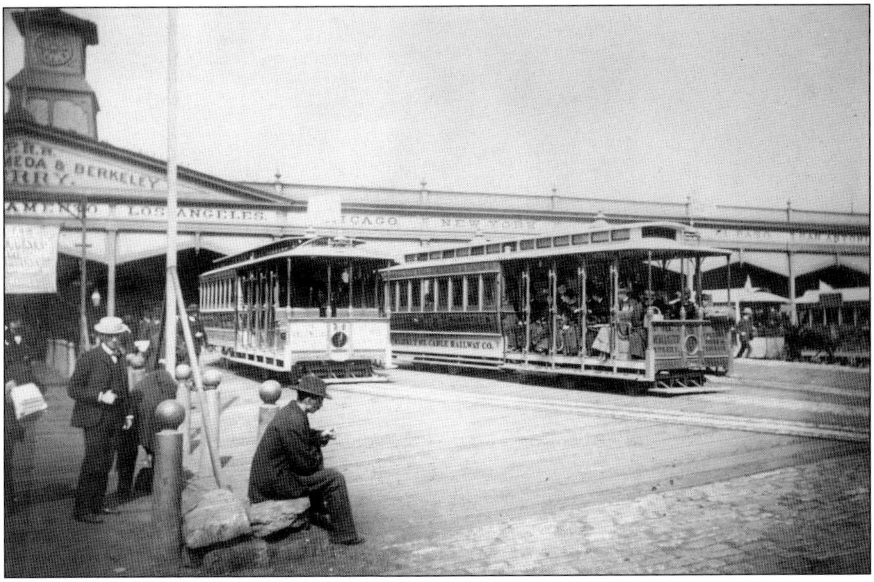

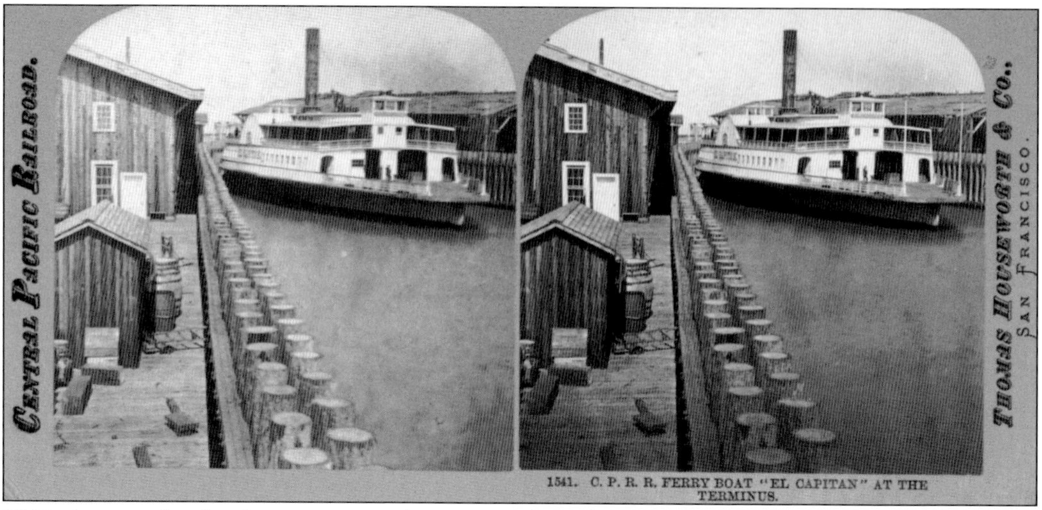

El Capitan, a side-wheel steam-powered passenger ferry that operated on San Francisco Bay, offered connecting service to San Francisco for train passengers arriving in Oakland. Built in 1869 by the Central Pacific Railroad in anticipation of the completion of the Transcontinental Railroad in 1869, it was the largest ferry on the bay at the time. (Library of Congress.)

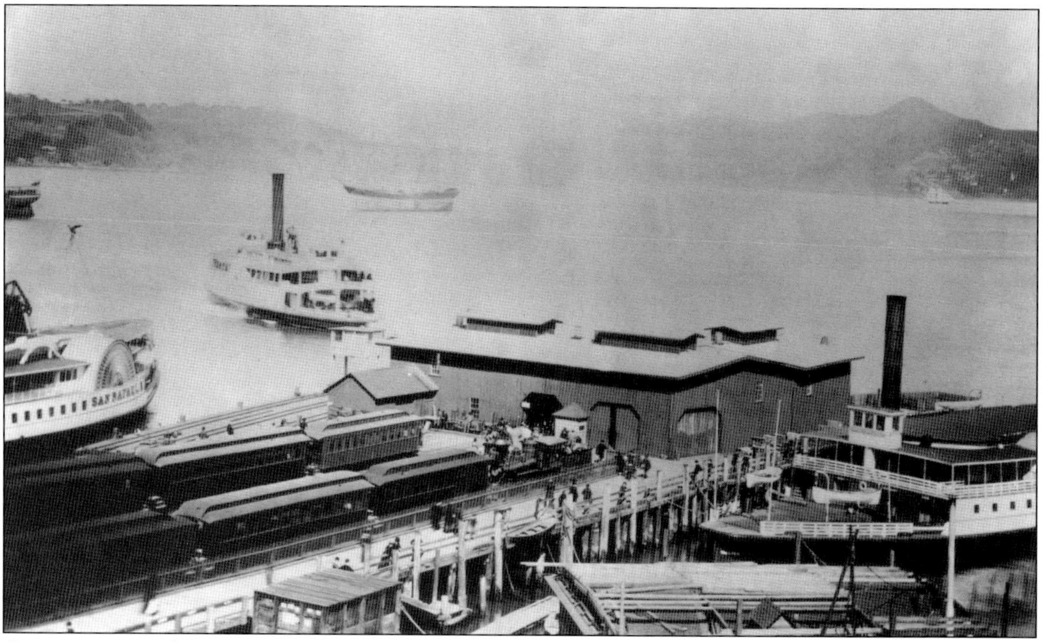

Commuters and excursionists could take ferries from San Francisco to the Sausalito ferry and train terminal (shown here in 1894) in Marin County. The trip took approximately 30 minutes. From Sausalito, passengers could board the North Pacific Coast Railroad, a narrow-gauge railroad that served Marin County towns before traveling north to Cazadero, California. (Anne T. Kent California Room, Marin County Free Library.)

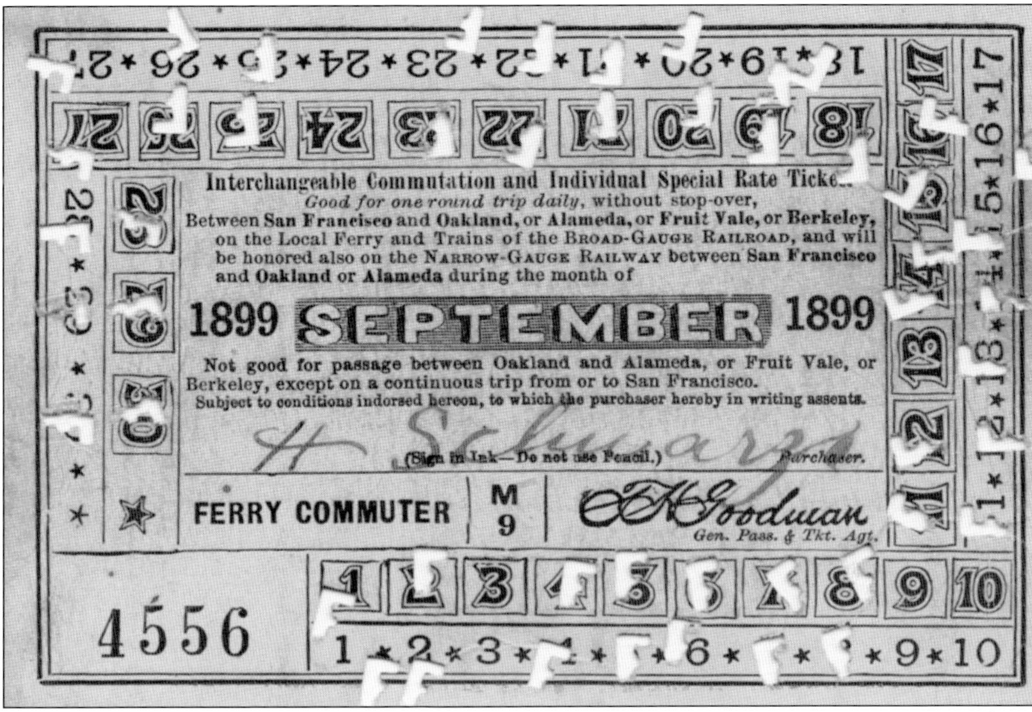

A well-used September 1899 ferry commuter ticket stipulates that it is "good for one round trip daily without stop-over, between San Francisco and Oakland, or Alameda, or Fruit Vale, or Berkeley, on the Local Ferry and Trains of the Broad-Gauge Railroad, and will be honored also on the Narrow-Gauge Railway." (Author's collection.)

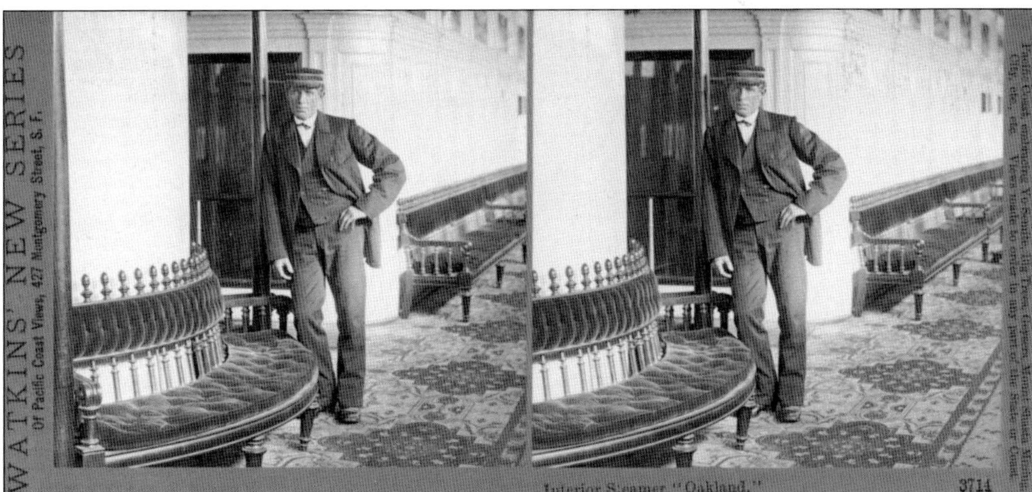

This photograph by Carleton Watkins (1829-1916) is of a crew member, perhaps a ferry steward, and shows the interior of the steamer *Oakland*. It is image 3714 in Watkins's New Series. Watkins, perhaps the best-known Western photographer, shot much of California and the western states. The *Oakland* ferry, in service from 1875 to 1940, was a side-wheel passenger ferry, which Southern Pacific rebuilt from the riverboat *Chrysopolis*. (California History Room, California State Library, Sacramento, California.)

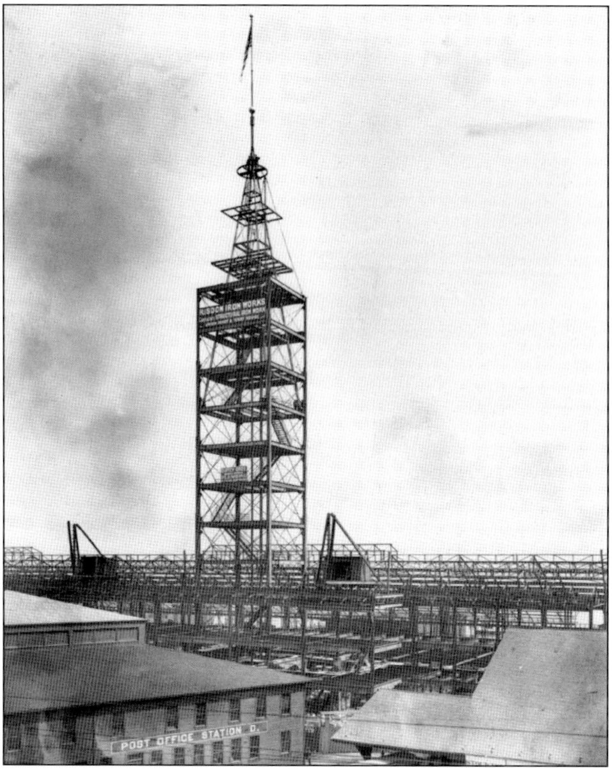

These photographs show the tower of the new Ferry Building. F.A. Koetitz, vice president and chief engineer of the Pacific Construction Company, which built most of the new building, described the tower's construction in *American Builders Review* (vol. 6, no. 1, January 1907): "Built with a steel frame enclosed, up to the cornice, by brick walls with a sandstone facing, the walls for each story being practically self-supporting. The frame above the main cornice was covered with galvanized iron, painted to match the stone. . . . The frame was constructed of steel columns, girders, beams and diagonal rods. . . . The foundation of the tower, as well as that of the building, consists of concrete piers on piles." (Both, SFMNHP, Bethlehem Steel Corp. P83-142a.4., 912.14635.)

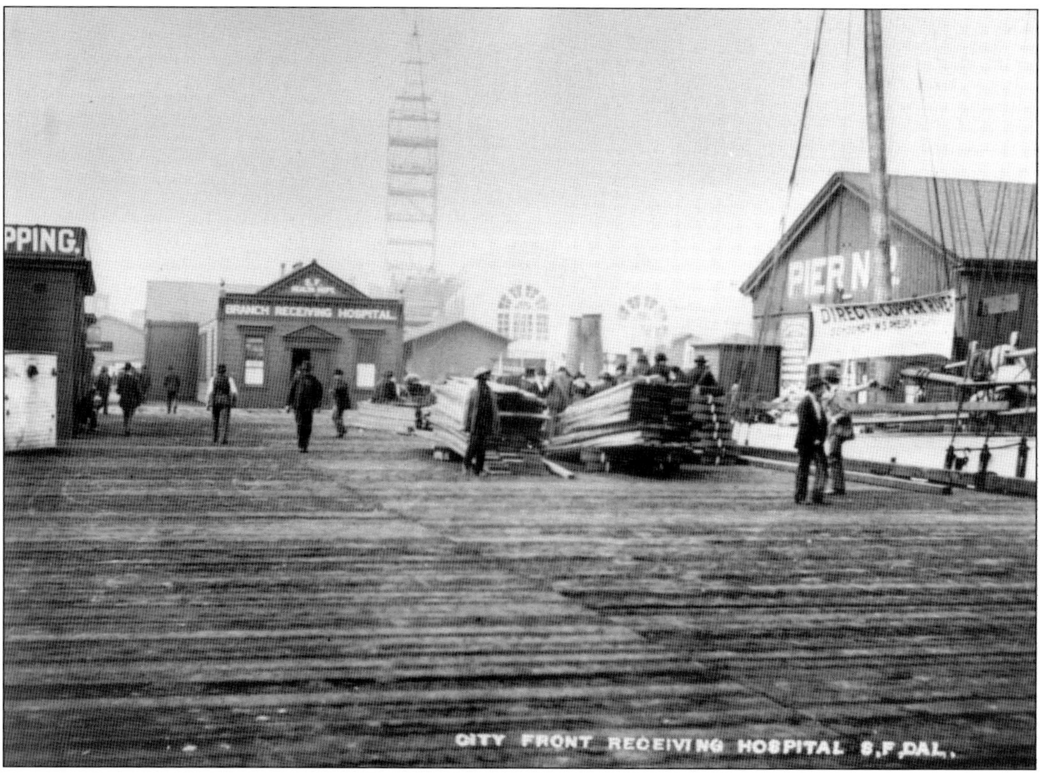

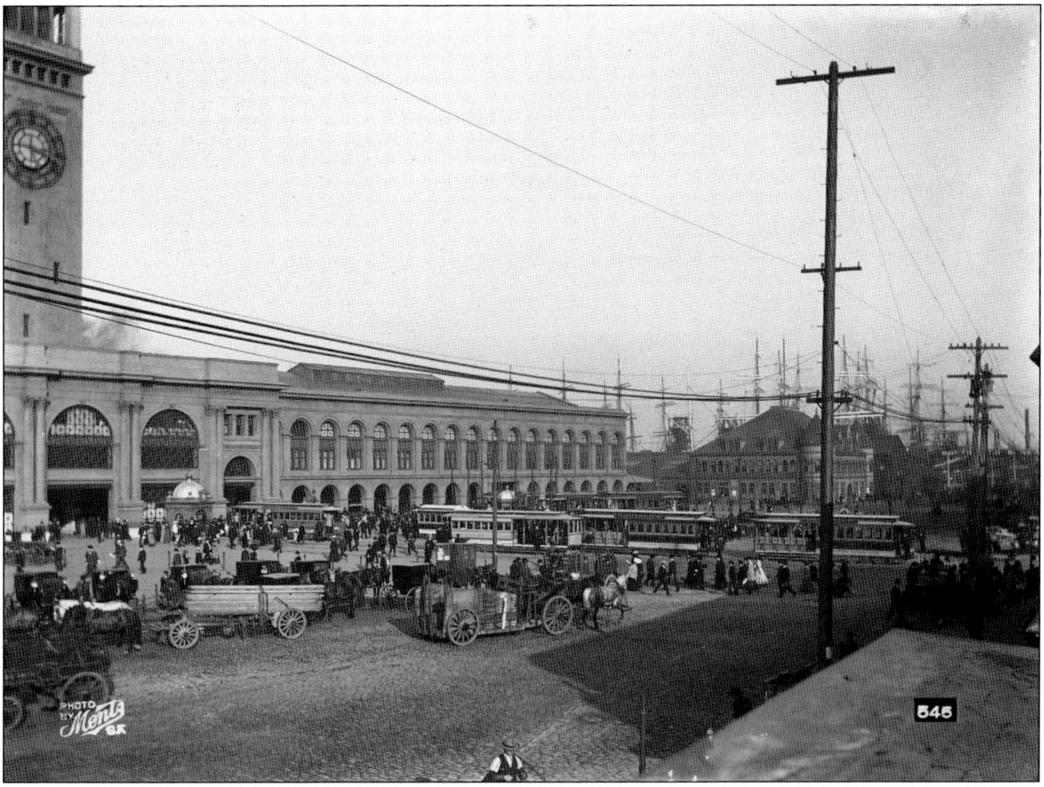

In this 1905 image, cable cars and horse-drawn carriages line the streets in front of the Ferry Building. Cable car 36 (Market Valencia line), cable car 158 (Market Haight line), cable car 206 (Market Hayes line), and cable car 278 (Market McAllister line) come and go with passengers. Each line's cars were painted a distinctive color so passengers could easily differentiate them. (Photograph by John Henry Mentz, SFMTA Photo Archive.)

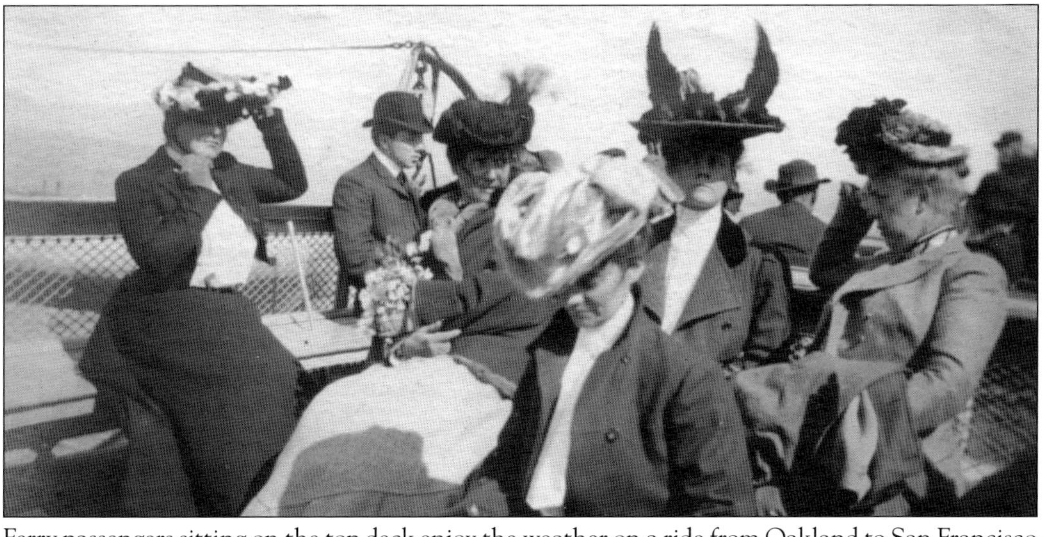

Ferry passengers sitting on the top deck enjoy the weather on a ride from Oakland to San Francisco around 1897. No woman of stature would venture out without her hat, and long hairpins held these elaborately trimmed hats in place in case a strong wind came up. (Author's collection.)

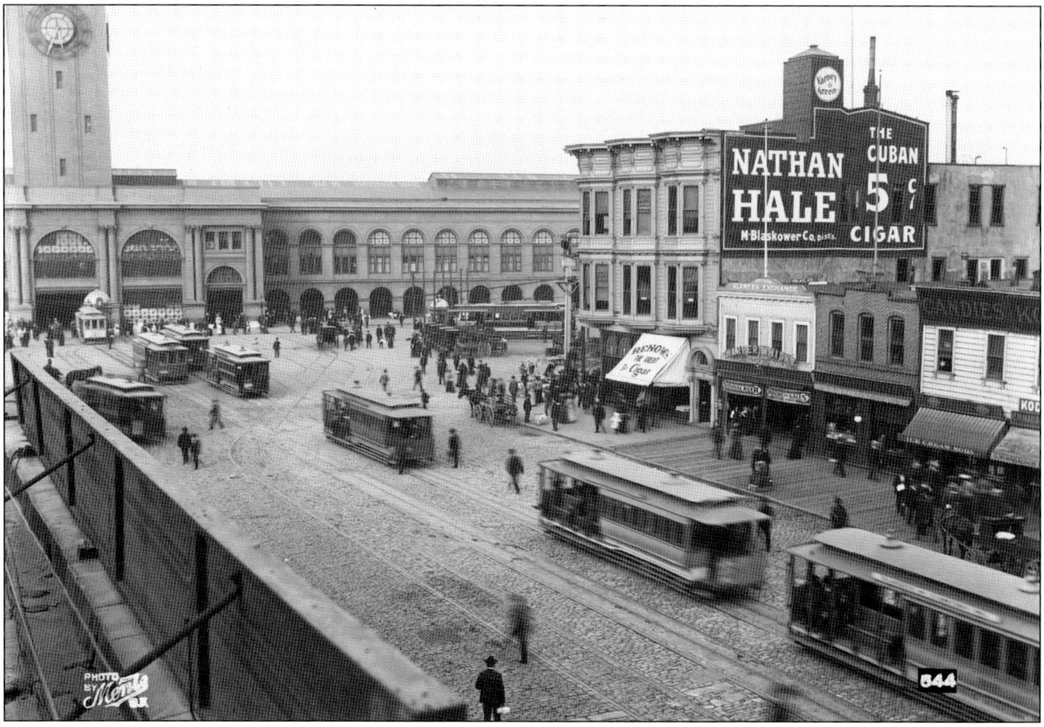

In 1905, cable cars approach the Ferry Building, while an advertisement, "Nathan Hale—The Cuban Cigar—5¢," looms above on the side of a nearby building. In the *Tobacco Leaf Journal* (vol. 42, 1905), an article titled "Facts from the Town of 'Frisco,'" notes, "The M. Blaskower Co. reports the Nathan Hale five-cent cigar selling remarkably well." Apparently, the advertising on the approach to the Ferry Building was successful. (Photograph by John Henry Mentz, SFMTA Photo Archive.)

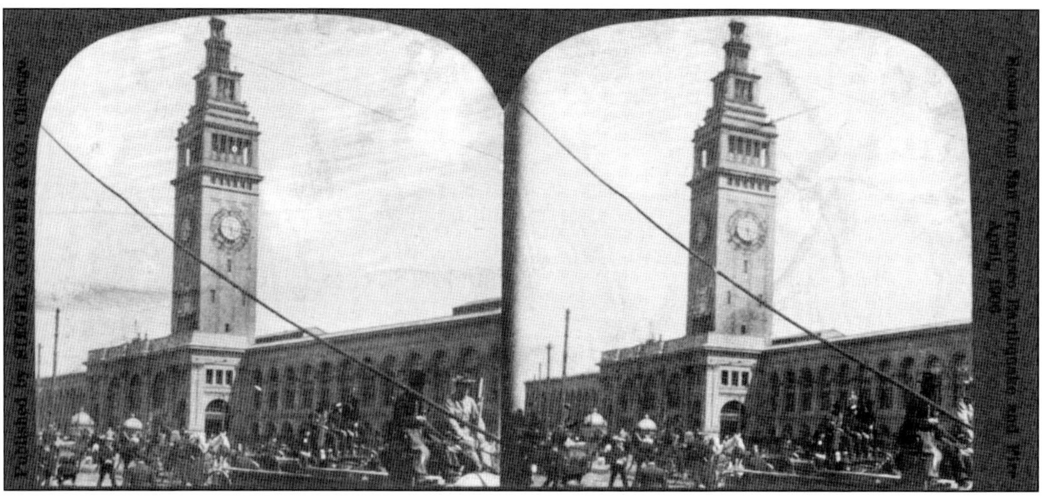

This stereograph of the Ferry Building in early 1906 captures it before the big earthquake hit in April. Stereoscopic views consist of two nearly twin photographs. Viewers look at the side-by-side images with a special viewing device. The brain combines the two flat images and "sees" a convincing three-dimensional image. (The Miriam and Ira D. Wallach Division of Art, Prints and Photographs, Robert N. Dennis Collection, New York Public Library.)

Two

The Earthquake and Its Aftermath

Everything changed on April 18, 1906. At 5:12 a.m., a powerful earthquake hit San Francisco. The earthquake (estimated at around 7.9 on the Richter scale) caused a lot of damage, but it was the subsequent out-of-control fires that caused the most destruction. Over 30 fires destroyed approximately 25,000 buildings on almost 500 city blocks. Fortunately, the Ferry Building was scarcely damaged by the quake, although the tower was damaged and the clock's hands stopped at 5:16 (it was running a bit fast).

Gen. Frederick Funston, in command of the city after the earthquake, ordered two fireboats that were close by to pump saltwater to fire engines to make sure the fire did not reach the building. If the Ferry Building burned, then food, medicine, and tents would not be able to get to the stricken city.

As one observer noted in the *New York Times* on April 28, 1906, "The Ferry Building's escape from flames was providential, as had it been destroyed, the ferries to Oakland would have had no place to put in and San Francisco would have been practically cut off."

Within two days of the earthquake, the US Army Corps of Engineers issued an order to demolish the Ferry Building, thinking it was unsafe; but ultimately, a committee of engineers inspected the building and found it structurally sound, thus vindicating the pioneering construction methods used. A May 1, 1906, *San Francisco Chronicle* article states that "immediately following the big quake, and until very recently, the thousands of passengers going through the building have shown some trepidation, while passing under the shadow of the lofty pile, which appeared to have a slight list. Had the tower fallen, its hundreds of tons of brick and stone would have crashed through everything to bedrock."

The Ferry Building stood firm as the symbol of the city as San Francisco faced the enormous task of rebuilding its infrastructure and taking care of its many displaced residents.

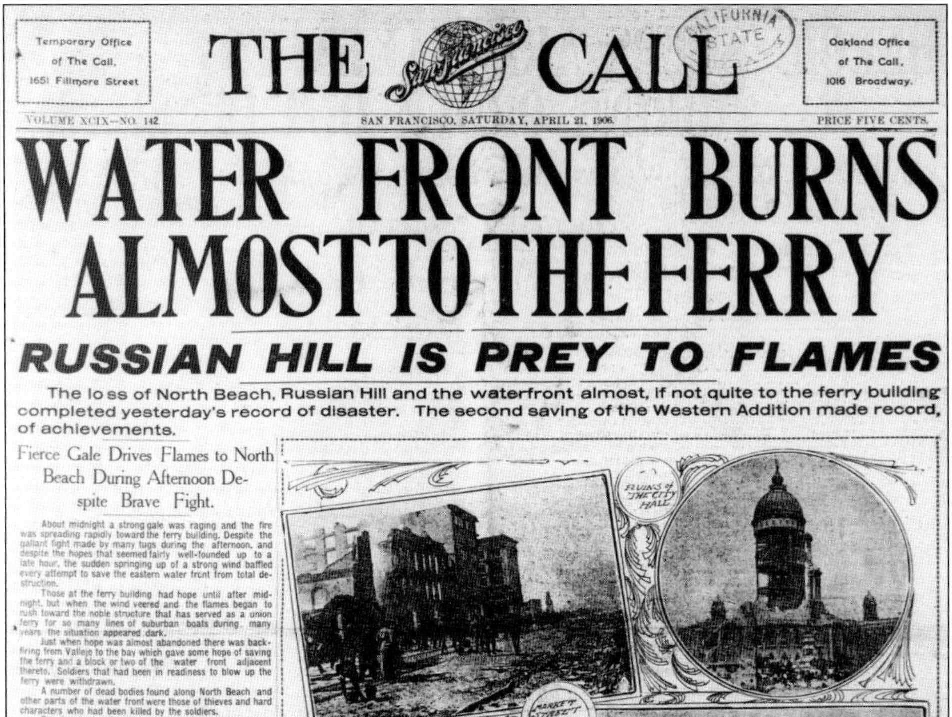

Temporary Office of The Call, 1651 Fillmore Street

THE San Francisco CALL

Oakland Office of The Call, 1016 Broadway.

VOLUME XCIX—NO. 142 | SAN FRANCISCO, SATURDAY, APRIL 21, 1906. | PRICE FIVE CENTS.

WATER FRONT BURNS ALMOST TO THE FERRY

RUSSIAN HILL IS PREY TO FLAMES

The loss of North Beach, Russian Hill and the waterfront almost, if not quite to the ferry building completed yesterday's record of disaster. The second saving of the Western Addition made record of achievements.

Fierce Gale Drives Flames to North Beach During Afternoon Despite Brave Fight.

About midnight a strong gale was raging and the fire was spreading rapidly toward the ferry building. Despite the gallant fight made by many tugs during the afternoon, and despite the hopes that seemed fairly well-founded up to a late hour, the sudden springing up of a strong wind baffled every attempt to save the eastern water front from total destruction.

Those at the ferry building had hope until after midnight, but when the wind veered and the flames began to rush toward the noble structure that has served as a union ferry for so many lines of suburban boats during many years the situation appeared dark.

Just when hope was almost abandoned there was backfiring from Vallejo to the bay which gave some hope of saving the ferry and a block or two of the water front adjacent thereto. Soldiers that had been in readiness to blow up the ferry were withdrawn.

A number of dead bodies found along North Beach and other parts of the water front were those of thieves and hard characters who had been killed by the soldiers.

One hundred and seventy-six prisoners from various branch county jails were sent to San Quentin, but the Warden refused to receive them, as they had not been sentenced. They were landed at Alcatraz and will probably be removed from there today to various jails adjacent to the bay. George D. Collins was among those thus transferred.

Two vital events marked yesterday in San Francisco—the breaking out of a great fire that consumed Russian Hill and most of the district between its apex and a point on the water front a few blocks north of the ferry building, and the subduing of the same blaze in its vicious attempts to creep back to the west and possibly invade the large section between Van Ness avenue and Golden Gate Park.

[illegible]

TUGS FIGHT BRAVELY.

The fight to save the water front after the blaze had crossed Russian Hill was waged entirely by a number of fire tugs that battled with vigor and did much to check the blaze from leaping at once to the foot of Market street.

[illegible]

WESTERN AREA SAVED.

[illegible]

PARDEE CALLS LEGISLATURE

Governor Pardee will call a special session of the State Legislature at once to prepare for relief measures for San Francisco.

Then they stopped, but burned in an easterly direction from Kearny street, destroying the two sections of the seawall and encircling Telegraph Hill. At the southern base of the hill lay Barbary Coast, which had until this time escaped the blaze. In a comparatively short time this far-famed district was laid in ashes and the fire reached out for that portion of the city on lower Broadway, Vallejo and Pacific streets that yet remained intact. The flames then crackled in the direction of the water front and made the work of demolition in this section of the town complete. The fire tugs were pressed into service and fought the fire as quickly as it reached East street.

MEIGGS WHARF GOES.

By 3 p. m. Meiggs wharf was in flames, which traveled fast toward the ferry. From the deck of the Vanguard, opposite Meiggs wharf, a Call man saw the burning of Meiggs wharf and the gallant fight of about twenty fire tugs, which pumped large streams of bay water ahead of the advancing flames and even in the very teeth of the fire.

[illegible]

Continued on Page 2, Columns 6 and 7.

RUINS OF THE CITY HALL AS THEY APPEARED YESTERDAY AFTERNOON; SCENE ON MARKET STREET LOOKING WESTWARD FROM EAST STREET AND VIEW OF RUINED DISTRICT EAST OF THE POST OFFICE.

WILL RISE AGAIN IN SPLENDOR

With Undaunted Spirit San Francisco Faces the Future, Confident That All Is Well.

San Francisco has demonstrated the courage and confidence of her citizens by declaring to the world that assistance will not be solicited from cities other that those in California. The spirit of the hour is that the city will rise again in renewed splendor and in such form that the dream of beautiful San Francisco will be realized.

The Mayor has invoked the Governor to call a special session of the Legislature and whatever aid the great State of California may extend to the metropolis of the commonwealth will be appreciated.

Continued on Page 2, Columns 3, 4 and 5.

On April 21, as the fire raged on, the *San Francisco Call* headline shouts, "Water Front Burns Almost to the Ferry." The article reports that the night before, a strong gale was raging and the fire was moving quickly towards the Ferry Building. Many fire tugs in the bay were fighting gallantly to stave off the spread of the fire, but the strong wind was a tough competitor. According to the article, "Those at the ferry building had hope until after midnight, but when the wind veered and the flames began to rush toward the noble structure that has served as a union ferry for so many lines of suburban boats during many years, the situation appeared dark. . . . The fight to save the water front after the blaze had crossed Russian Hill was waged entirely by a number of fire tugs that battled with vigor and did much to check the blaze from leaping at once to the foot of Market street [*sic*]." (Library of Congress.)

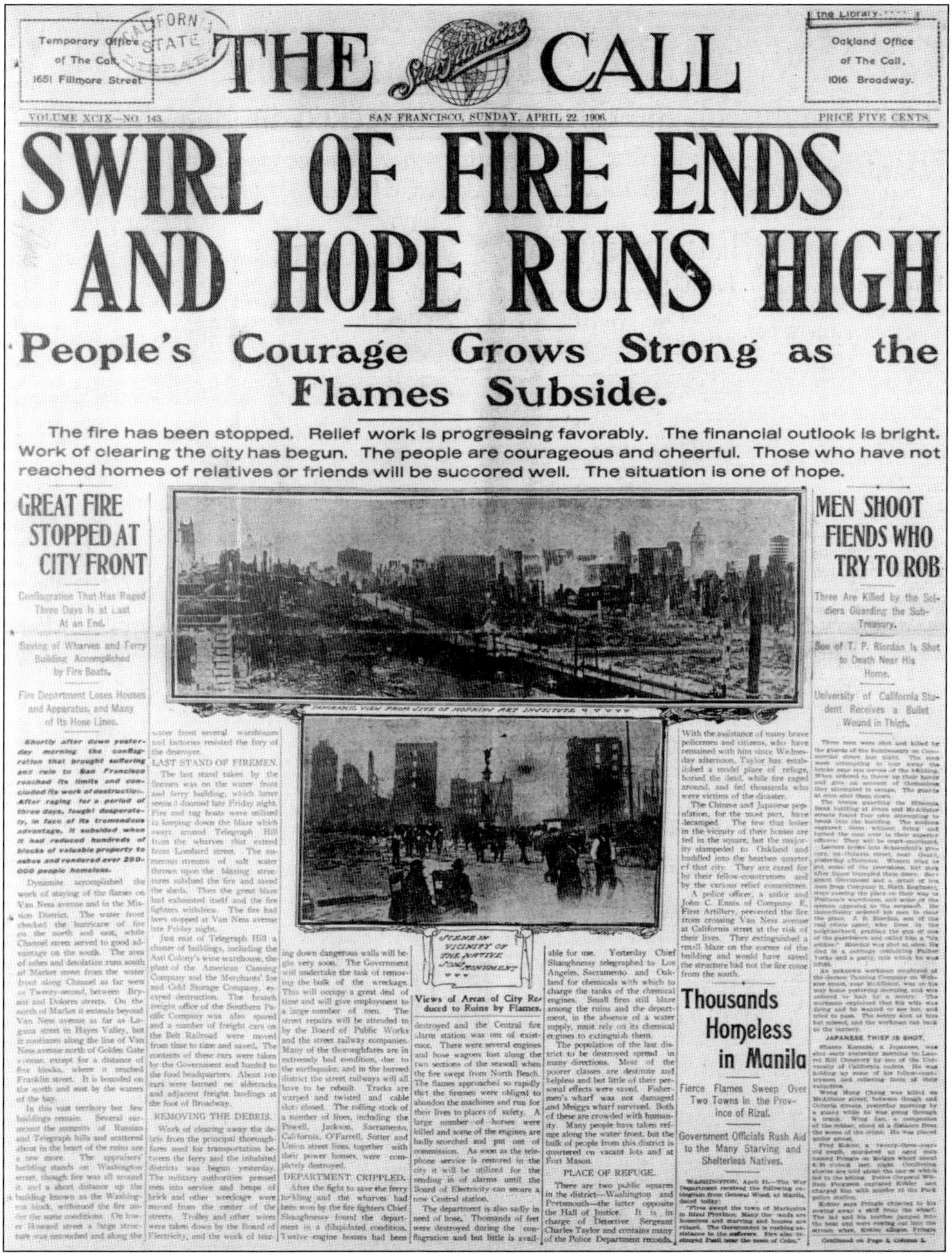

Temporary Office of The Call, 1651 Fillmore Street

THE San Francisco CALL

Oakland Office of The Call, 1016 Broadway.

VOLUME XCIX—NO. 143. SAN FRANCISCO, SUNDAY, APRIL 22, 1906. PRICE FIVE CENTS.

SWIRL OF FIRE ENDS AND HOPE RUNS HIGH

People's Courage Grows Strong as the Flames Subside.

The fire has been stopped. Relief work is progressing favorably. The financial outlook is bright. Work of clearing the city has begun. The people are courageous and cheerful. Those who have not reached homes of relatives or friends will be succored well. The situation is one of hope.

GREAT FIRE STOPPED AT CITY FRONT

Conflagration That Has Raged Three Days Is at Last At an End.

Saving of Wharves and Ferry Building Accomplished by Fire Boats.

Fire Department Loses Houses and Apparatus, and Many of Its Hose Lines.

MEN SHOOT FIENDS WHO TRY TO ROB

Three Are Killed by the Soldiers Guarding the Sub-Treasury.

Son of T. P. Riordan Is Shot to Death Near His Home.

University of California Student Receives a Bullet Wound in Thigh.

Views of Areas of City Reduced to Ruins by Flames.

Thousands Homeless in Manila

Fierce Flames Sweep Over Two Towns in the Province of Rizal.

Government Officials Rush Aid to the Many Starving and Shelterless Natives.

On April 22, four days after the earthquake, the *San Francisco Call* newspaper declared, "People's Courage Grows Strong as the Flames Subside." The newspaper article, headlined "Great Fire Stopped at City Front," states, "The last stand taken by the firemen was on the water front and ferry building, which . . . seemed doomed late Friday night. Fire and tug boats were utilized in keeping down the blaze which swept around Telegraph Hill from the wharves that extend from Lombard Street. The numerous streams of salt water thrown upon the blazing structures subdued the fire and saved the sheds. Then the great blaze had exhausted itself and the fire fighters withdrew." The port was saved from much of the fire's devastation, which was important as it was an essential area during the emergency and while the city recovered. (Library of Congress.)

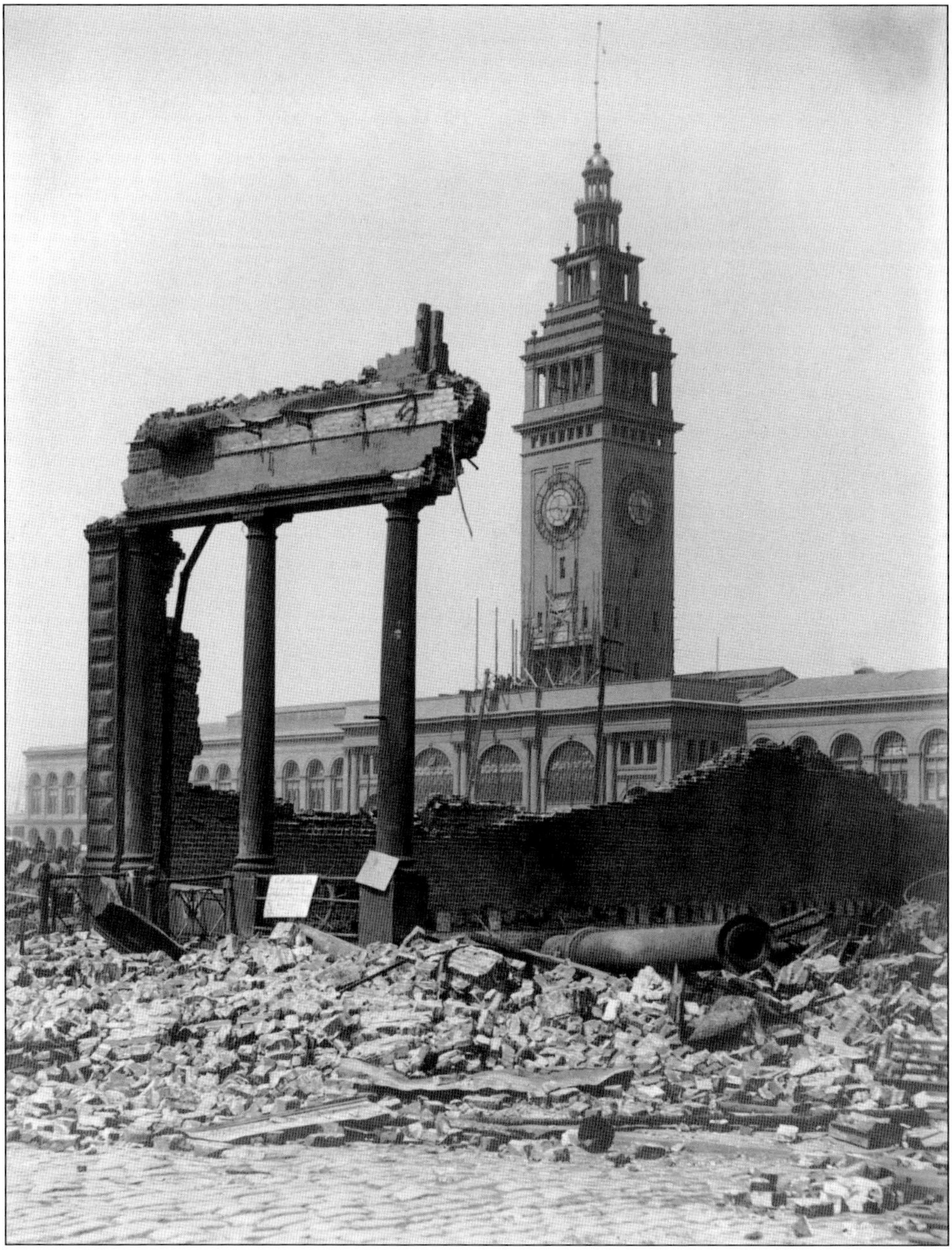

After the disaster, the Ferry Building stands proudly behind ruins. In this photograph, taken from Steuart Street, the clock is at 5:16 a.m. and scaffolding and men are at the base of the tower. The workmen were probably inspecting the extent to which the Colusa sandstone facing had been destroyed. The three lower stories sustained the most damage. Once the port engineers decided that the tower was sound and did not need to be razed, they located 5,000 feet of cable car wire that they used to wrap the tower and secure it while waiting for a wooden scaffolding to be built and reconstruction to begin. An area in front of the depot was roped off, and the refuse from the tower was dumped there. It was more than a year before repairs were done, and the damaged sandstone replaced with concrete. (Photograph by W.J. Street, Anne T. Kent California Room, Marin County Free Library.)

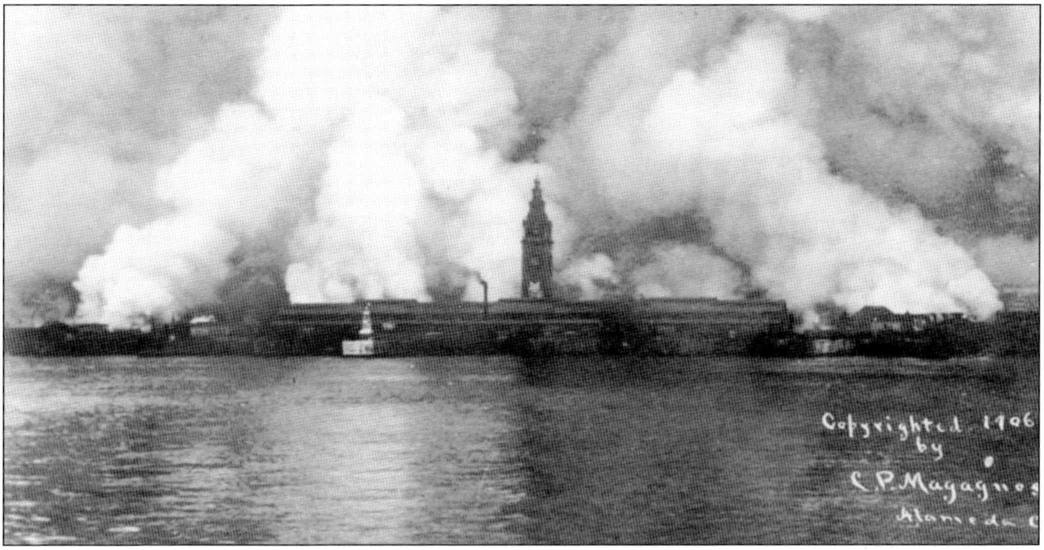

Charles B. Sedgwick, an eyewitness and editor of the *British-Californian*, described the fire (seen here from the bay): "Never shall I forget the sight. It was weirdly beautiful. A thousand banners of flame were streaming in the cloudless sky from spires and domes and lofty roofs . . . magnificent in irresistible power." (San Francisco History Center, San Francisco Public Library.)

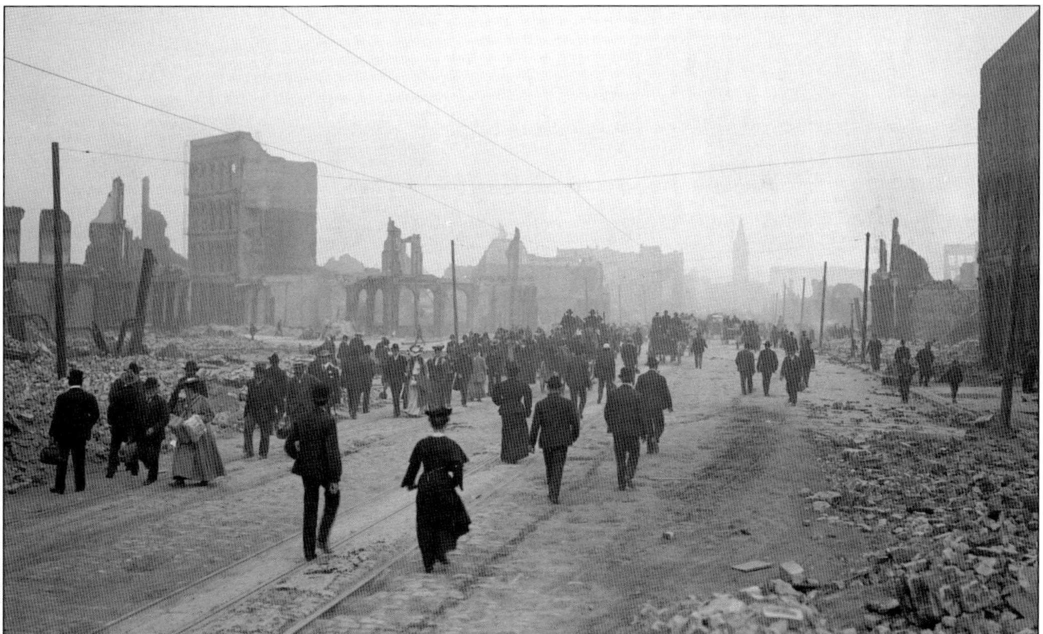

In *History of the Earthquake and Fire in San Francisco: An Account of the Disaster of April 18, 1906 and its Immediate Results*, by Frank W. Aitken and Edward Hilton and published in 1906, the authors write, "Crowds collected on Market Street to see if any damage had been done to the big buildings. They sauntered along easily, and laughed at the strange appearance of rooms exposed by the falling of the front walls . . . An occasional businessman hurried along, anxious to protect his records. But for the most part the procession was one of curious sightseers." (Library of Congress.)

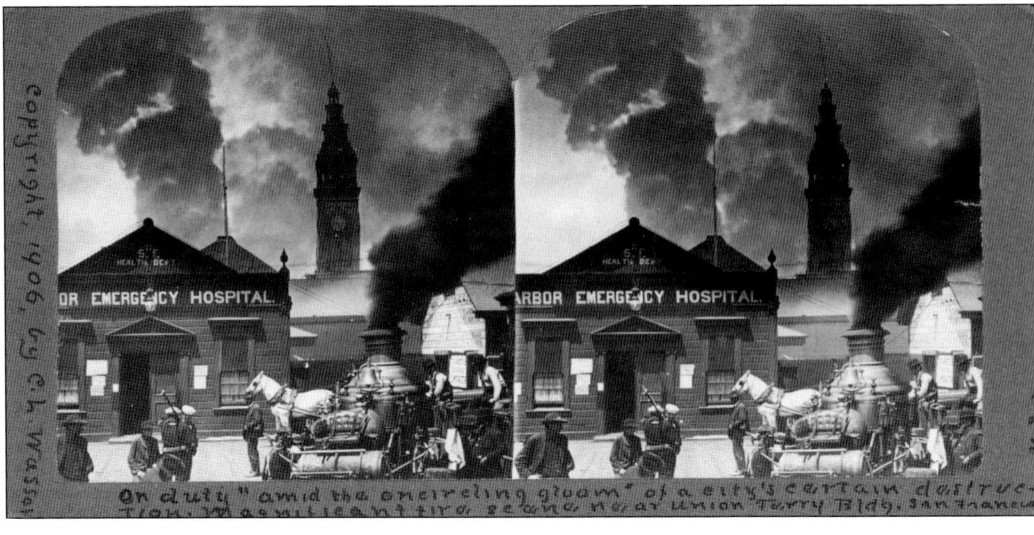

The Harbor Emergency Hospital (above), adjoining the Howard Street Wharf near the Ferry Building, was one of the only undamaged hospitals. The Virtual Museum of San Francisco features the account of Dr. George Blumer, who volunteered at the hospital after the quake: "During the 48 hours after the quake this hospital had a patient every two minutes. I recall seeing one patient with smallpox who was temporarily isolated out on a wharf, one sailor with a gunshot wound received while preventing looting, and a good many drug habitués, mostly courtesans from the Barbary Coast district, who could not get their morphine from the usual sources and would come to the hospital and beg for it." Crowds trying to leave the stricken city gathered at the Ferry Building (below). (Both, Library of Congress.)

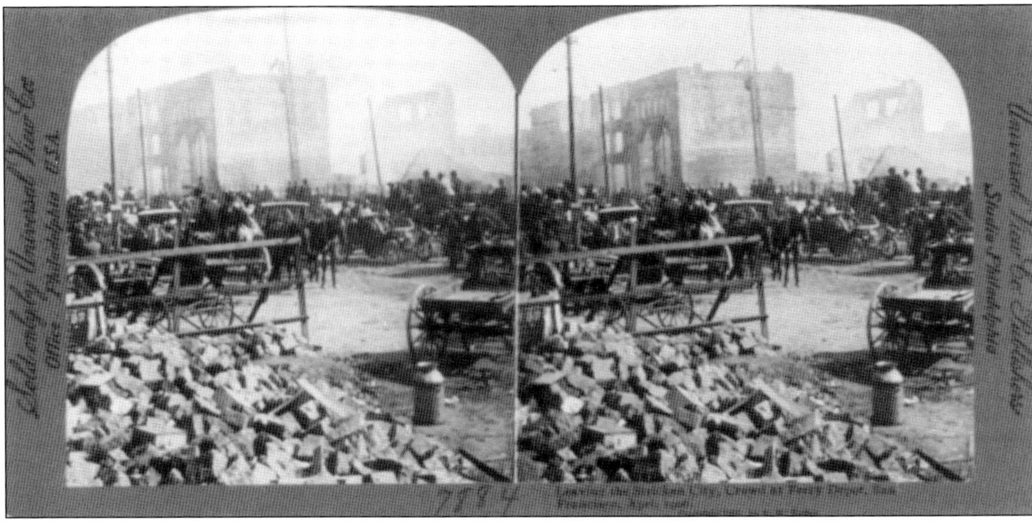

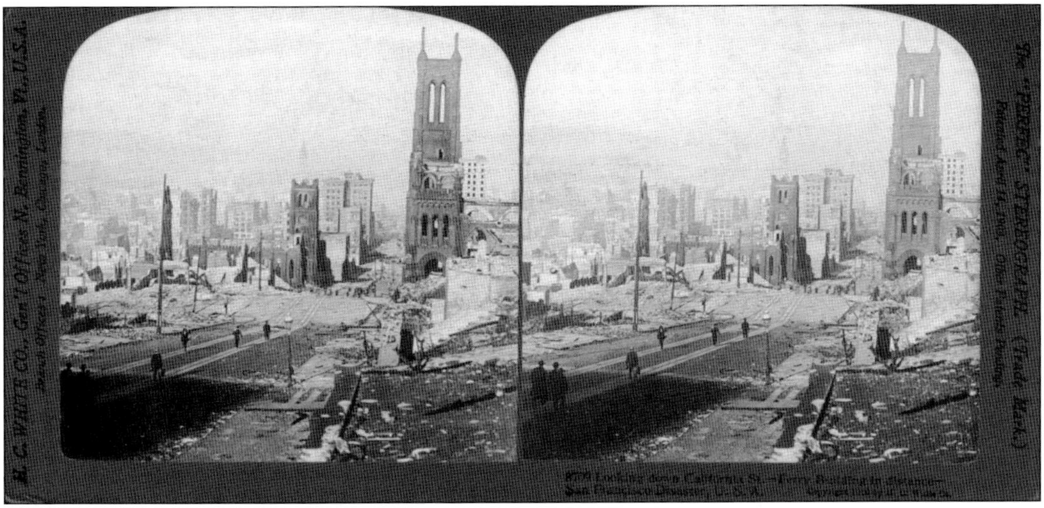

The fires burned continuously during Wednesday and Thursday (when the main progress was checked) and to a small extent on Friday and Saturday, from April 18 to 21, 1906. Squads of dynamiters set charges, and with a roar and a cloud of dust, a building would fall. Unfortunately, many charges were set by unskilled hands, and the fire was scattered. The above stereograph shows the view up California Street after the fire, with the Ferry Building in the distance. The stereograph below, taken from the Ferry Building tower, shows the damage on Market Street. (Both, the Miriam and Ira D. Wallach Division of Art, Prints and Photographs, Robert N. Dennis Collection, New York Public Library.)

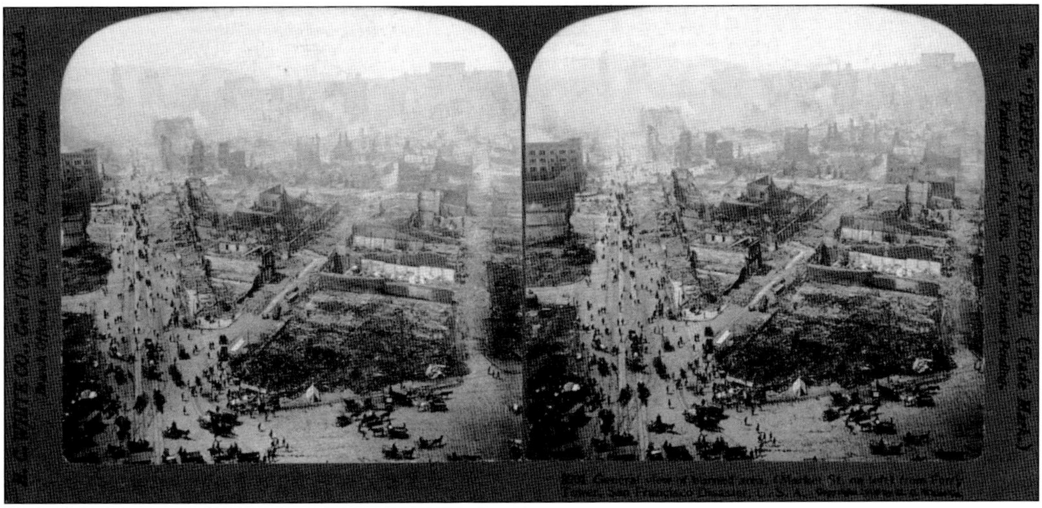

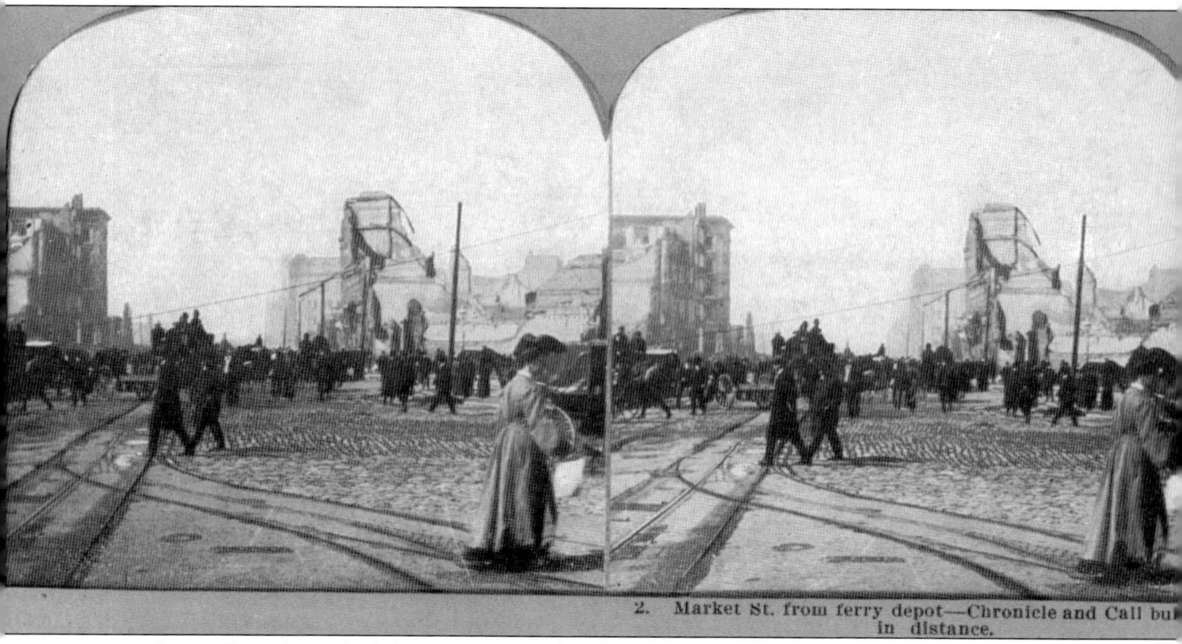

As the earthquake rocked the city, hundreds of buildings south of Market Street were either thrown down or badly damaged. In the ensuing inferno, the entire district south of Mission was a mass of fire, which leapt from block to block. According to a 1906 press release from Southern Pacific, "The fire began in a region of closely built frame structures along narrow streets in the older residence section. . . . From small beginnings the flames unfolded as a fan in the district south of Market Street, and then attacking the business section crept up the hills to the broader streets, where the stubbornly fighting fire department, with improvised weapons, stopped them." This stereograph shows Market Street from the Ferry Building, with the Chronicle and Call Buildings in the distance. (The Miriam and Ira D. Wallach Division of Art, Prints and Photographs, Robert N. Dennis Collection, New York Public Library.)

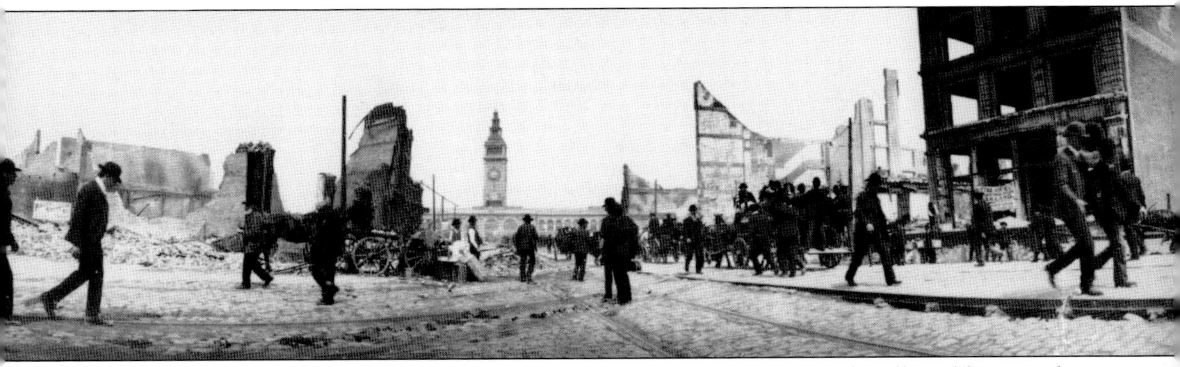

The fire had swept up Fifth Street, destroying the Emporium, Chronicle, and Call Buildings and sending bursts of flame hundreds of feet into the air. Thieves burgled wrecked stores and deserted homes, and rowdies broke into saloons and helped themselves to liquor. Troops began patrolling the streets and Mayor Eugene Schmitz issued his "shoot to kill" order. In this photograph, taken 10 days after the quake and fire, the Ferry Building stands in the distance and a man in shirtsleeves sells fruit. Charles Sedgwick, one of the eyewitnesses and editor of the *British-Californian*, observing the earthquake's aftermath on Market Street, wrote, "Now the grand old street was scarcely recognizable—a sad scene of destruction. Buildings by the dozen were half down; great pillars, copings, cornices and ornamentations had been wrenched from the mightiest structures and dashed to the ground in fragments." (SFMNHP, a12, 27, 902NL.)

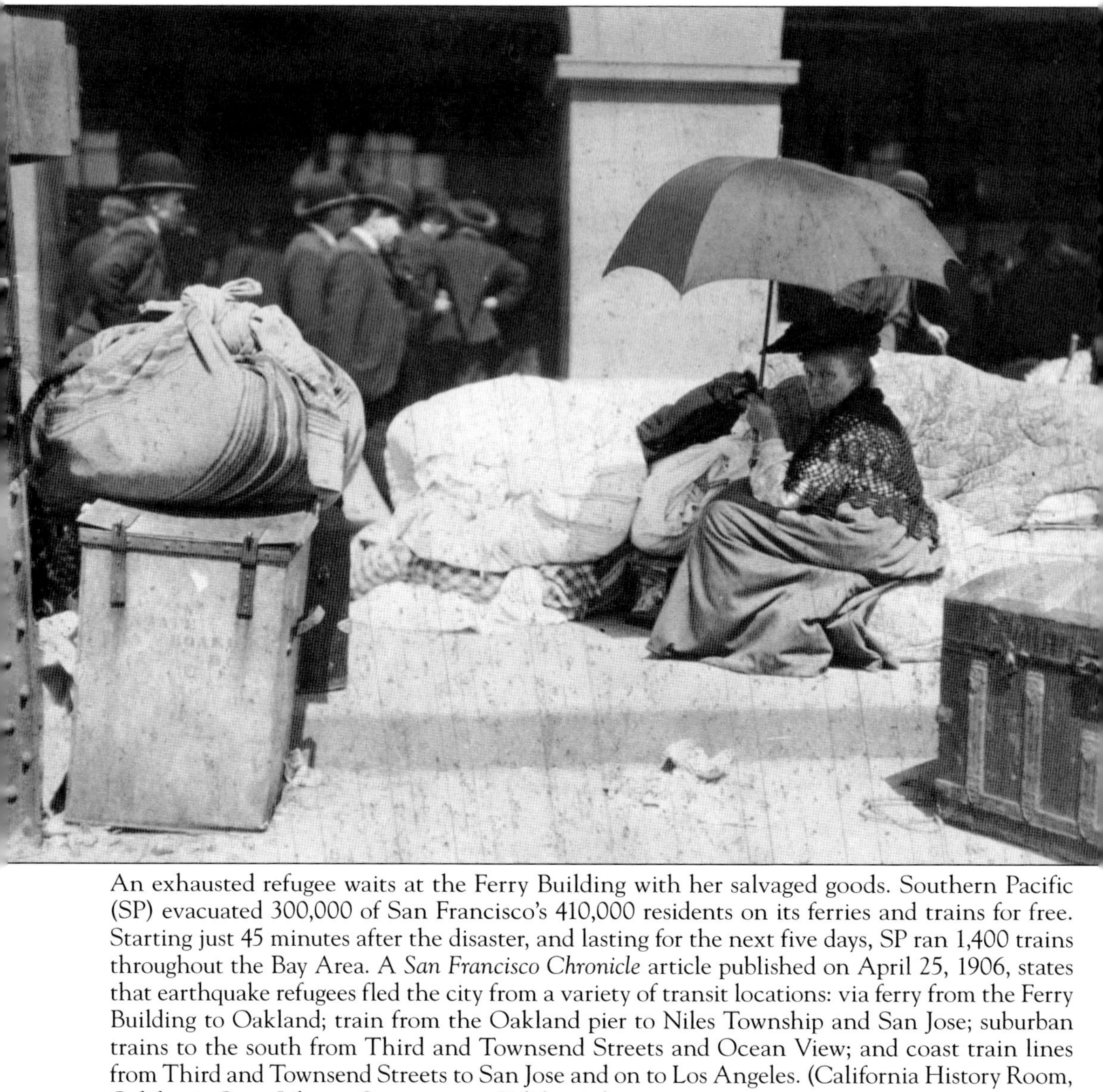

An exhausted refugee waits at the Ferry Building with her salvaged goods. Southern Pacific (SP) evacuated 300,000 of San Francisco's 410,000 residents on its ferries and trains for free. Starting just 45 minutes after the disaster, and lasting for the next five days, SP ran 1,400 trains throughout the Bay Area. A *San Francisco Chronicle* article published on April 25, 1906, states that earthquake refugees fled the city from a variety of transit locations: via ferry from the Ferry Building to Oakland; train from the Oakland pier to Niles Township and San Jose; suburban trains to the south from Third and Townsend Streets and Ocean View; and coast train lines from Third and Townsend Streets to San Jose and on to Los Angeles. (California History Room, California State Library, Sacramento, California.)

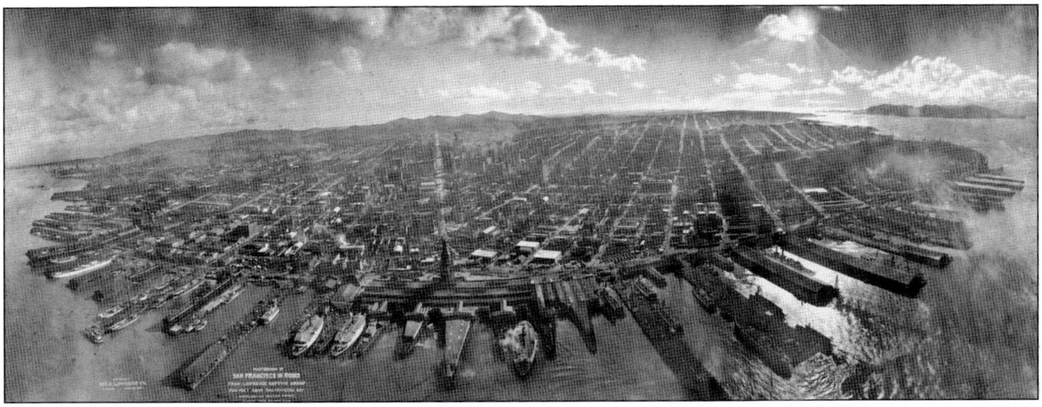

San Francisco lies in ruins on May 28, 1906, about six weeks after the earthquake and fire. This photograph was taken from a camera suspended on a kite, perhaps 1,000 feet above the city. The tower of the Ferry Building is visible at the bay end of Market Street, which can be clearly seen all the way to the foothills of Twin Peaks. (Library of Congress.)

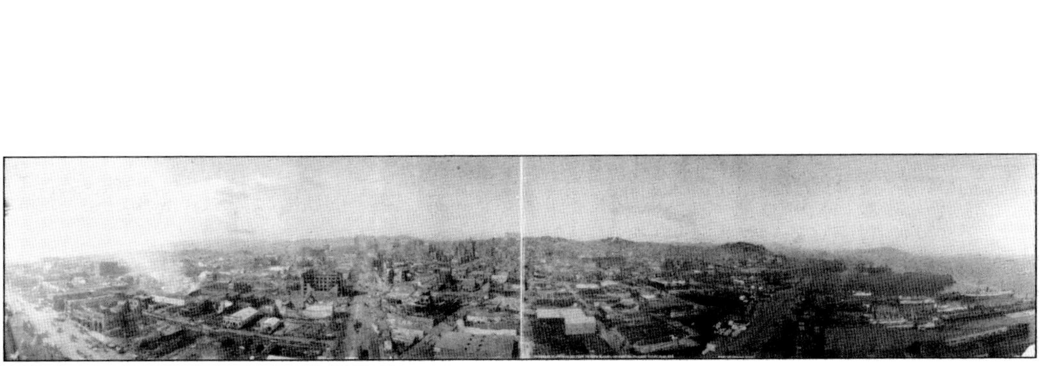

In this panoramic photograph, taken from the tower of the Ferry Building, one can see Market Street straight ahead, and to the left and right is East Street. At first, European insurance companies refused to pay claims for fire damage for many San Francisco policyholders, believing that it was the quake that caused the damage (they did not insure for earthquakes). (Library of Congress.)

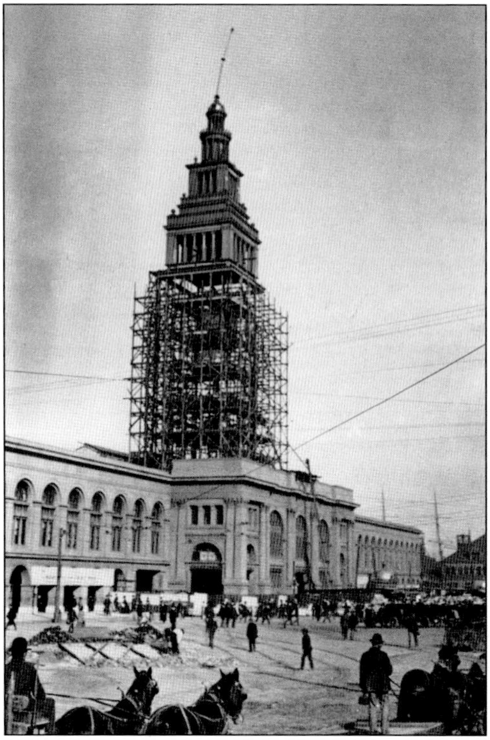

In these photographs, crews are busy repairing the streetcar loop and the Ferry Building tower facade in October 1906. F.A. Koetitz, chief engineer for Pacific Construction Company, which oversaw the reconstruction, wrote in *American Builders Review*, published January 1907: "The upper portion of the tower was intact . . . it was decided to reduce its weight by taking down all the stone and brickwork, then to repair the steel frame, and to replace the covering with materials of lighter weight. The steel work was carefully repaired; all broken parts were removed and renewed; the separated columns and girders were riveted back to place; all injured rods were repaired, and the tower was brought to proper plumb ready for the covering." (Left, SFMNHP, A12, 36,669n, BD Johnson; below, photograph by John Henry Mentz, SFMTA Photo Archive.)

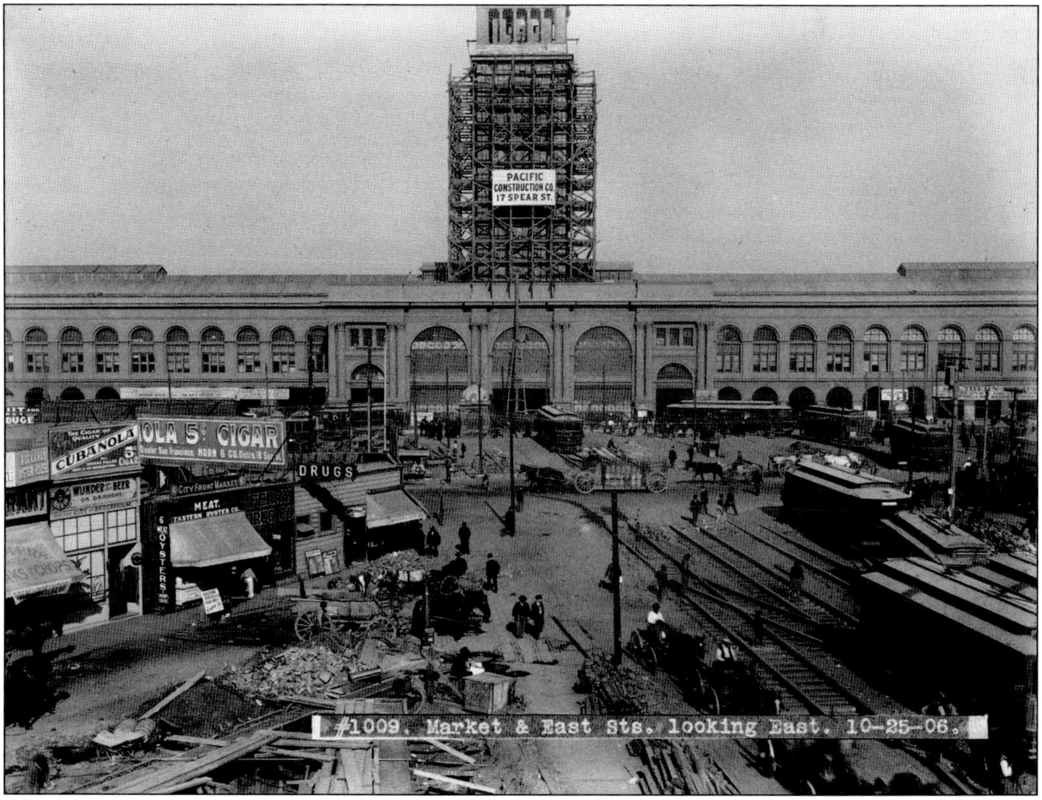

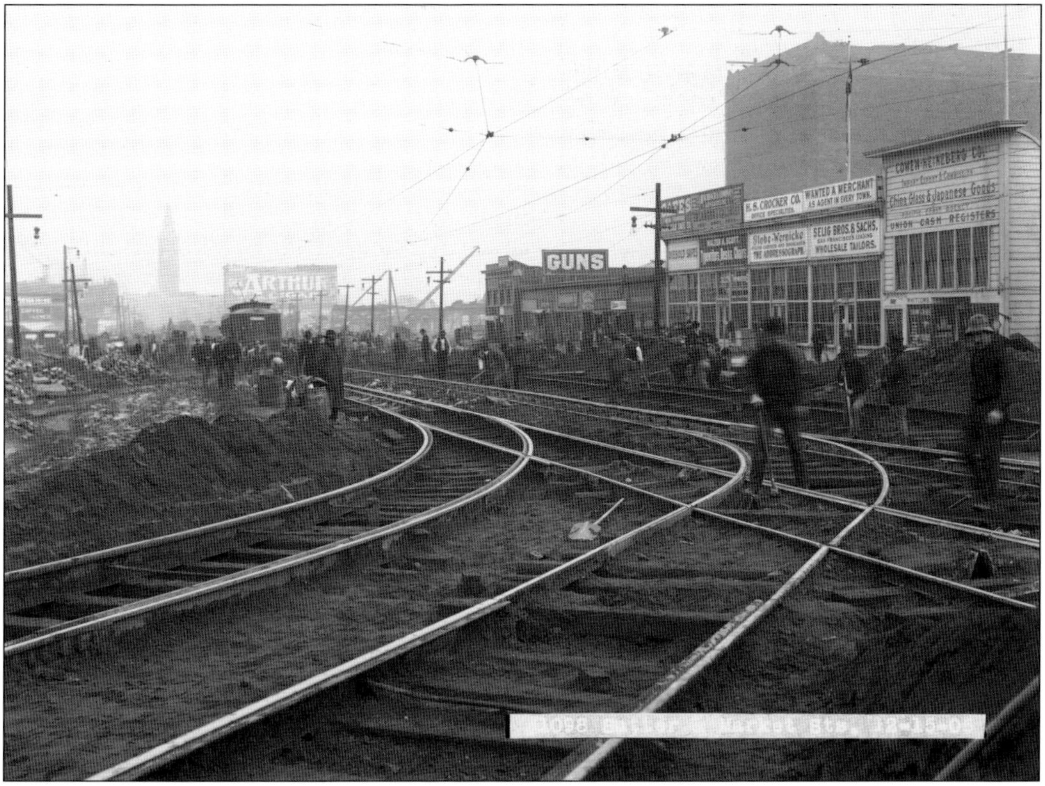

Market Street, the main boulevard leading up to the Ferry Building, has had rail transit service since 1860. First steam trains, followed by horse cars, and then after that, cable cars provided service until the morning of April 18, 1906. Electric streetcars had also begun operating in San Francisco in 1892, and it was estimated that it cost twice as much to build and six times as much to operate a line with cable cars rather than electric streetcars. The earthquake's destruction turned out to be the perfect opportunity for United Railroads (URR), who owned most of the cable car lines, to replace them with electric streetcar lines, which had not been allowed previously. In these photographs, taken in 1906 and 1907, one can see the rubble and overhead streetcar lines. (Both photographs by John Henry Mentz, SFMTA Photo Archive.)

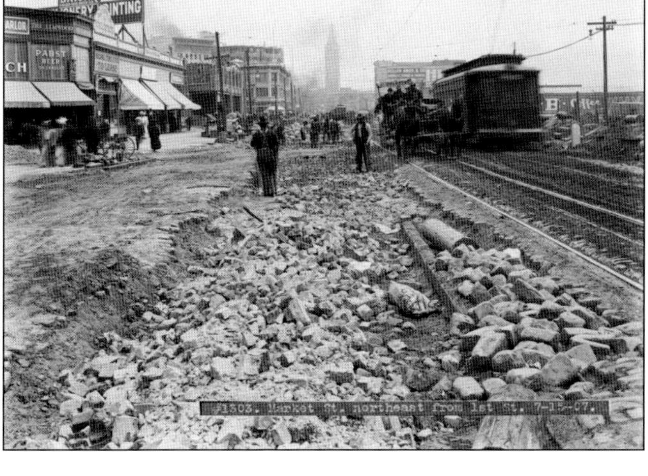

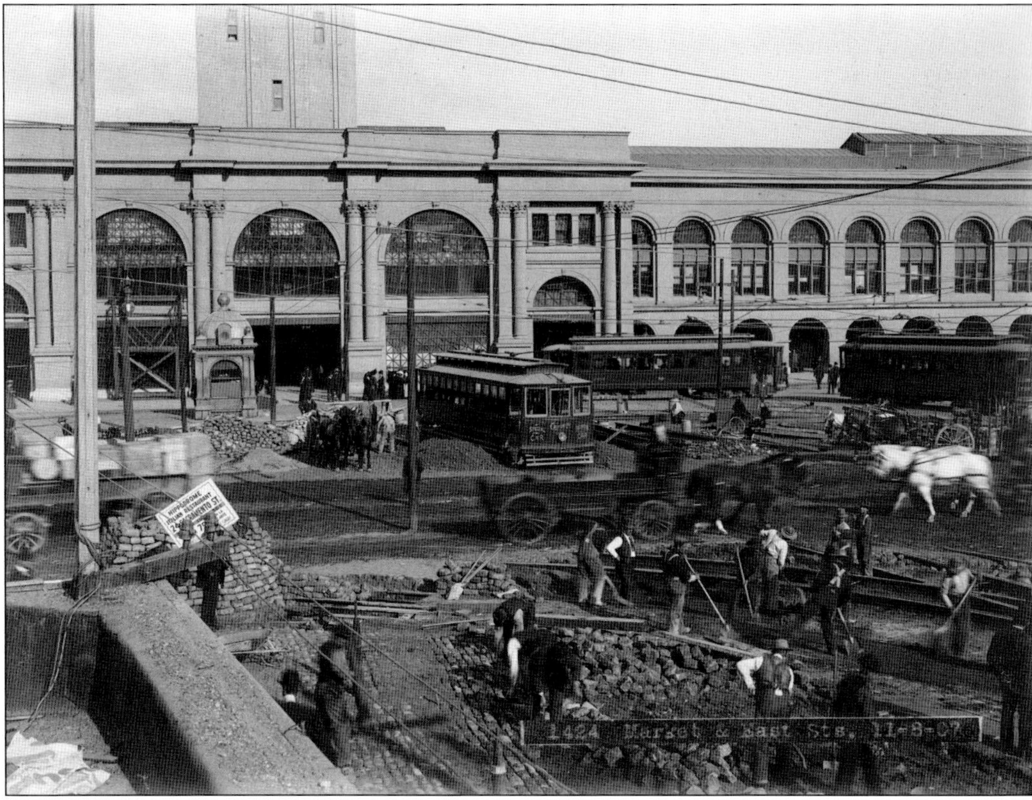

Before the earthquake and fire, Patrick Calhoun, president of United Railroads, wanted to convert unprofitable cable lines to electric operations, but there was public opposition to overhead trolley lines and provisions of some of the railway franchises restricted them to operating as either cable or horse car lines. After the earthquake, Calhoun and his subordinates bribed the board of supervisors with $200,000 to get an ordinance passed saying the cable lines could be converted to electrified street railways. To get public support for the conversion, Calhoun claimed that URR's cable lines would have to be completely reconstructed. URR retained only the cable lines that operated on grades too steep for electric streetcars. (Both photographs by John Henry Mentz, SFMTA Photo Archive.)

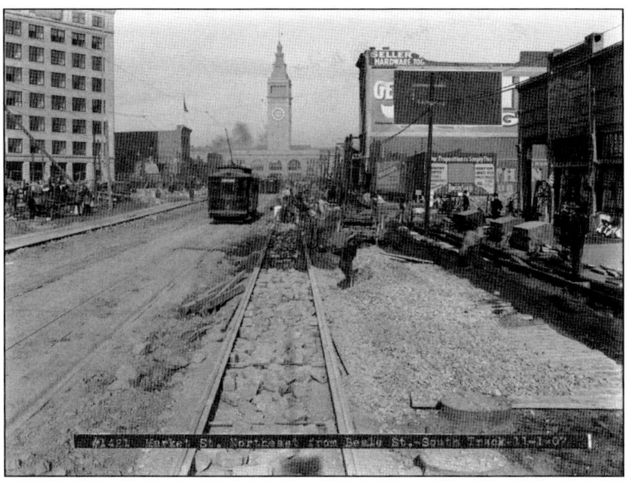

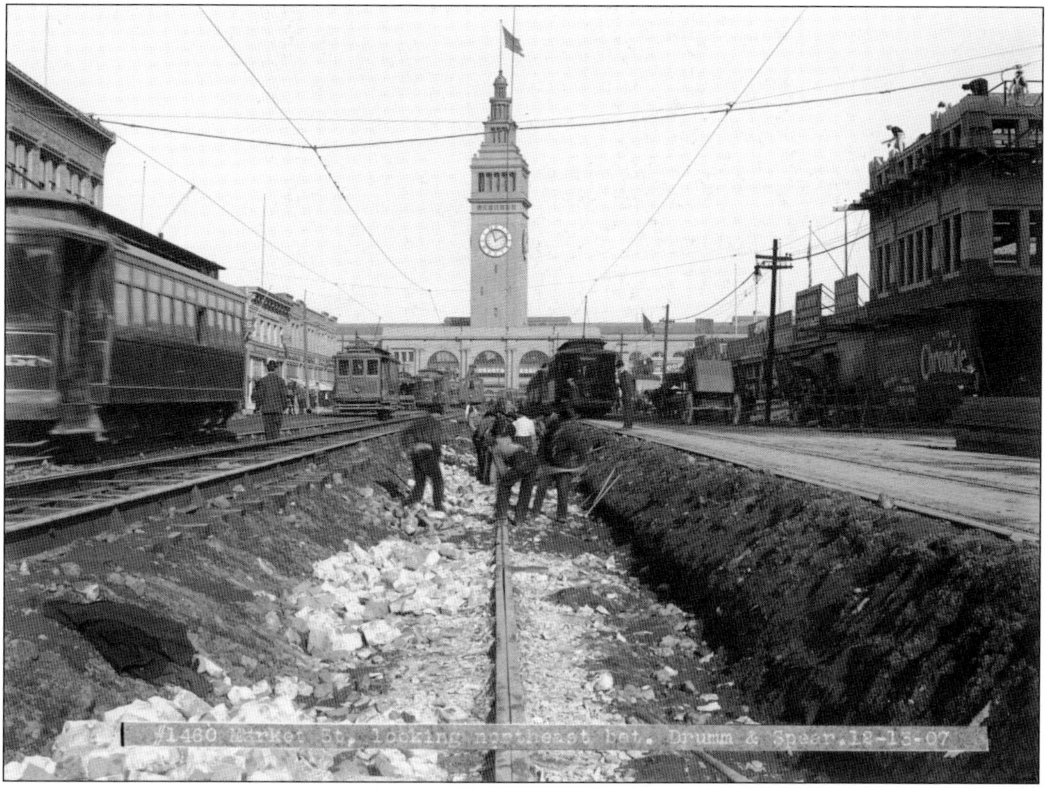

After the quake, streetcar tracks were bent and twisted out of shape, and the streets in places had sunk three or four feet, or great humps had appeared four or five feet high. In the photograph above, the Ferry Building looks on as new streetcar tracks are installed in December 1907. In the image below, workers remove a turntable pit in front of the Ferry Building in March 1908. Turntables reduced the time required to reverse the cars. The turntable dispatched cars onto three separate spur tracks, which allowed cars to travel on Market Street efficiently. (Both photographs by John Henry Mentz, SFMTA Photo Archive.)

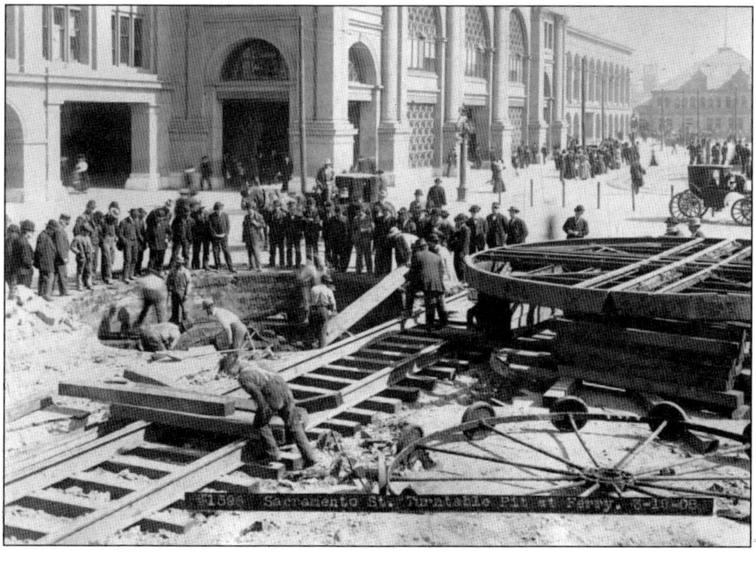

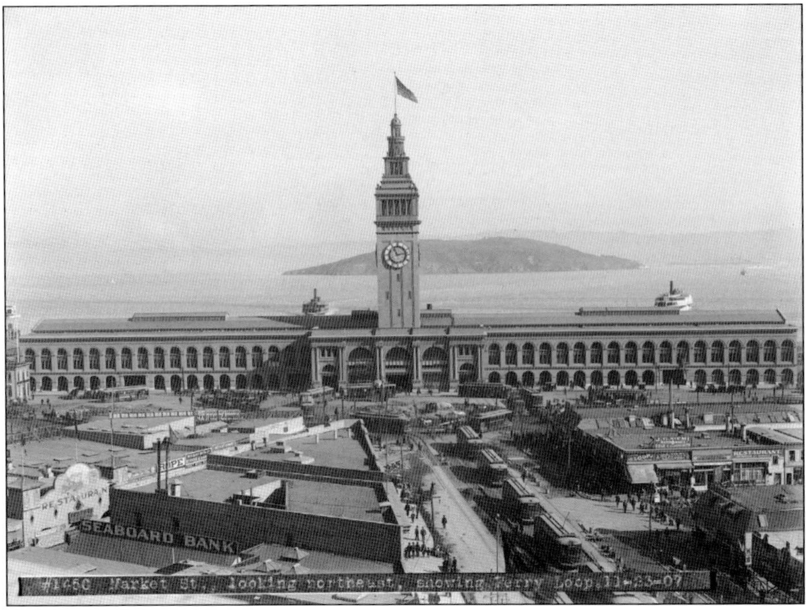

In November 1907, the Ferry Building looks all cleaned up. Streetcars come into the loop to deposit and pick up passengers, and ferries come and go. There is still some rubble in the streets more than a year and a half after the earthquake and fire. (Photograph by John Henry Mentz, SFMTA Photo Archive.)

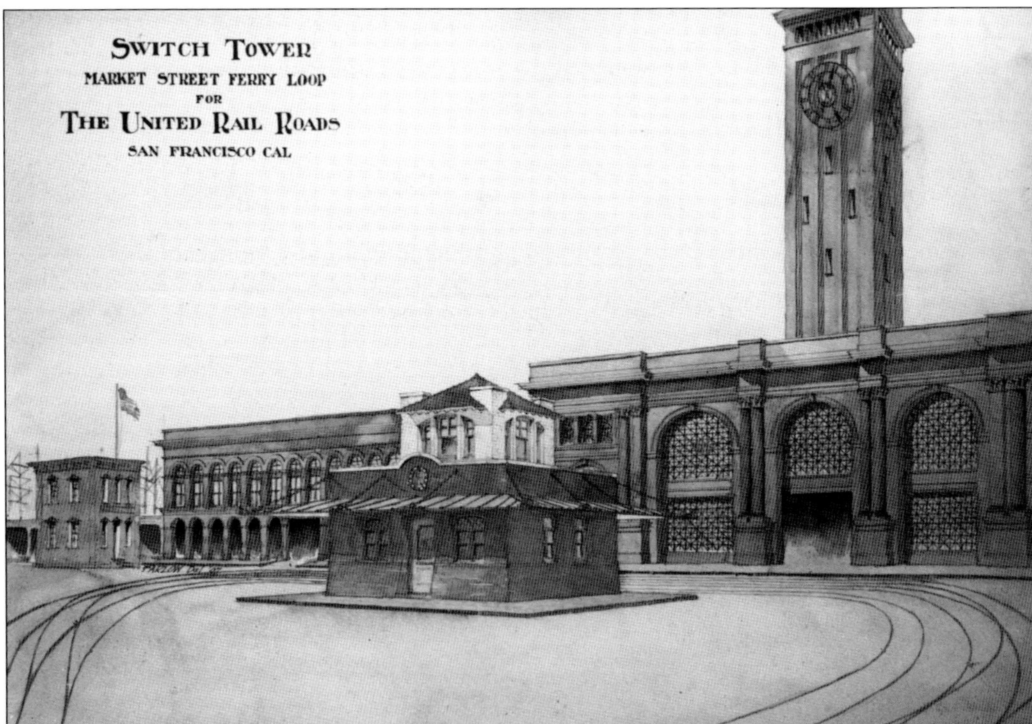

This 1907 drawing shows a proposed design for a new switch tower at the Ferry Building. With no traffic lights, cable car and streetcar drivers relied on the signals to start and stop. Progress on the new switch building was slow; however, as it was not until quite a few years later, in 1925, that the switch tower seen in the 1907 photographs was replaced with a new tower. (Photograph by John Henry Mentz, SFMTA Photo Archive.)

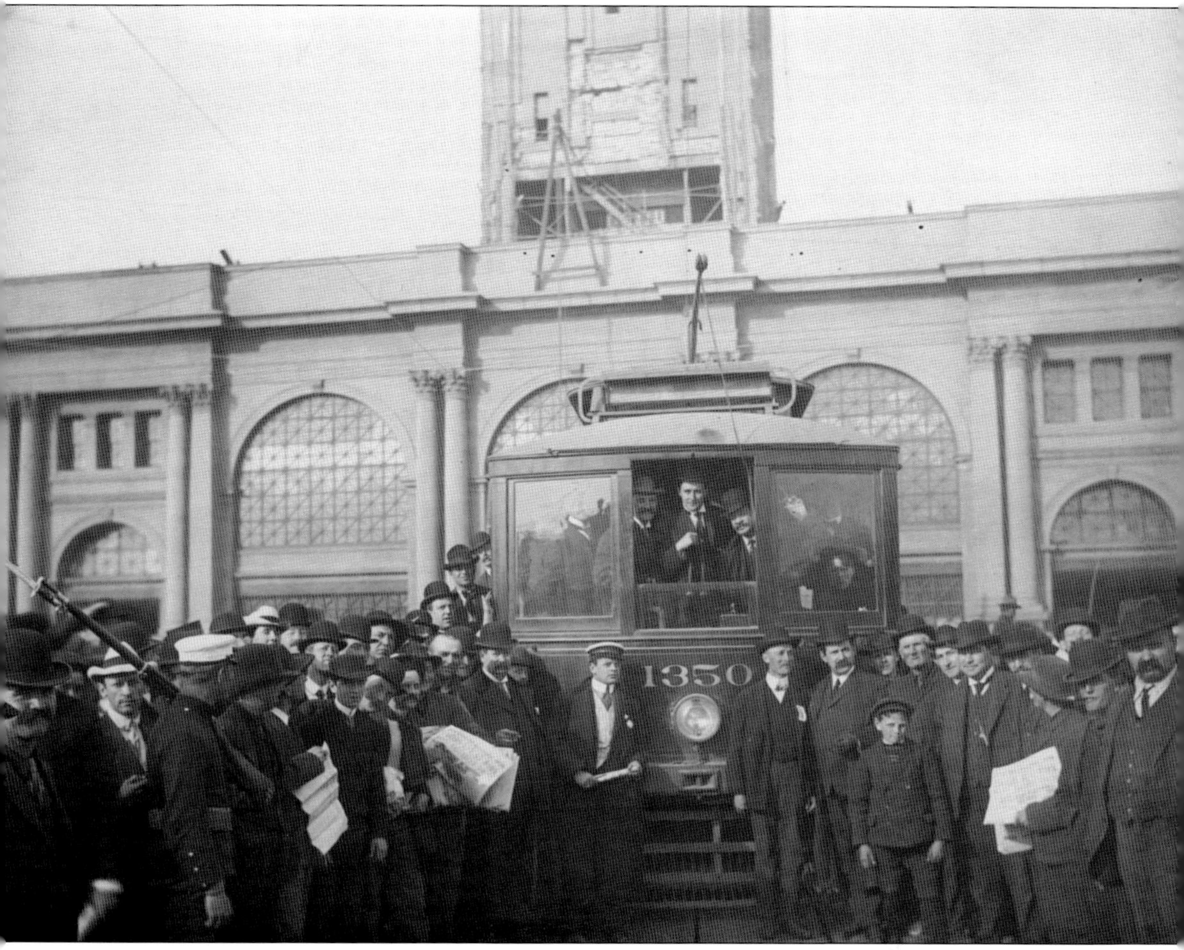

On May 2, 1906, just two weeks after the earthquake, the first regular streetcar, Car No. 1350, gets ready to depart from the Ferry Building. The fellow at the front of the car is Patrick Calhoun, head of United Railroads, and Mayor Schmitz was on board. The car ran on the cable car tracks and was powered by electricity from temporary wires that had been strung overhead. Since it was so urgent to resume streetcar service after the quake, United Railroads was granted a temporary permit allowing the company to install overhead trolley wires on Market and Sutter Streets. (There was strong sentiment against overhead lines, and many preferred that they be placed in underground conduits, a more expensive option.) For a few days, once service was restored following the quake, riders could ride for free. (Photograph by John Henry Mentz, SFMTA Photo Archive.)

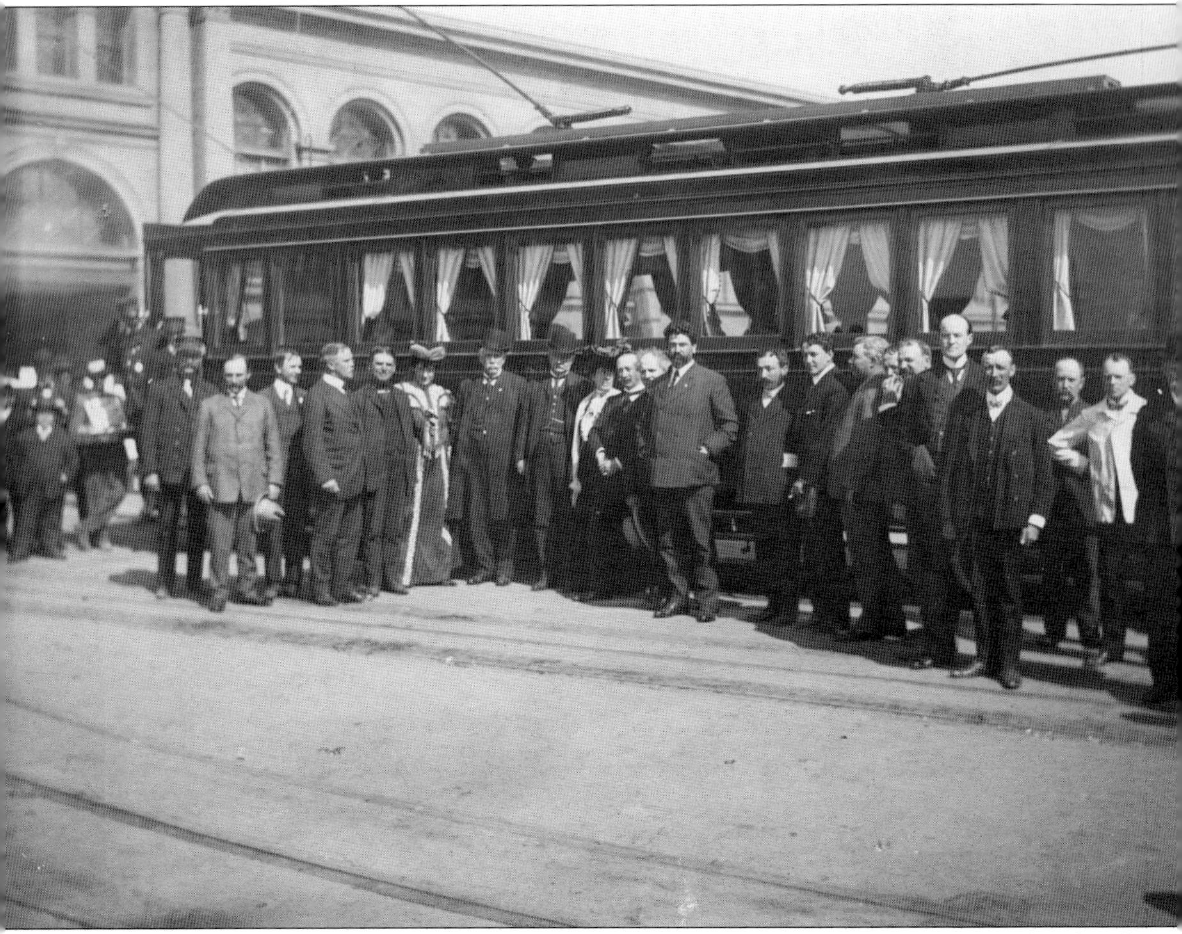

On May 3, another streetcar took off from the Ferry Building; this time it was the United Railroad's private-party streetcar, the *San Francisco*, with Mayor Schmitz at the controls. After a stop at the Ferry Building for this commemorative photograph, the car went on Market to Valencia. There was streetcar service on Market to Castro and on Market and Valencia to Twenty-Eigth Street within the next few days. Private trolley cars were quite fashionable and often used for evening parties to go to a restaurant and the theater and then on to the Cliff House or Beach Chalet. A typical private-party car might have a cherrywood interior, velour curtains, and a fancy sideboard, plus moss green carpet, rattan chairs, a buffet, and an ice chest (to chill champagne for after-theater parties). (Photograph by John Henry Mentz, SFMTA Photo Archive.)

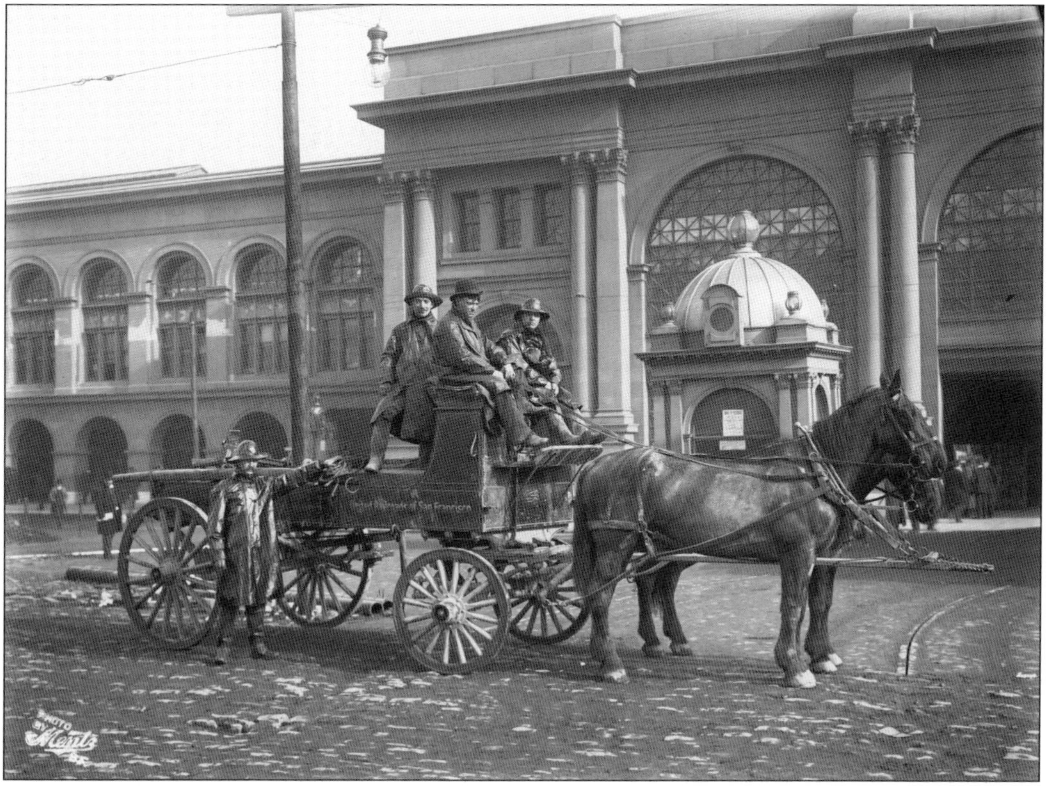

In early 1907, firemen pose on an emergency wagon in front of the Ferry Building. On the side of the wagon, it says, "United Railroads of San Francisco," so perhaps this was the rail company's fire wagon standing by in case of emergency. The old starter tower is in the background. (Photograph by John Henry Mentz, SFMTA Photo Archive.)

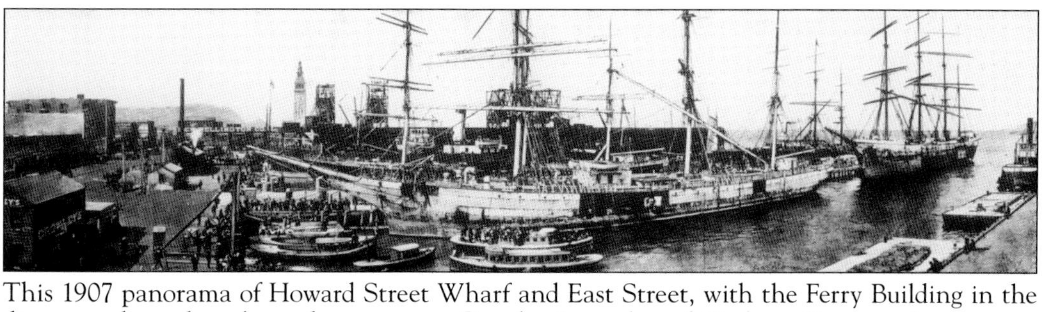

This 1907 panorama of Howard Street Wharf and East Street, with the Ferry Building in the distance, shows how busy the port was. Crowley Launch and Tugboat Company's two-story boathouse is in the lower left. Crowley's launches are taking people to see the warships USS *Maryland*, *Colorado*, *West Virginia*, and *Pennsylvania*. (SFMNHP, A12, 24,032nl.)

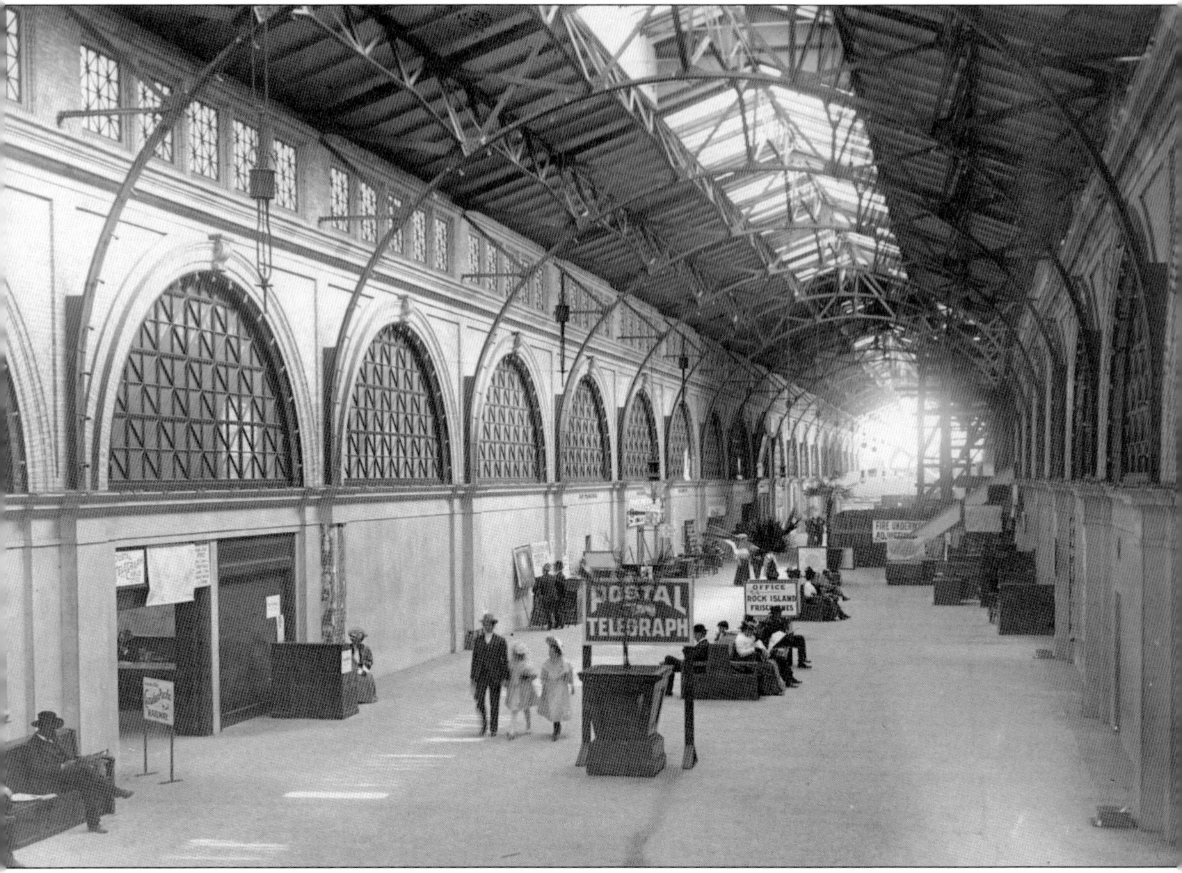

After the earthquake had displaced the ticket agents for the railroads from their offices in the burned section of the city, they established temporary offices in the nave of the Ferry Building. A *San Francisco Chronicle* article, "Ticket Agents in Ferry Nave," published on May 13, 1906, notes, "The various foreign lines have a committee on location, consisting of the following general agents: Stern of the Canadian Pacific, Ritchie of the Chicago and Northwestern, Canfield of the Chicago, Milwaukee, and St. Paul, Shotwell of the Gould lines and Stokes of Cook & Boas. . . . It is generally agreed . . . that inasmuch as the Ferry Building is conveniently located in respect to the business district, and that the great volume of passenger traffic in and out of the San Francisco flows through the Ferry Building, no more convenient location for freight and passenger offices could be secured than that now occupied in the nave of the Ferry Building." (California History Room, California State Library, Sacramento, California.)

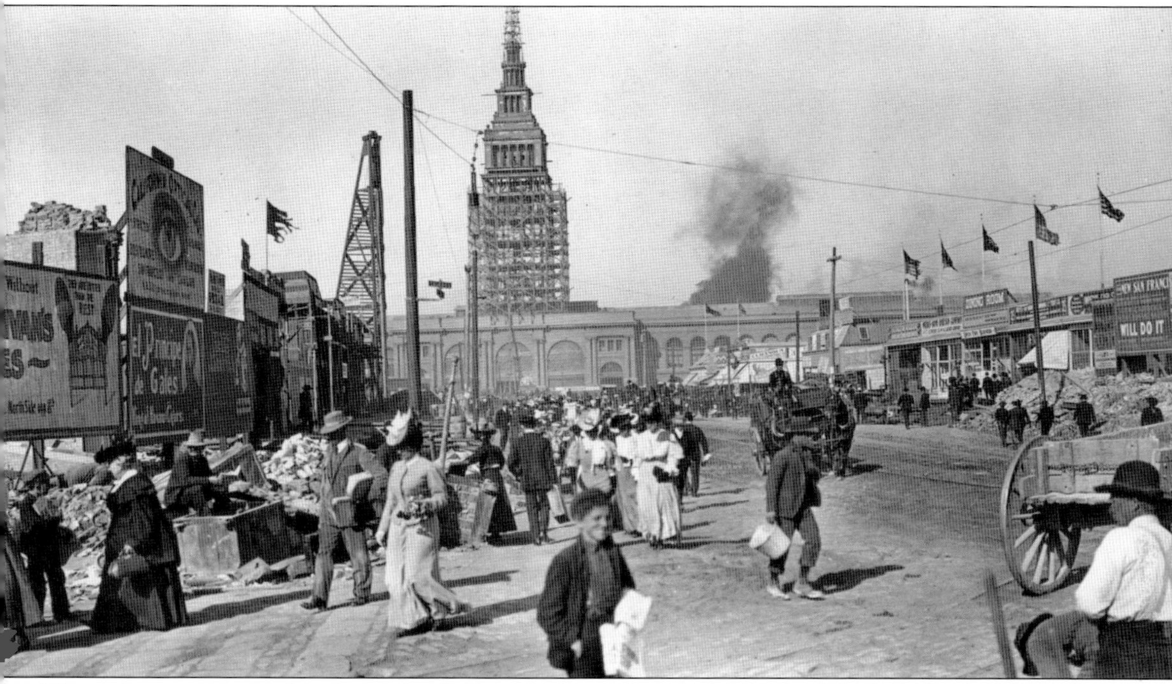

This is a scene on Market Street (with the Ferry Building in the background) during the violent streetcar strike of 1907. More than 1,500 members of the streetcar Carmen's Union struck against the URR on May 5, 1907, demanding an eight-hour day and $3 per day. The URR brought in strikebreakers who were well trained in both the operation of streetcars and the use of firearms. The strike had little support in the press, and it was highly unpopular with most of the public. It was a violent strike. At least six men died of gunshot wounds, over 25 people were killed in streetcar accidents, and more than 1,100 were injured. The strike was broken on September 12, when the General Campaign Strike Committee, acknowledging that the URR had defeated the union, ended its boycott of the company. The strike was officially ended the next March, with the union giving up its charter and dissolving as an organization later that year. (SFMNHP, 1907 A22, 34,197n.)

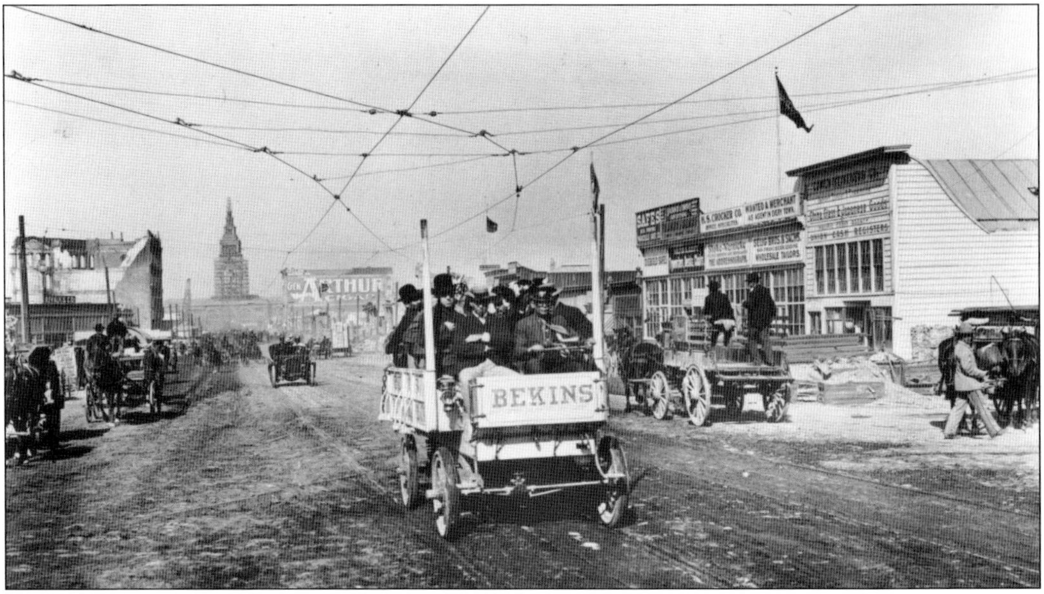

Here is another image from the streetcar strike, with passengers loaded into a cart. There was violence on both sides during the strike. It caused more deaths than any other strike in the history of San Francisco, and it was probably the most violent streetcar workers' strike in any American city. (SFMNHP, 1907 A22, 16,336n.)

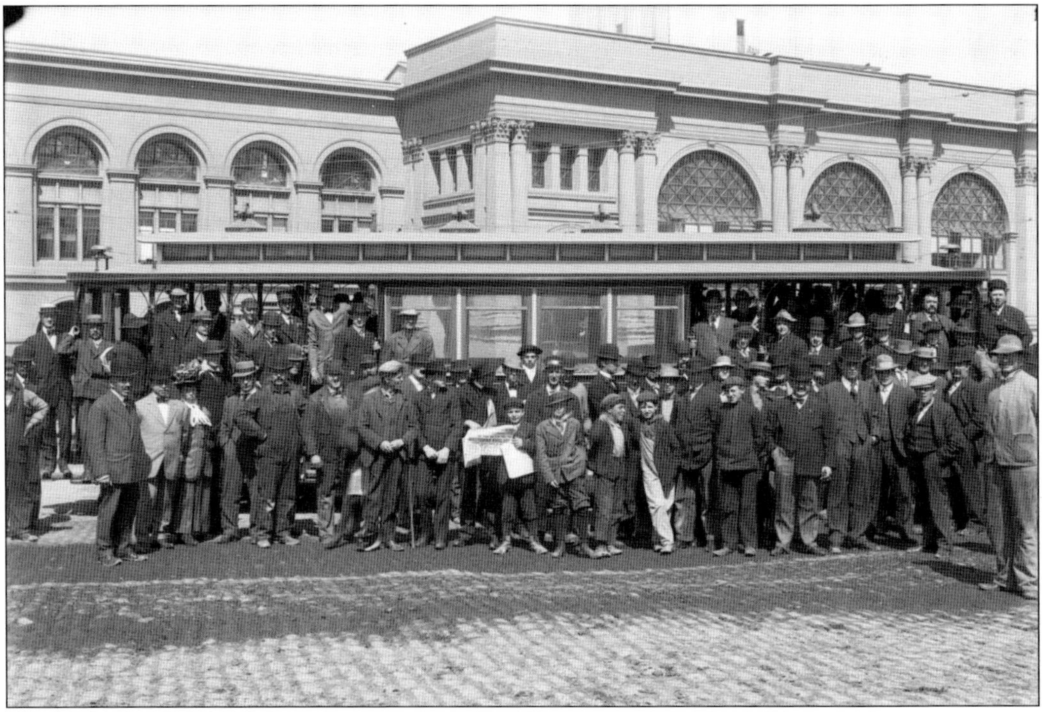

A group of men, many in bowlers, poses on the new Sacramento Street line cable car in June 1908. As electric streetcars replaced cable car lines, by 1912 only eight cable car lines remained, all with steep gradients impassable to electric streetcars. (Photograph by John Henry Mentz, SFMTA Photo Archive.)

Three

A Stunning Landmark

To build a large terminus over water with a limited budget and in earthquake country presented significant engineering and logistical challenges. In November 1892, after the electorate approved by a narrow margin the $600,000 bond issue to build the "Union Depot and Ferry House," the port selected its architect (A. Page Brown) and contractors. The building process did not always go smoothly. Over the next couple of years, the project was delayed by various lawsuits and misfortunes, including the loss of more than 3,000 piles during a gale while the piles were en route from Coos Bay, Oregon, and a lawsuit about the Colusa stone that was to be used on the facade.

A. Page Brown's original design called for a building 840 feet in length, but when costs ran too high for cement, it was decreased to 660 feet. The Ferry Building's steel frame was constructed atop 5,000 Oregon pine piles and a reinforced concrete foundation. In an 1898 report to the Board of State Harbor Commissioners, Edward R. Swain, who served as supervising architect and finished the building after the untimely death of architect Brown, states, "There were used in the construction of the building about 5,000,000 pounds of steel and cast iron; 2,000 cubic feet of granite; 30,000 square feet of marble; 53,000 cubic feet of sandstone; 1,450,000 common brick; and 125,700 square feet of expanded metal and concrete floor arches. There are also about 40,000 square feet of mosaic flooring, and 375,000 pounds of galvanized iron, including roofing."

In the end, as noted in the *San Francisco Chronicle* on January 11, 1895, the Ferry Building was acknowledged as "a magnificent structure and a matter of pride not only to this city, but also to the entire State . . . a fitting entrance to the metropolis. . . . This city has gone beyond the provincial period and is becoming metropolitan, and with this advancement comes the new ferry depot."

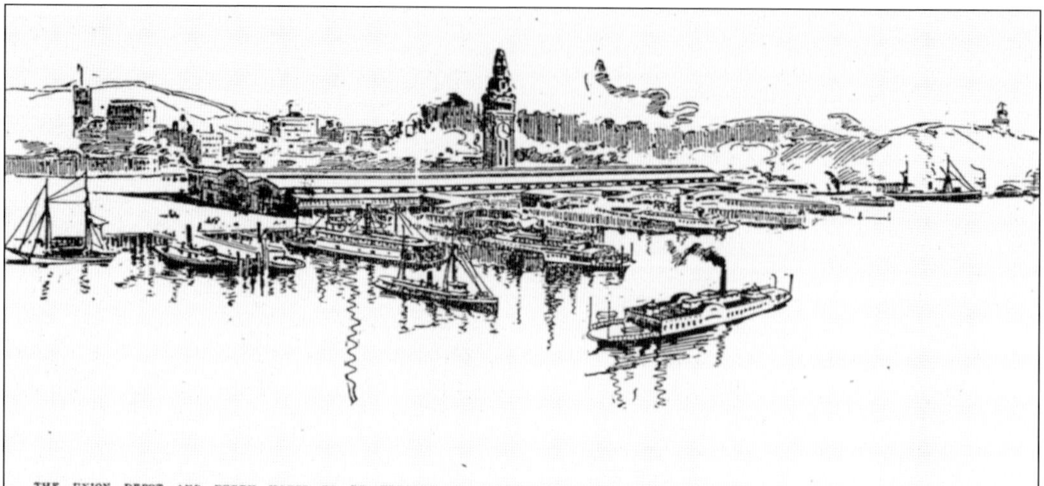

THE UNION DEPOT AND FERRY HOUSE TO BE ERECTED AT THE FOOT OF MARKET STREET—FROM THE DESIGN BY A. PAGE BROWN.

A. Page Brown, in his 1893 proposal to the port commissioners, included an eight-foot-wide-by three-foot-tall painting by Charles Gratham, showing the proposed Union Depot and Ferry House from the water. The *San Francisco Chronicle* then asked Gratham to produce an illustration from his painting, seen here. In an article dated January 11, 1895, the *San Francisco Chronicle* describes the illustration: "It gives a comprehensive view of the new ferry building and its slips, with the steamers passing to and fro and the grand clock looming up above." In the illustration below, also from the *San Francisco Chronicle*, one can see the grand entrances at either end that were in Brown's original plan, but when the bids for the foundations came in much higher than expected, the port commissioners decided to delete them to keep costs under control. (Both, San Francisco Public Library.)

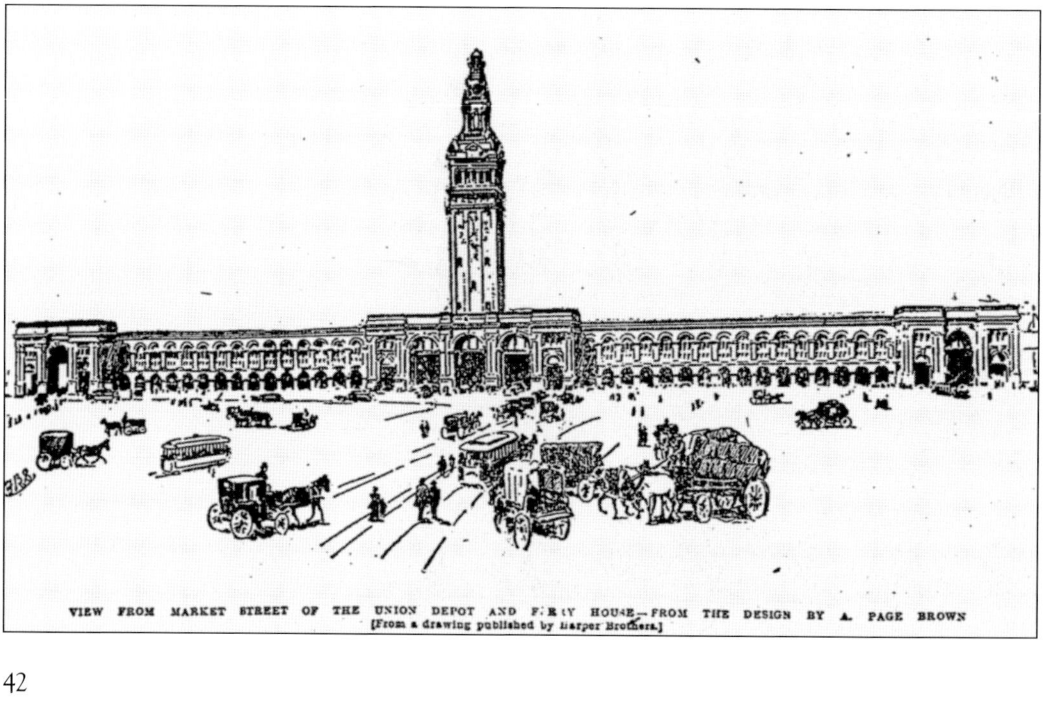

VIEW FROM MARKET STREET OF THE UNION DEPOT AND FERRY HOUSE—FROM THE DESIGN BY A. PAGE BROWN
[From a drawing published by Harper Brothers.]

Pile drivers, known as pile butts, were some of the many workers who built the waterfront. Some pile drivers, most likely members of the Pile Drivers, Bridge and Structural Iron Workers Union No. 77, pose in front of a pile-driving rig in ferry slip No. 3 behind the Ferry Building. Even with advances in machinery, materials, and construction methods, driving piles was hard and dangerous work. As labor historian Archie Green notes in his discussion of pile-driver history (*Wobblies, Pile Butts, and Other Heroes: Laborlore Explorations*, published in 1993), pile drivers were responsible for "construction, reconstruction, repairing, removing, and wrecking of wharves, piers, docks, bridges, viaducts, towers, masts . . . pile driving in all its branches; cutting off and capping of piles, abutments, foundations, submarine or other work. . . . Operation of all derricks, tools or machinery necessary in performing any of the aforesaid work." (Both, SFMNHP, Kebb/Baker Photos p77-011 [151-155].)

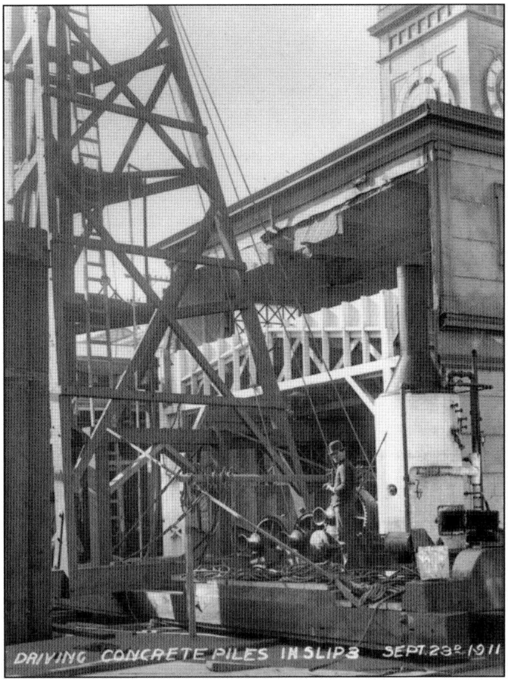

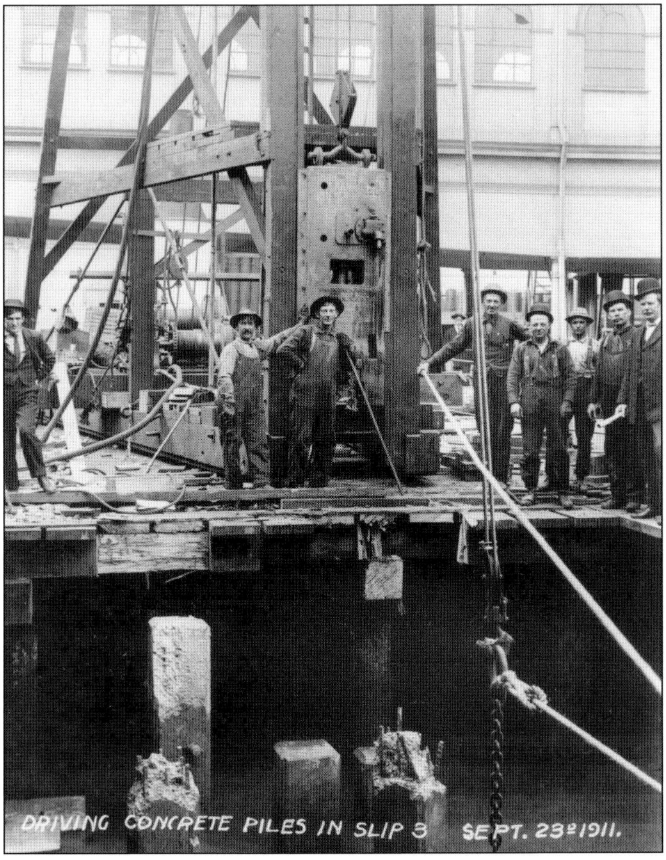

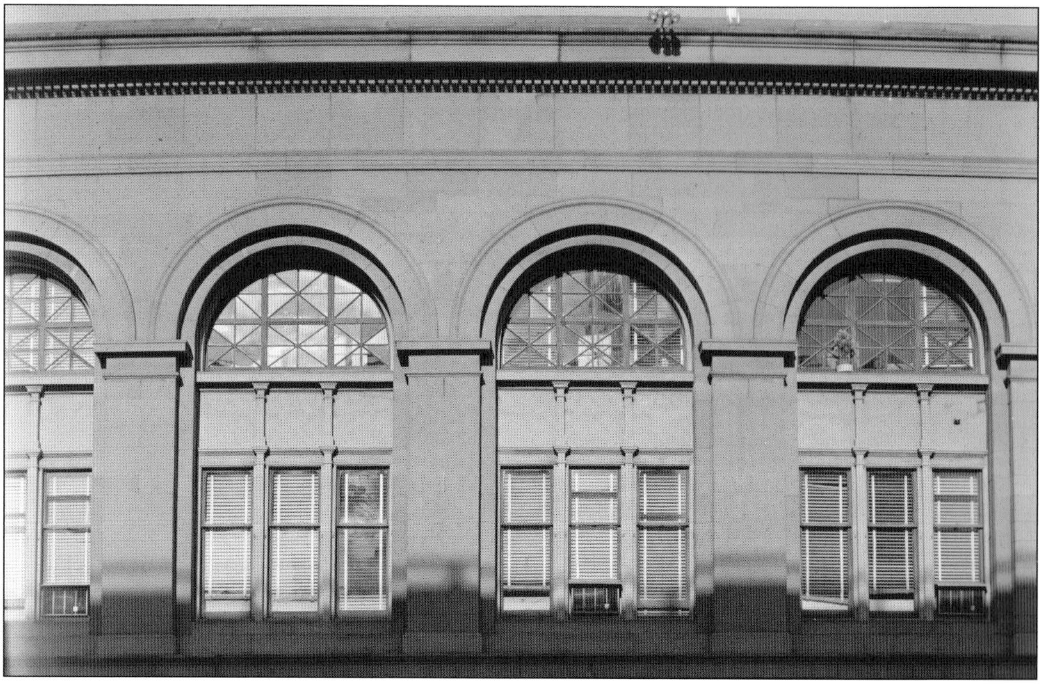

The Ferry Building's windows and skylight are among its most distinctive features. The arched *clathri*, or lattice of bars, sit atop each set of triple windows. The original building had 220 clerestory windows. Clerestory windows are used on an upper zone of a wall, to admit light to the center of a lofty space. (Library of Congress.)

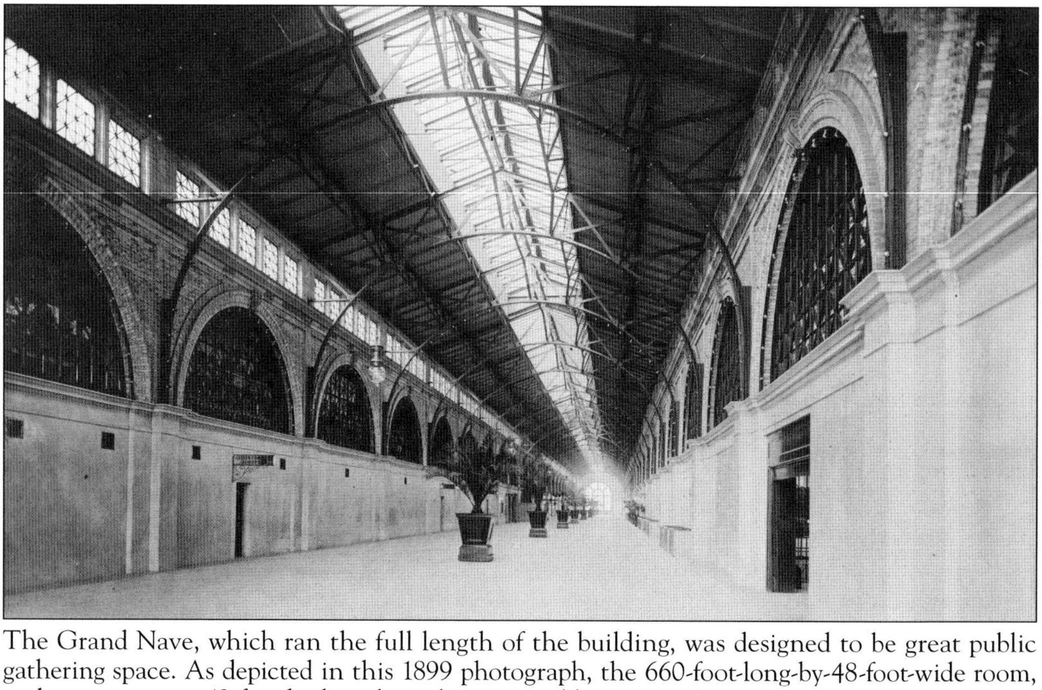

The Grand Nave, which ran the full length of the building, was designed to be great public gathering space. As depicted in this 1899 photograph, the 660-foot-long-by-48-foot-wide room, with its two-story, 42-foot-high ceiling above a marble mosaic floor, was an elegant room from the start. It was used for many exhibits and banquets. (Library of Congress.)

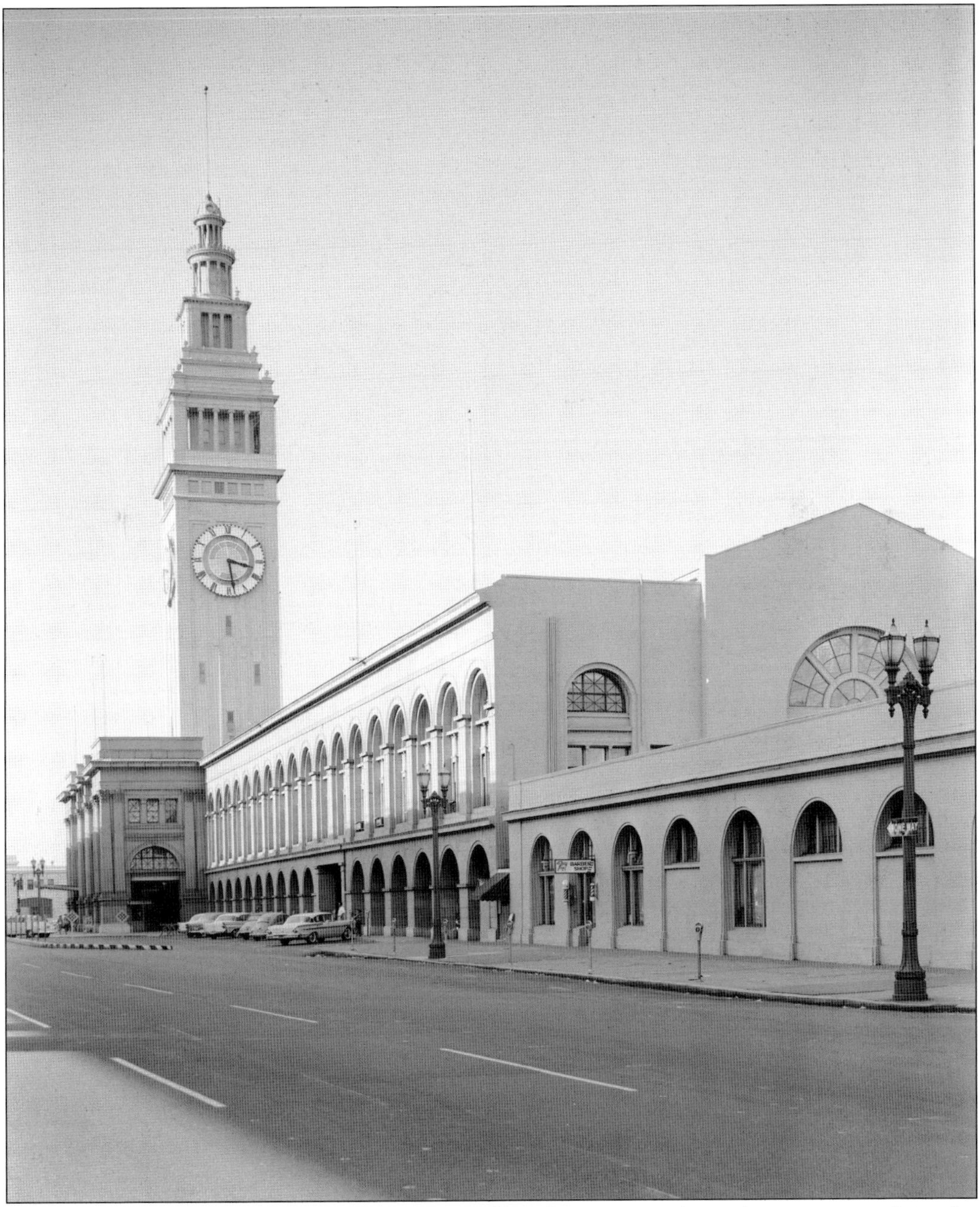

A. Page Brown traveled to Europe in 1892 to collect depot views. According to an article in the *San Francisco Examiner*, published on August 2, 1895, "He returned with what is pronounced the finest collection of depot views ever seen in this country. Included in the pictures was one of the Saint-Lazare depot in Paris, and this was decided as being best suited [as a possible design for the Ferry Building]." An 1898 report to the Board of State Harbor Commissioners notes, "There has been no attempt at decorative features in the design, the outline and proportion giving simplicity, elegance, and grandeur, which if carried out, will make the building compare favorably with the great structures of similar character which have been erected during the last few years about New York harbor and other points in this country and Europe." (Library of Congress.)

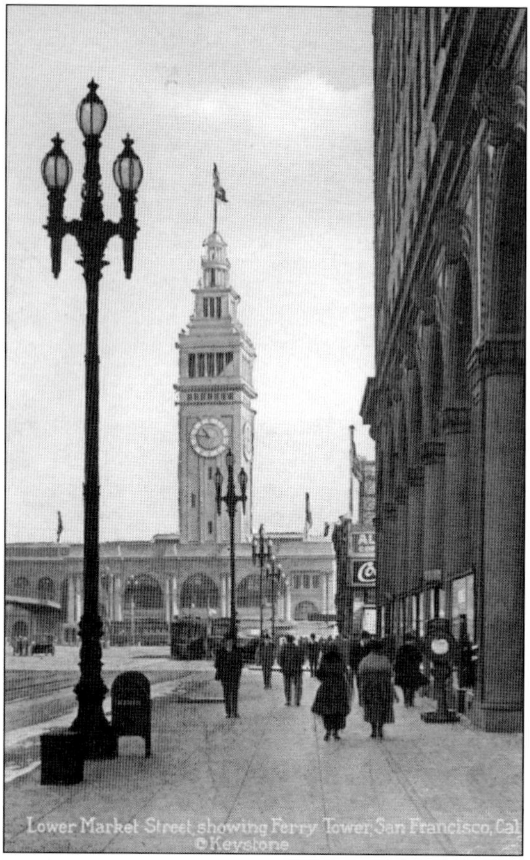

Pedestrians walk towards the building from lower Market Street. Architect Brown designed the tower to be directly on axis with both Market and Commercial Streets, and aligned with the Embarcadero. It is visible all along Market Street, from the hills to the north, south, and west, as well as from the water and the Bay Bridge. (Author's collection.)

This cornerstone at the Ferry Building lists A. Page Brown as architect, and Edward R. Swain as supervising architect. Brown was in a horse-and-buggy accident that severely injured him in October 1895, and he died in January 1896. When Brown could not supervise the construction of the new building, as his contract with the harbor commissioners stipulated, Swain stepped forward. (Joe Mabel.)

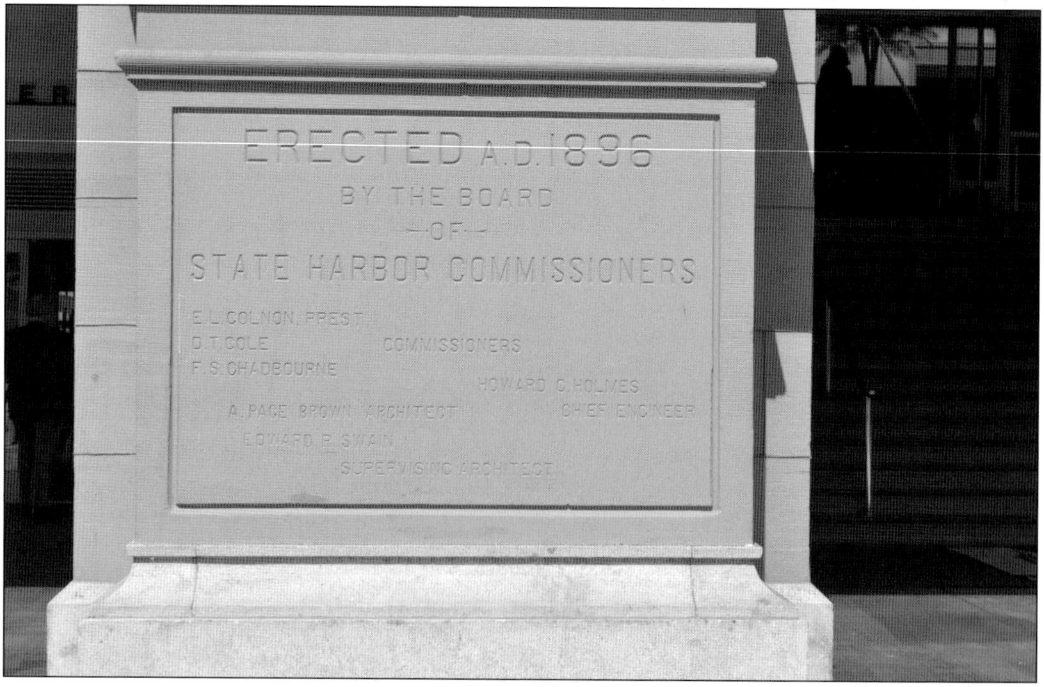

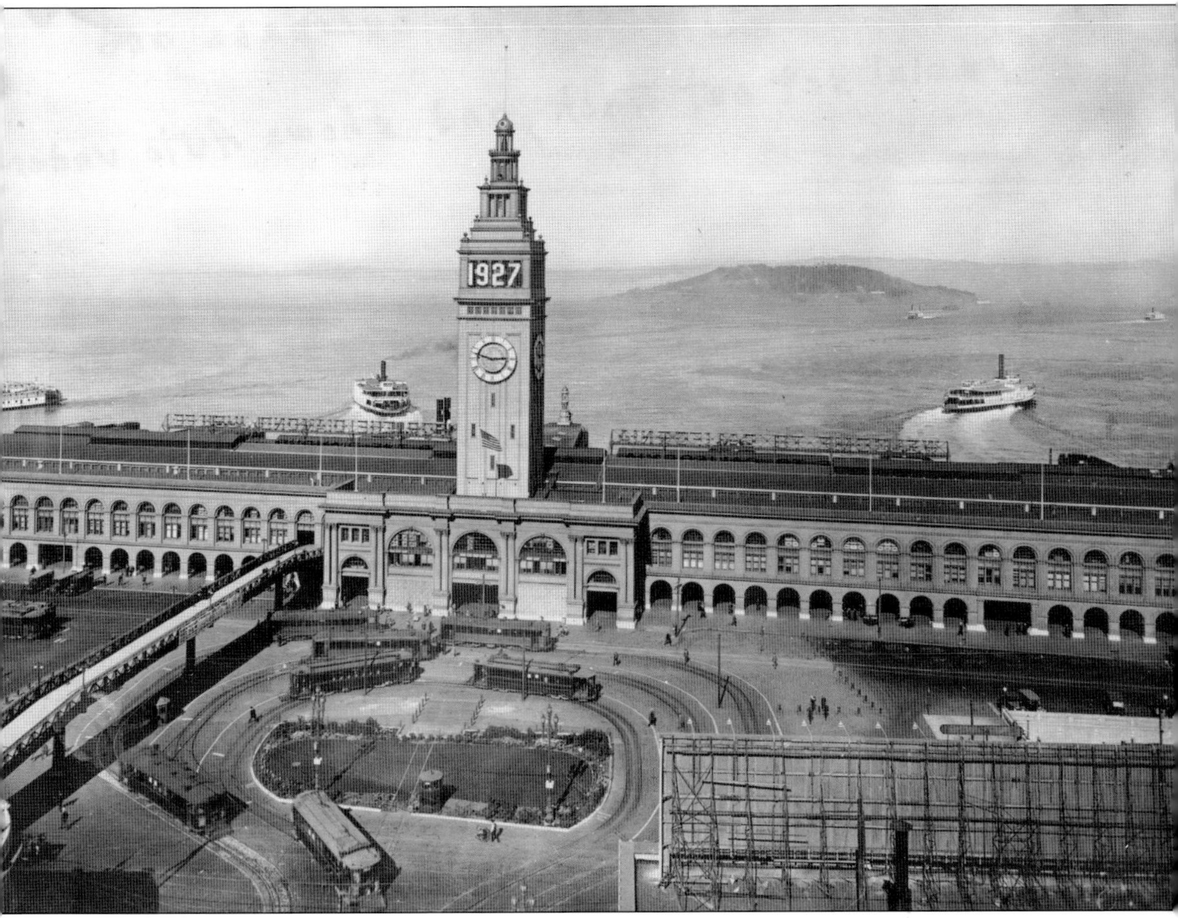

The 1920s and 1930s were busy times for San Francisco transportation. Ferryboats connected via the Ferry Building to four steam railroads and five interurban systems with 29 streetcar and cable car lines. In this image, the double streetcar loop is in front of the building with the pedestrian overpass at left, which was built in 1917 to allow passengers to walk directly into the second-floor level to avoid the cars and trams in front of the building. Out of range of the photograph is the 958-foot automobile subway that extended from Mission to Merchant Streets and opened in 1925. It helped manage the congestion in front of the Ferry Building and, by 1926, was used by over 11,000 vehicles a day. Some ferries carried both automobiles and passengers, and drivers could line up and then drive though express sheds onto the lower automobile deck of the ferry. (Photograph by John Henry Mentz, SFMTA Photo Archive.)

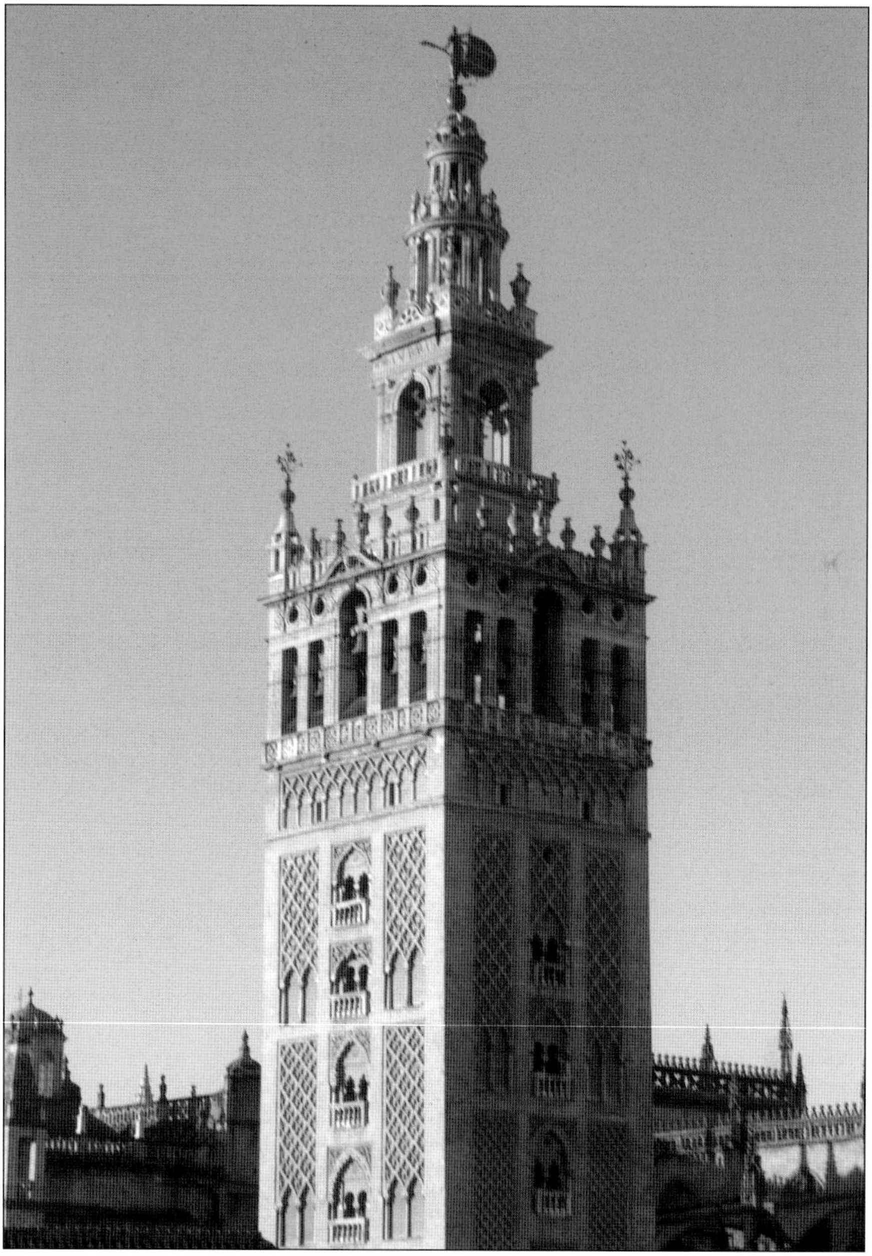

Architect A. Page Brown supposedly modeled the Ferry Building's 245-foot clock tower on the Giralda Tower of the Cathedral of Seville, shown here. The Giralda Tower, completed in 1198 and 342 feet high, was originally built as a minaret during the Moorish period. Spaniards added a Renaissance-style top. As historian Kevin Starr notes in *Inventing the Dream: California through the Progressive Era*, "The Spanish tower asserted an element of imagination, of lightness and grace, which San Francisco also had need of in its skyline." Other buildings in the United States that have or have had replicas of the Giralda include the Wrigley Building in Chicago (1920), the second Madison Square Garden in New York City (1890; demolished in 1926), the Biltmore Hotel in Coral Gables, Florida, (1926), and the Terminal Tower in Cleveland (1930). (Miguel Hermoso.)

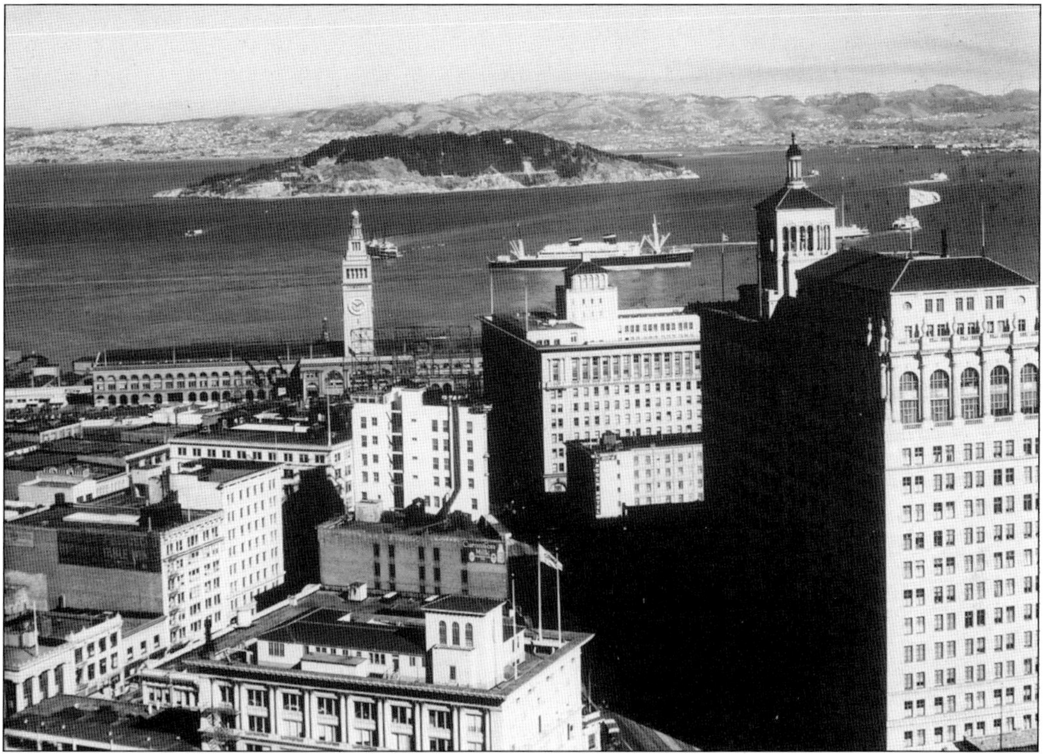

In this aerial photograph of the San Francisco Bay, taken from the Shell Building (100 Bush Street) in the early 1930s, one can see five ferries and Yerba Buena Island. Market Street is in the center, with California Street coming in on the left. (SFMNHP, Morton & Co. Studio A20.39,700.)

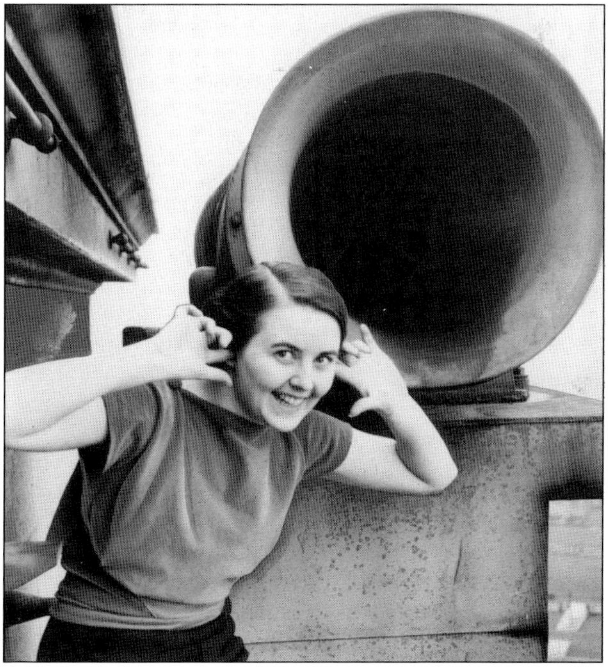

The electric siren on the tower, capable of an instant blast, was installed in 1919. It was used to mark big events and dockworker shifts. Invented by Harry C. Heath, the siren could be heard all the way to Mount Diablo. Mary Dakin, pictured here in 1933, playfully plugs her ears just in case the siren goes off. (San Francisco History Center, San Francisco Public Library.)

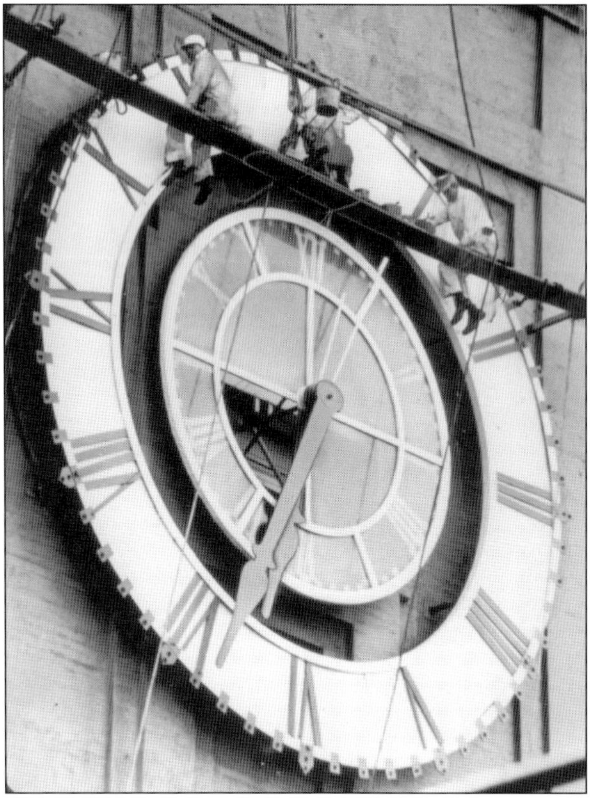

The Ferry Building clock incorporates four 22-foot-diameter clock dials, with 11-foot-long minute hands. It was installed in 1898 as a pendulum clock by the J. Howard Clock Company of Boston. Originally a 900-pound weight and pendulum system, it needed to be wound every seven days. In 1919, it was transformed into an electric clock, powered by an independent battery system. However, the weights and pendulum are still there and can be used to keep the clock going if something happens to the batteries. (Both, San Francisco History Center, San Francisco Public Library.)

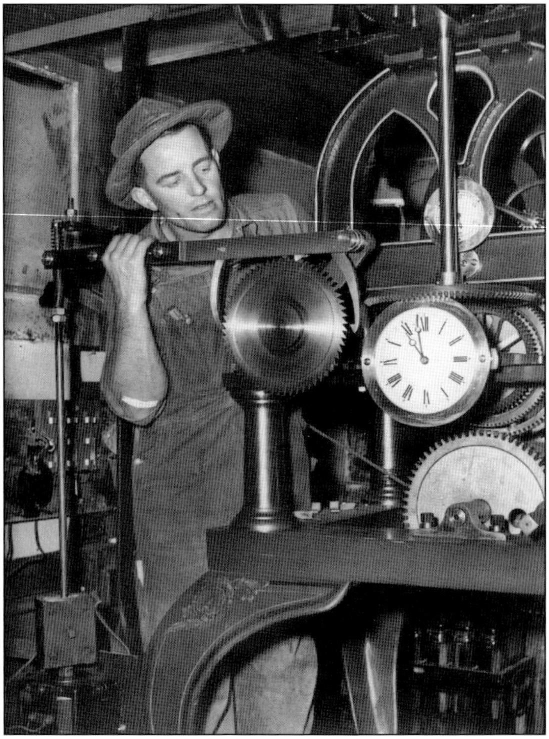

Four

Celebrations and Daily Life

Architect A. Page Brown, although he did not live to see the Ferry Building finished, envisioned that the structure would be a stunning public space. Brown believed that all great cities needed covered promenades like the Grand Nave, where San Francisco's urban population could easily circulate. The large nave, with its 24 steel trusses and a skylight, has been the scene of many gatherings, from fairs to celebrate California's citrus crops to receptions for visiting US presidents.

As historian Kevin Starr observes in *Inventing the Dream: California Through the Progressive Era* (published in 1998), "Brown wanted an aerial pageant of steel and skylight and space, intended to sweep above a continuous pageant of human activity. . . The ferry depot was thus San Francisco's actual and symbolic point of linkage with the outside world . . . a building that would serve as a citywide point of reference, an architectural expression of San Francisco's dawning ambition to become a center of world trade and a busy point of arrival and departure for international traffic."

Over the years, in addition to the thousands of daily commuters going in and out of the building, there have been parades that start at the Ferry Building and proceed up Market Street to celebrate holidays, victorious sports teams, and returning soldiers, to protest wars and controversial labor practices, and for countless other occasions that merit a gathering of San Franciscans.

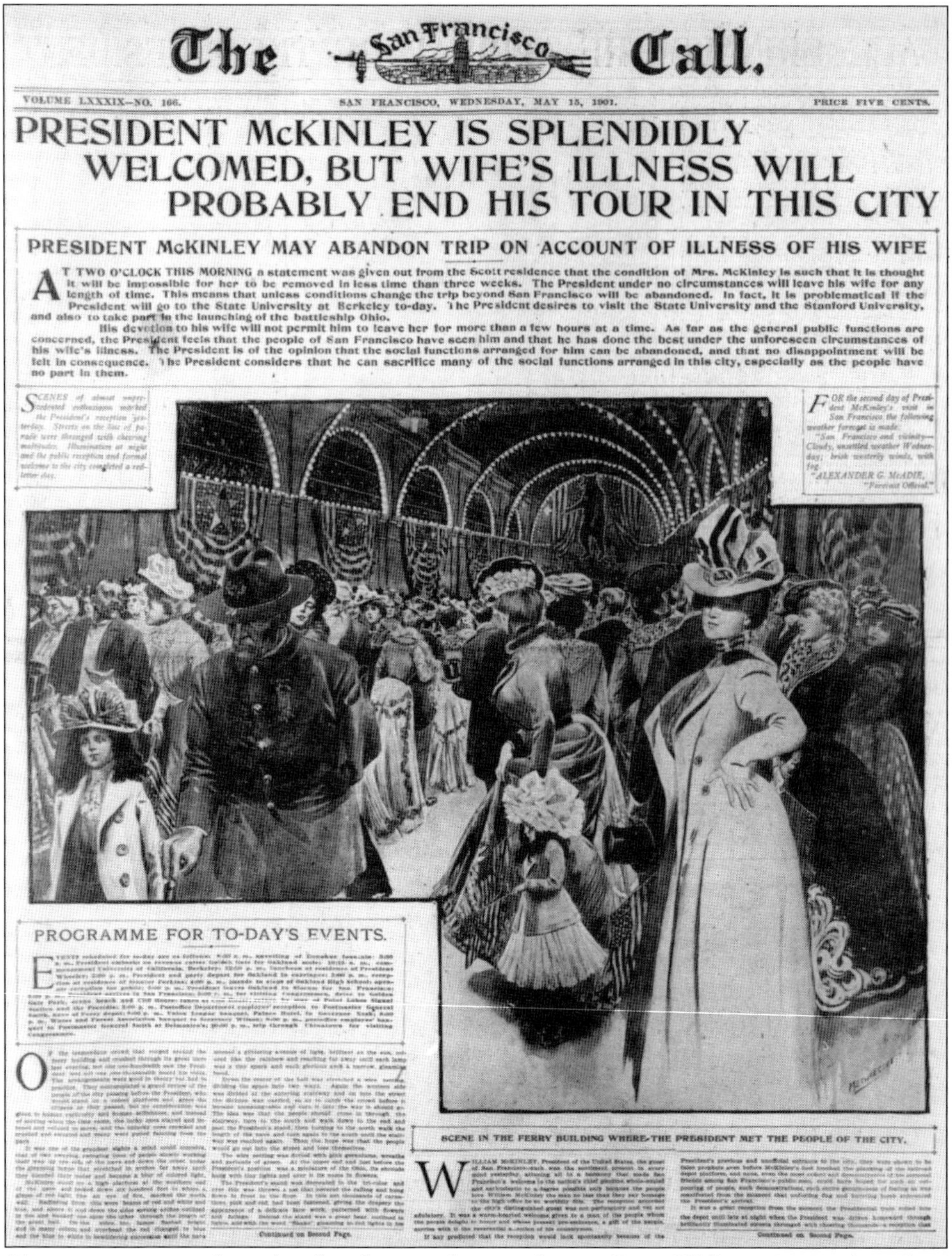

The San Francisco Call.

VOLUME LXXXIX—NO. 166. SAN FRANCISCO, WEDNESDAY, MAY 15, 1901. PRICE FIVE CENTS.

PRESIDENT McKINLEY IS SPLENDIDLY WELCOMED, BUT WIFE'S ILLNESS WILL PROBABLY END HIS TOUR IN THIS CITY

PRESIDENT McKINLEY MAY ABANDON TRIP ON ACCOUNT OF ILLNESS OF HIS WIFE

AT TWO O'CLOCK THIS MORNING a statement was given out from the Scott residence that the condition of Mrs. McKinley is such that it is thought it will be impossible for her to be removed in less time than three weeks. The President under no circumstances will leave his wife for any length of time. This means that unless conditions change the trip beyond San Francisco will be abandoned. In fact, it is problematical if the President will go to the State University at Berkeley to-day. The President desires to visit the State University and the Stanford University, and also to take part in the launching of the battleship Ohio.

His devotion to his wife will not permit him to leave her for more than a few hours at a time. As far as the general public functions are concerned, the President feels that the people of San Francisco have seen him and that he has done the best under the unforeseen circumstances of his wife's illness. The President is of the opinion that the social functions arranged for him can be abandoned, and that no disappointment will be felt in consequence. The President considers that he can sacrifice many of the social functions arranged in this city, especially as the people have no part in them.

SCENES of almost unprecedented enthusiasm marked the President's reception yesterday. Streets on the line of parade were thronged with cheering multitudes. Illumination at night and the public reception and formal welcome to the city completed a red-letter day.

FOR the second day of President McKinley's visit in San Francisco the following weather forecast is made: "San Francisco and vicinity—Cloudy, unsettled weather Wednesday; brisk westerly winds, with fog. "ALEXANDER G. McADIE, "Forecast Official."

PROGRAMME FOR TO-DAY'S EVENTS.

SCENE IN THE FERRY BUILDING WHERE THE PRESIDENT MET THE PEOPLE OF THE CITY.

Continued on Second Page.

Continued on Second Page.

San Franciscans turned out by the thousands to welcome Pres. William McKinley, the 25th president of the United States, to San Francisco in 1901. In the Ferry Building nave, the president stood on an elevated stand decorated with white carnations from 8:00 to 11:00 p.m., while well-wishers filed by waving small American flags. "Every person attending the reception is requested to come prepared for this unique compliment to the Nation's chief . . . Myriads of little red, white and blue electric globes will brighten the long tesslated hall," reads an article in the May 14, 1901, issue of the *San Francisco Call*. American flags and evergreen garlands were strung along the arched ceiling. A mile of Market Street was aglow with Japanese lanterns lighting the approach to the Ferry Building, while 1,200 National Guardsmen and 125 policemen were stationed in and around the building to manage the crowds. (Library of Congress.)

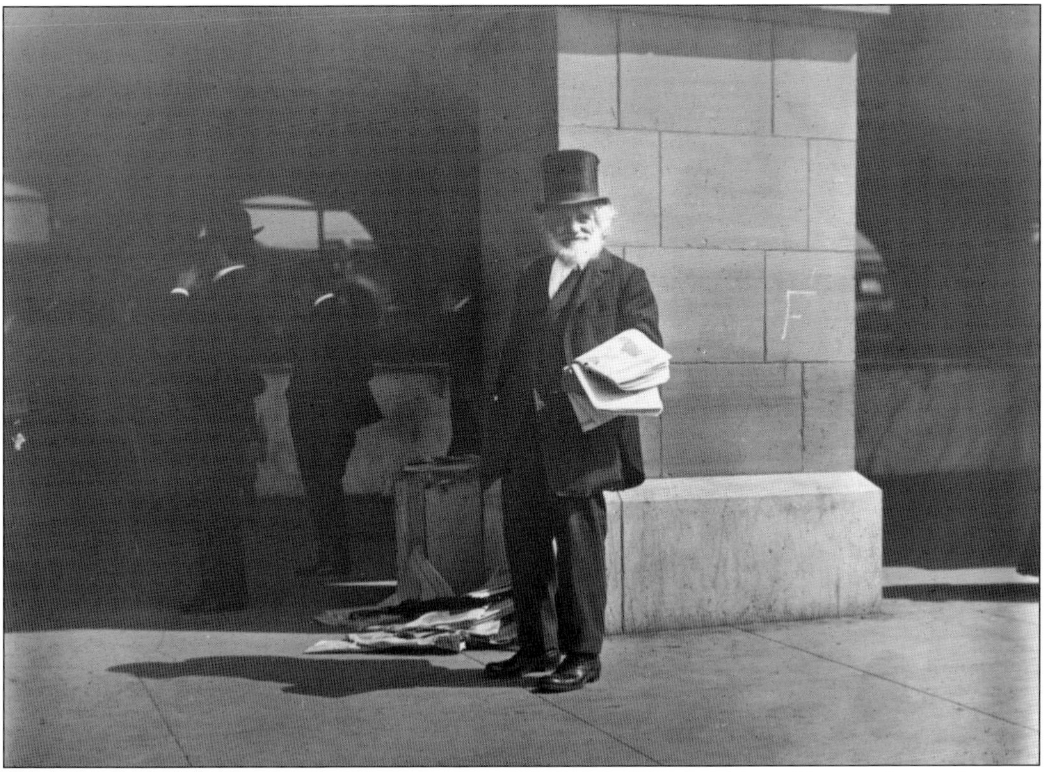

The Ferry Plaza was a prime place for news vendors to sell their papers. Here, a dapper-looking newspaper vendor in a top hat sells the latest edition at the entryway to the Ferry Building, next to one of the Corinthian columns, around 1900. As thousands of commuters arrived, they could pick up a paper to read on the ferry. (OpenSFHistory/wnp13.201.)

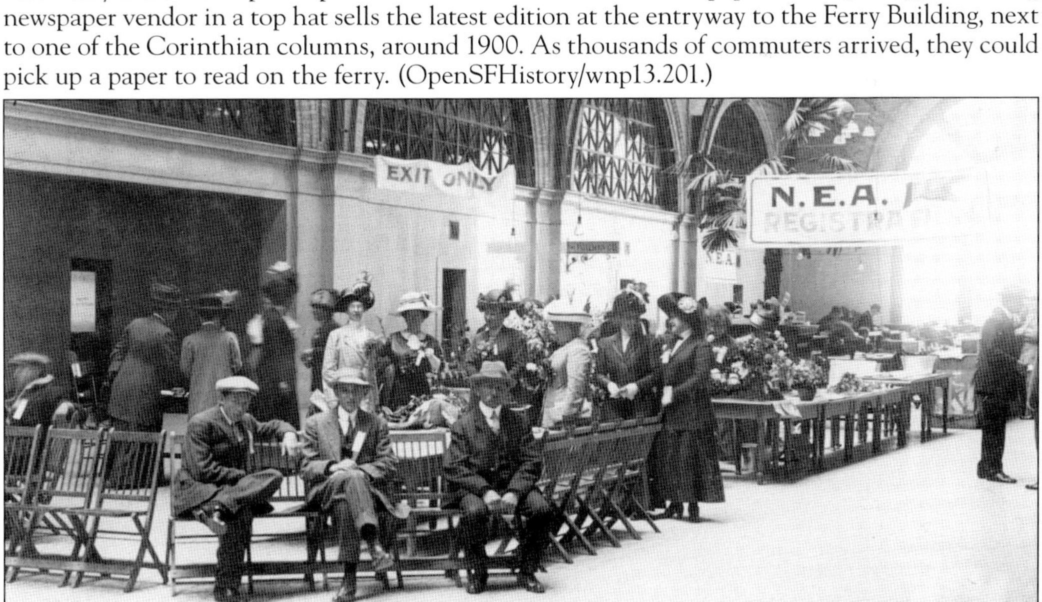

Registration tables are set up in the south end of the Grand Nave for members of the National Education Association around 1911. Light pours in from the windows as the ladies chat and the men wait. The Ferry Building was perfectly situated for gatherings like this. (Author's collection.)

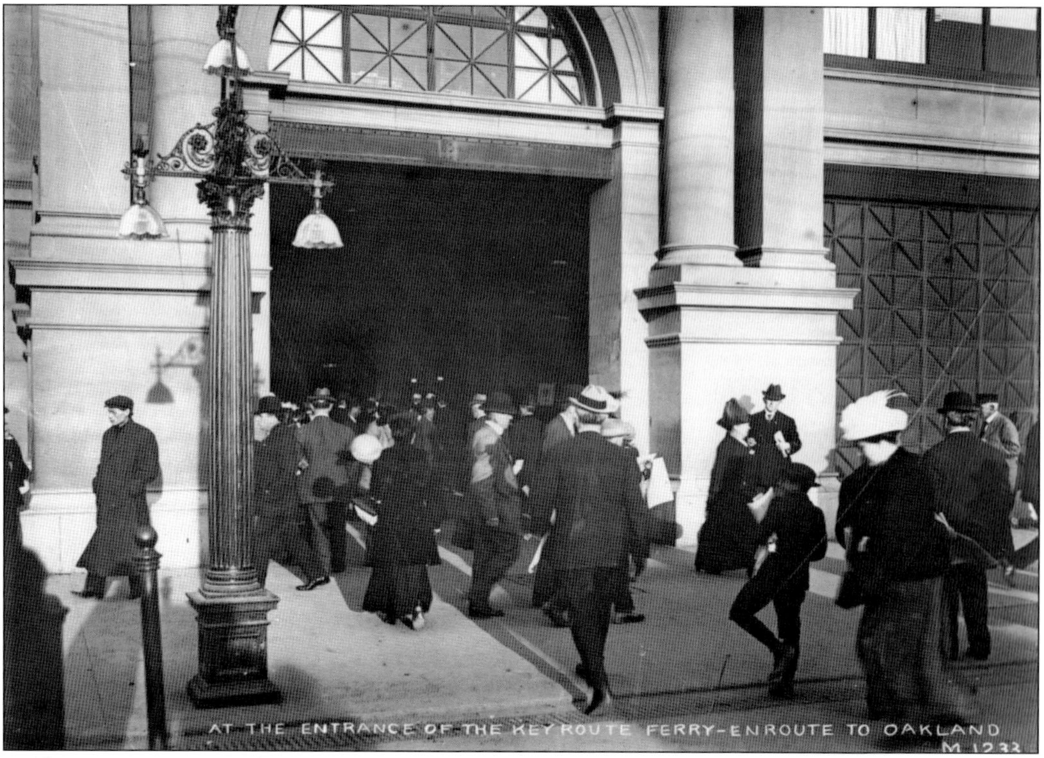

In these c. 1910–1915 photographs, passengers pass through the graceful archways to enter the building. The 28-foot-tall arches, with glazed latticework in repetitive patterns flanked by pairs of 35-foot Corinthian columns, extend from the ground nearly to the top of the building, creating a beautiful, distinctive entryway. Once in the building, as noted in the *San Francisco Chronicle* issue on January 11, 1895, prior to the building's opening, "The beauty of the entire arrangement for travelers will be that everything will be under cover. A passenger can come over from San Rafael, leave the upper deck of the steamer, walk along the corridor, go to the ticket office and procure transportation to Oakland, board the proper steamer on the upper deck and be under cover all the time. The system of receiving and delivery baggage . . . will be of great benefit, especially to those who are obliged to use the ferry system in traveling from one part of the State to another." (Above, SFMNHP, p80-124, 20nl; below, San Francisco Port Commission.)

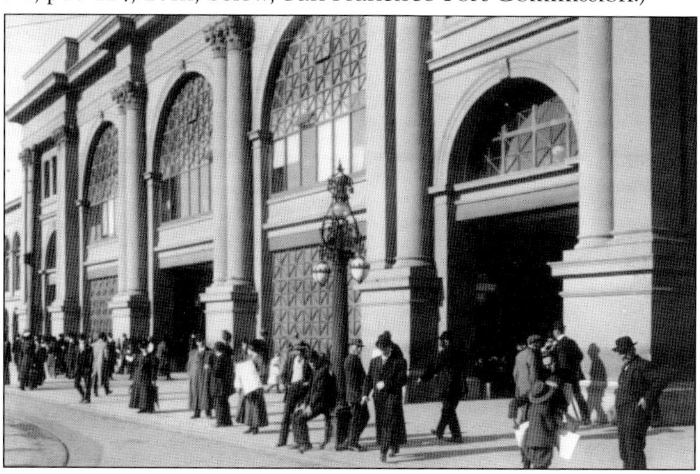

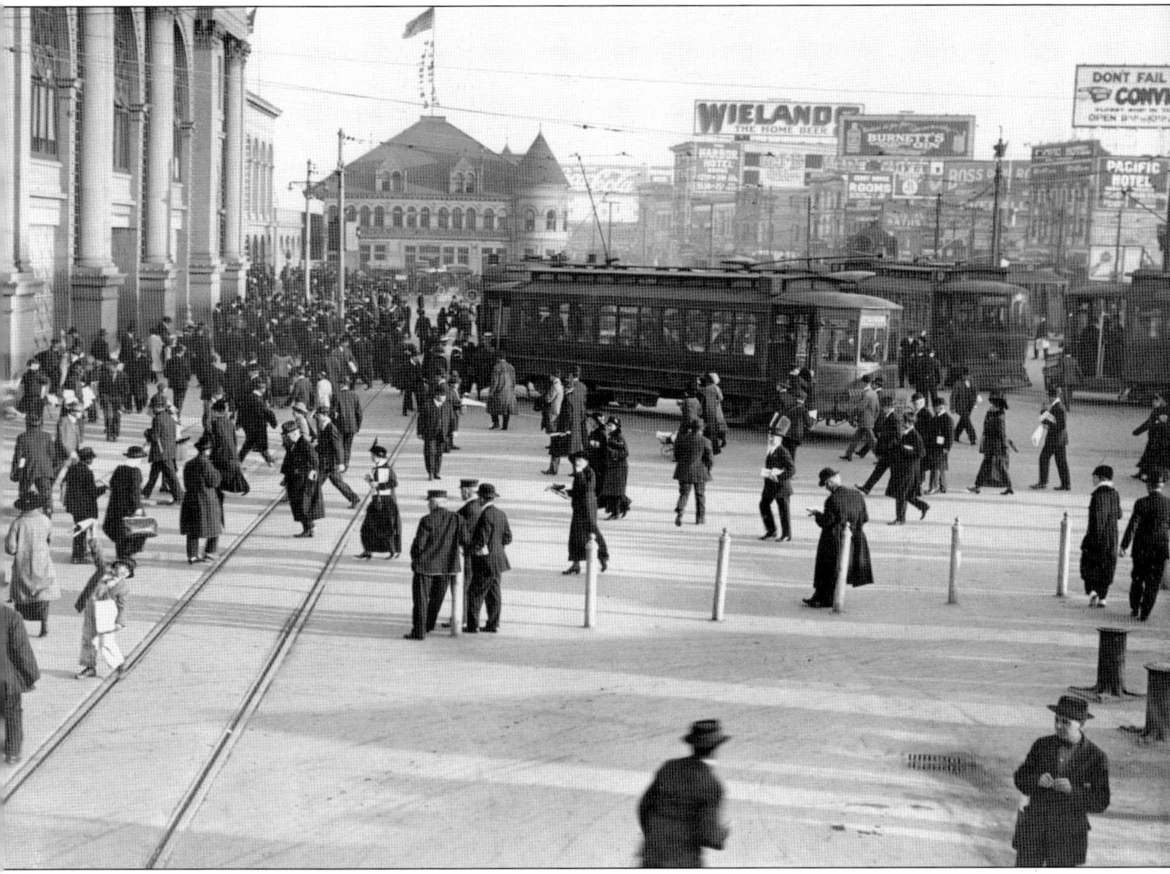

A moment in time is captured on March 2, 1915, at 5:20 p.m. In 1913, about 60,000 commuters passed through the Ferry Building in the morning and again in the evening, riding the 23 ferry boats that made 180 trips a day. In 1915, the Panama-Pacific International Exposition (PPIE) was in full swing, having opened in late February. Throngs of commuters rush to catch their ferries home, crossing the State Belt Railroad tracks that run in front of the Ferry Building. The castle-like, turreted post office (built in 1905 and replaced in late 1915) is in the background, with flags flying, probably in celebration of the PPIE. It was the busiest post office in San Francisco, as all transcontinental mail came through this office, which had direct pier-level access for waterfront deliveries. Billboards for Boss of the Road overalls, Wieland's Home Beer, and Burnett's London Gin advertise their wares for commuters and tourists alike. (SFMNHP, Ted Wurm Collection, Neg. 163.)

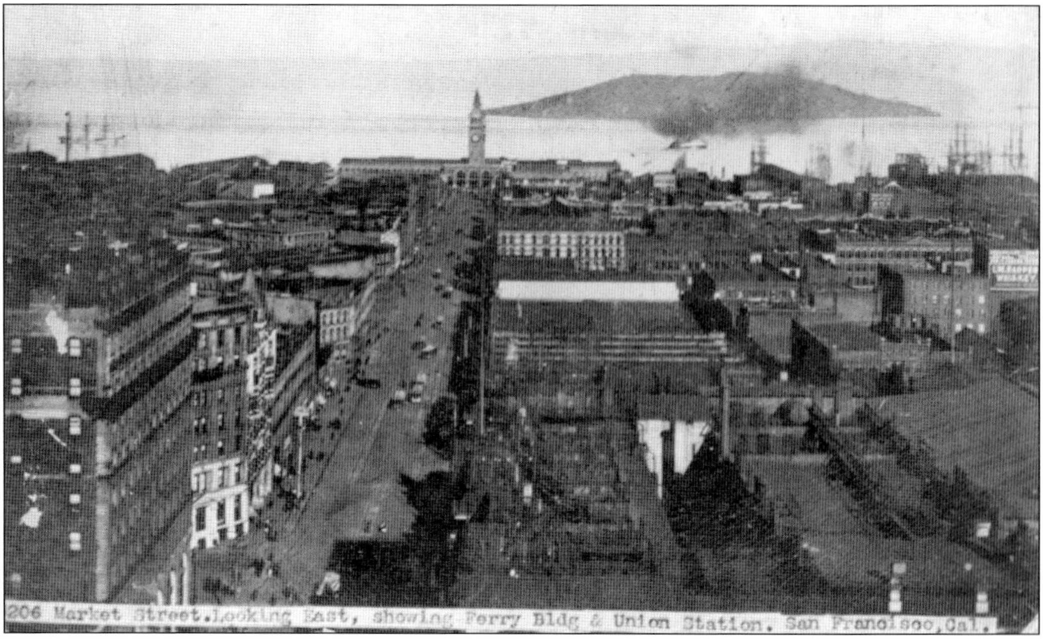

The Ferry Building's location at the foot of Market Street made it a visual anchor point for city celebrations. The 1906, pre-earthquake postcard above shows how dramatic the building's clock tower looked on the horizon. Soldiers parade down Market Street in 1899 with the Ferry Building in the background in the image below. The parade was to welcome the soldiers back from the Philippines, where they fought in the Philippine-American War (1899–1902). These "Fighting First" boys, as they were known, were among the first infantry units to fight in the war, and arrived back in San Francisco on July 13, 1899, where they were met with a hero's welcome, including a banquet in the nave of the Ferry Building. (Above, author's collection; below, Golden Gate NRA, Park Archives, Martin Berhman Negative Collection, GOGA 35346 CB-019.)

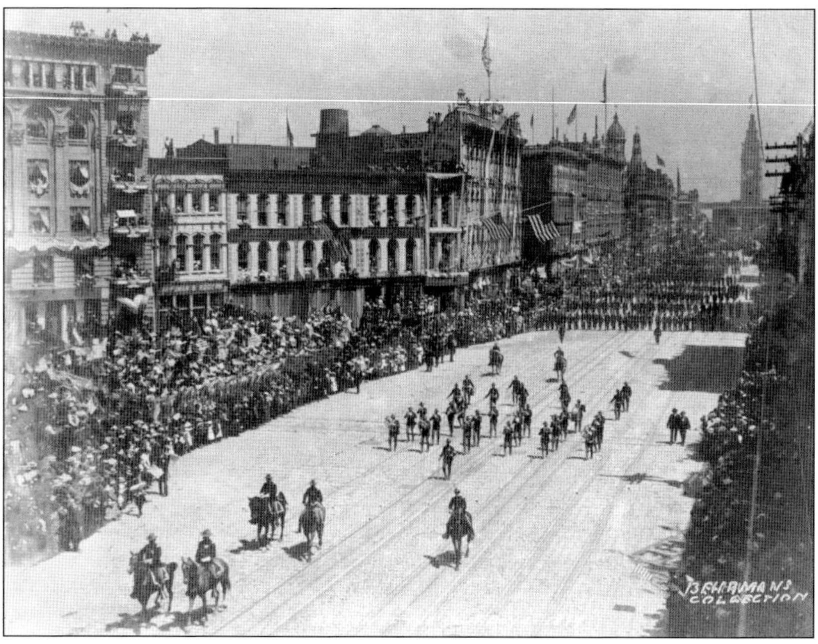

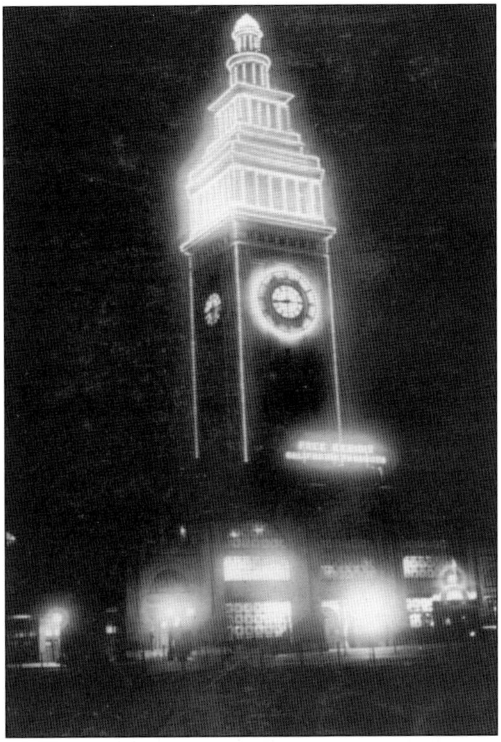

In late November 1902, a citrus fair, sponsored by the State Board of Trade, officially opened in the Ferry Building nave. To celebrate, the tower was illuminated. The electric sign reads, "Free Exhibit. California Products." Fifteen thousand people a day attended the 10-day fair, the largest citrus fair held in the state, including tens of thousands of schoolchildren. As reported in the *San Francisco Chronicle* on November 28, 1902, during the fair, "the Stockton Boys' Band, a juvenile organization of 30 pieces, played a musical programme, which included several instrumental solos . . . the youthful bandsmen sounded a resounding welcome to the public and played to gladden the hearts of the 300 Stockton people who came down for the occasion." (Right, San Francisco Port Commission; below, California History Room, California State Library, Sacramento, California.)

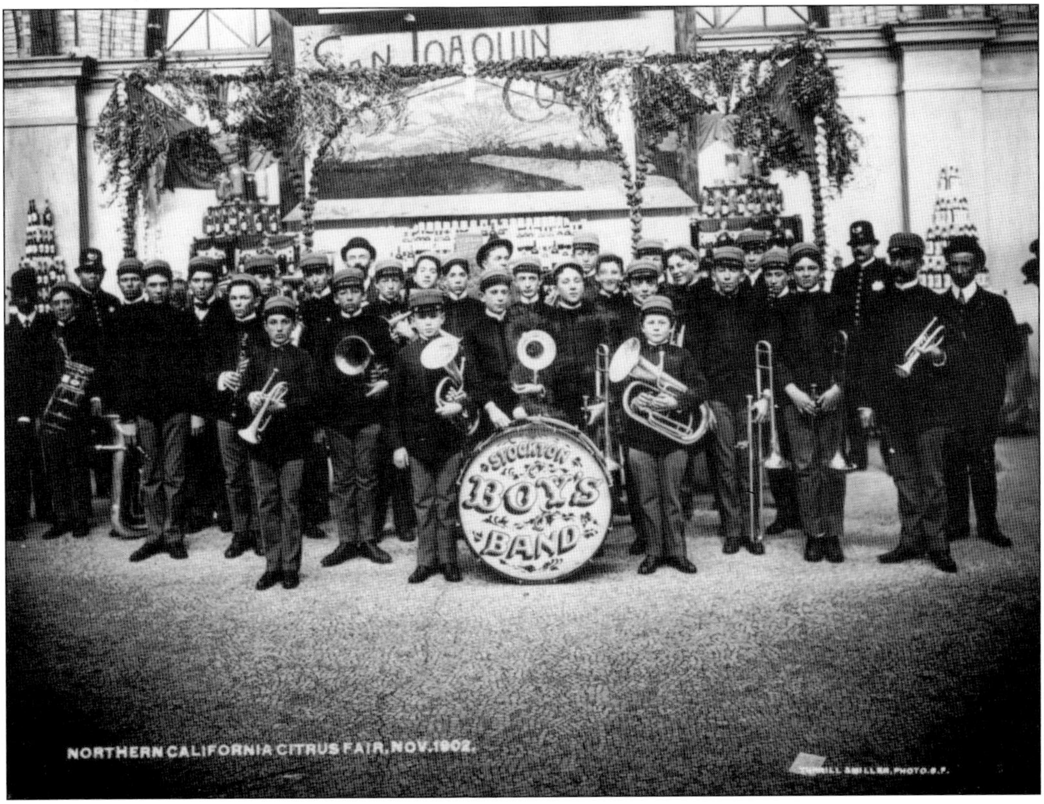

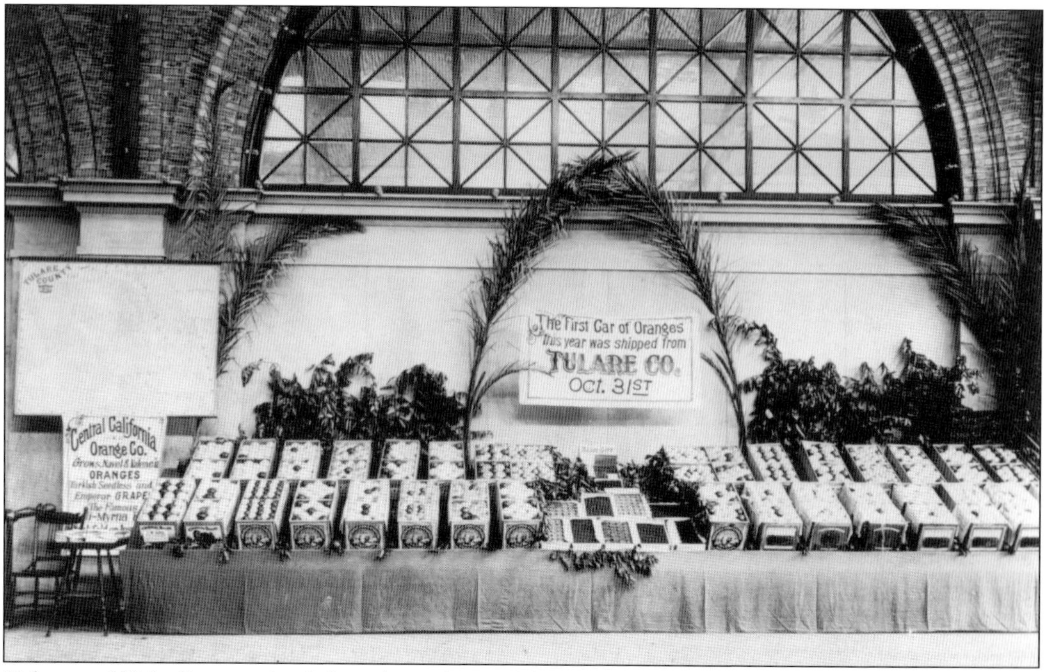

Tulare and Yolo Counties' exhibits show the wealth of their agricultural offerings. The date ("Oct. 31st") on Tulare's booth is to prove that counties in Central and Northern California could ship their fruits ahead of counties in Southern California, which was one of the goals of the exhibition. In the words of secretary J.A. Filcher of the State Board of Trade, published in the *San Francisco Chronicle,* on November 16, 1902, "The fair . . . will prove that the entire territory of California below an altitude of 1,000 feet and within a certain distance from the coast is a great citrus belt. Hitherto the counties adjacent to Los Angeles have assumed that the citrus belt is confined to that locality. The fair will be an evidence that this is not true." (Both, California History Room, California State Library, Sacramento, California.)

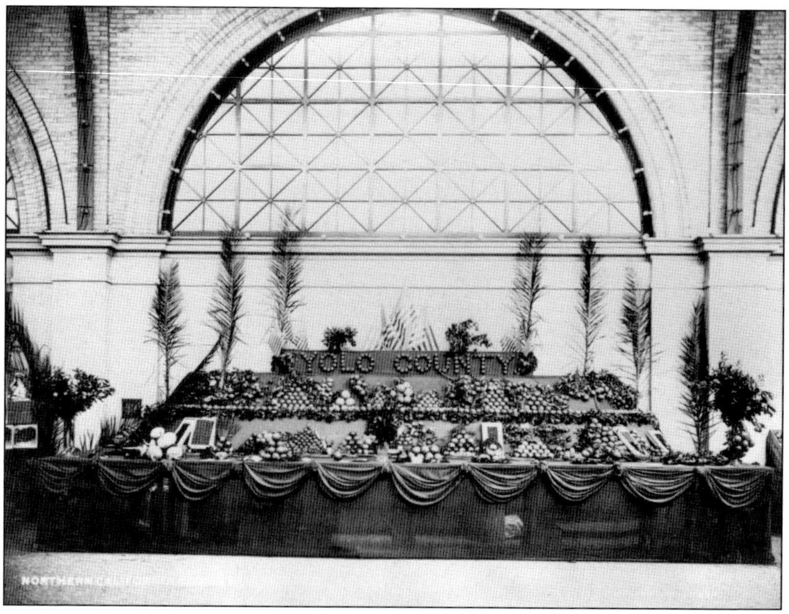

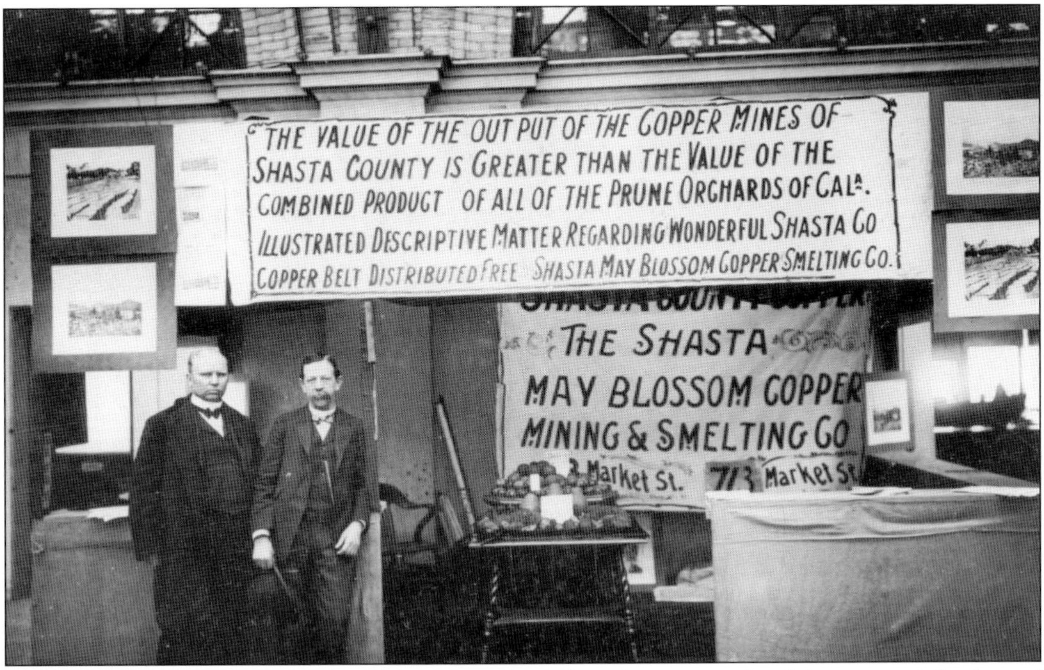

Most counties at the fair displayed citrus products, but there were also "flowers and displays of California perfumery and copper mines and California wines," according to the *San Francisco Chronicle* on November 26, 1902. Shasta County's sign declares, "The value of the output of the copper mines of Shasta County is greater than the value of the combined product of all the prune orchards of Cala." (California History Room, California State Library, Sacramento, California.)

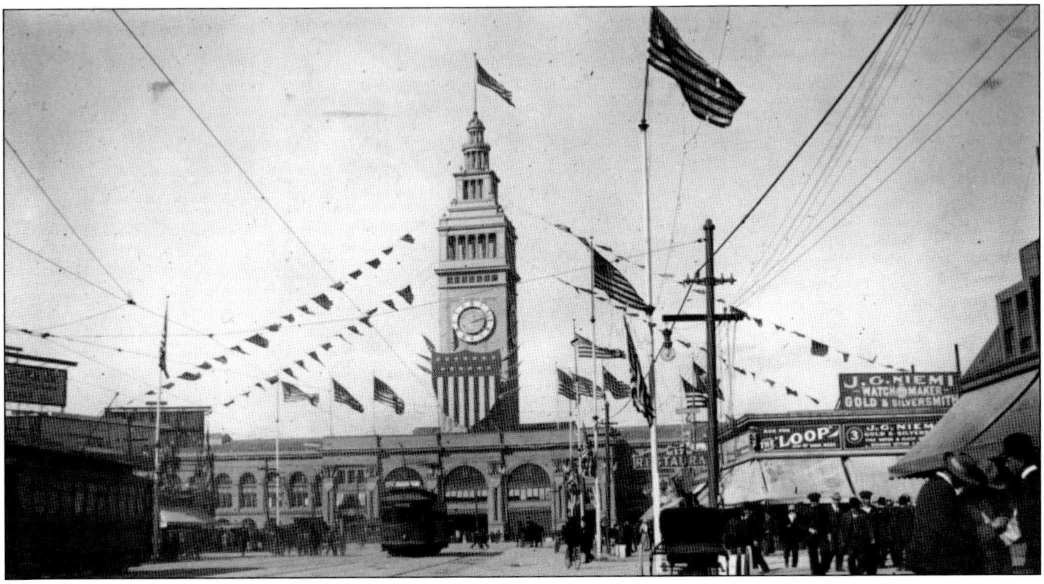

The Ferry Building celebrates the arrival in San Francisco of the "Great White Fleet" in May 1908: 16 American warships, support vessels, and 14,000 men. Painted white and gold, the ships cruised worldwide (43,000 miles, 20 ports of call on six continents). Pres. Theodore Roosevelt's aim was not only to promote goodwill, but also to show the world that the United States had become a major sea power. (SFMNHP, A12, 4523n.)

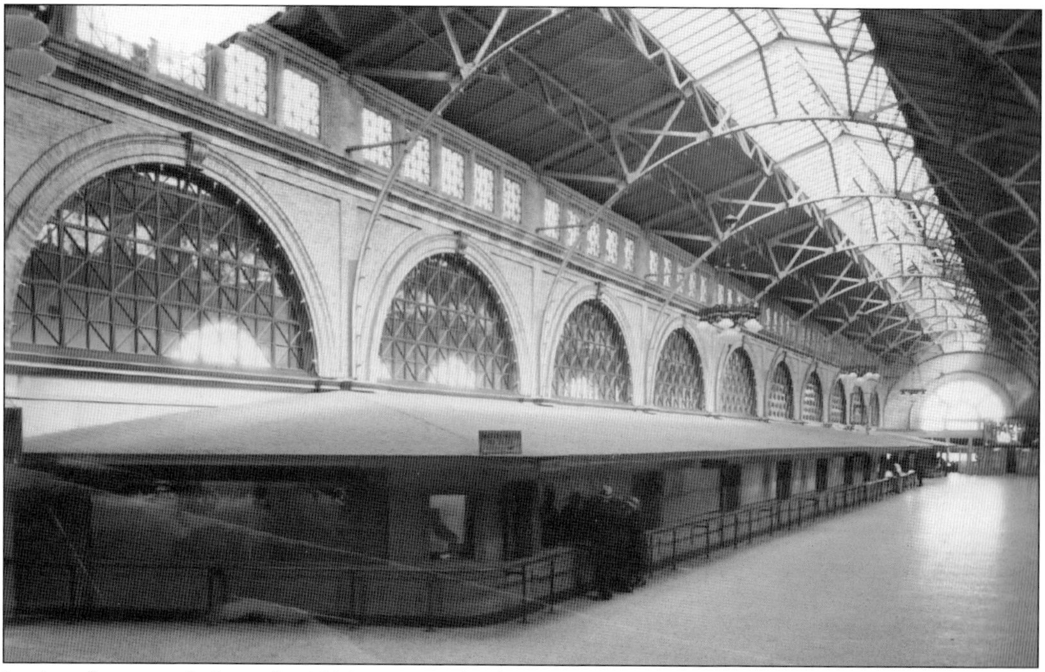

In this photograph from the 1920s, visitors look at "Paradise in Panorama," a 450-foot-long-by-18-foot-wide California diorama—a scale model of the entire state—that was on display along the bay side of the nave from 1924 until 1955. (National Register of Historic Places.)

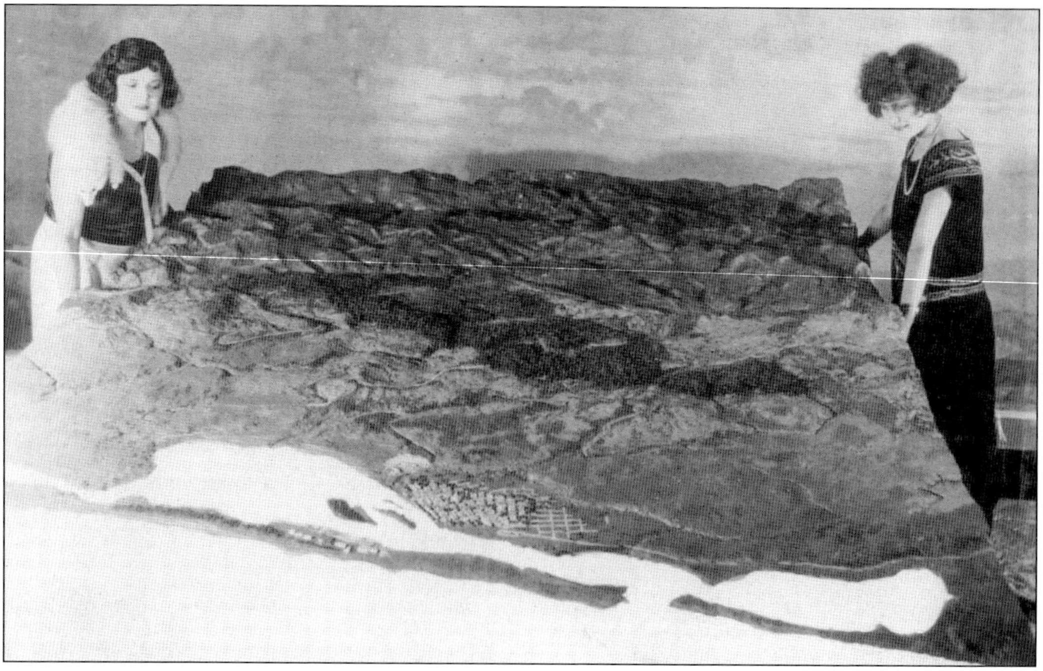

The three-dimensional relief map, when it was unveiled to great fanfare in 1924, was the largest map in the world. Department store mogul Reuben Hale came up with the idea for the map. It was created in 14 months by 25 artists, geographers, and craftsmen in a rented movie studio in Glendale, California. (Neil Malloch.)

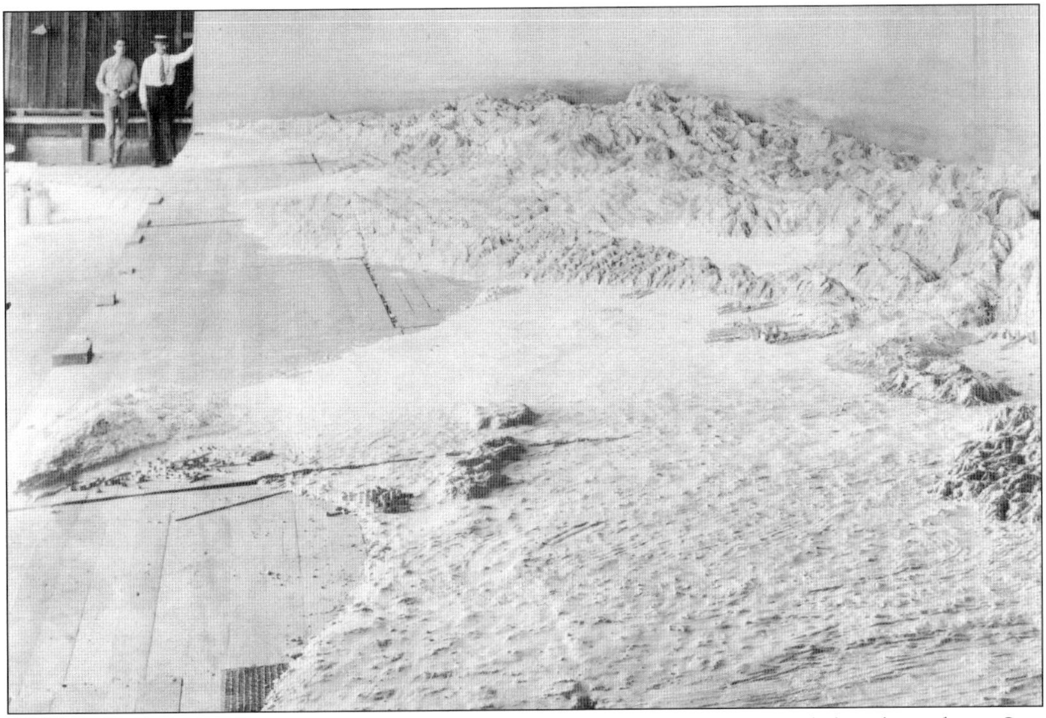

The map, which cost $147,000, was built in four-by-seven-foot sections and then brought to San Francisco in six box cars. Built to a linear scale of six inches to one mile, it had almost 600,000 models of buildings, bridges, roads dams, ships, railroads, river, mountains, and towns. Over 1,000 business and government leaders attended its unveiling in November 1924. (Neil Malloch.)

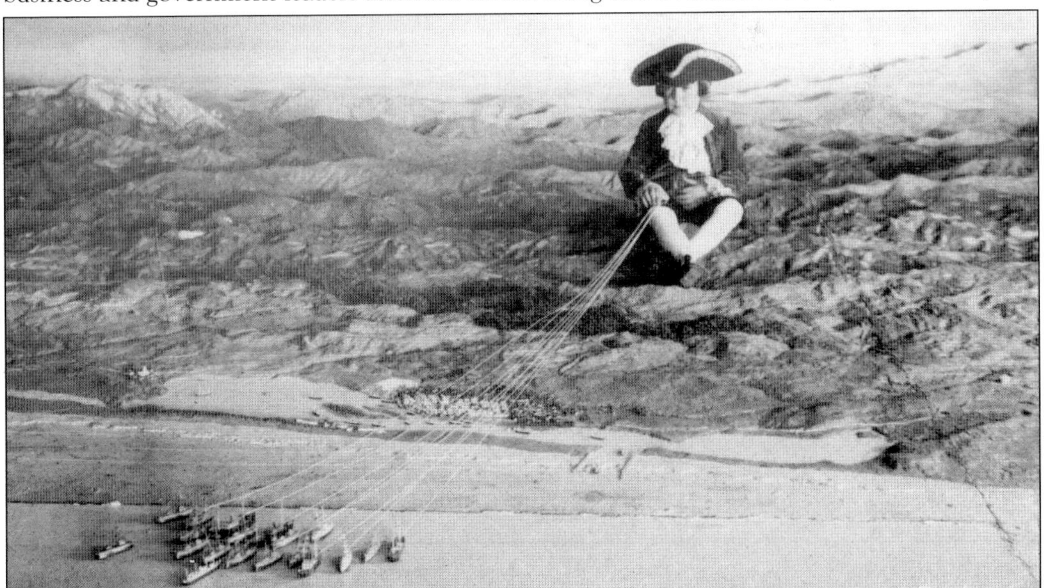

Millions of ferry commuters viewed the map in the 30 years it was on display. Damaged in the mid-1950s during a remodeling project at the Ferry Building, it was cut up into sections and put into storage in 1960. The Port of San Francisco now has it stored in 230 crates (which weigh about 70 tons total) at a warehouse. (Neil Malloch.)

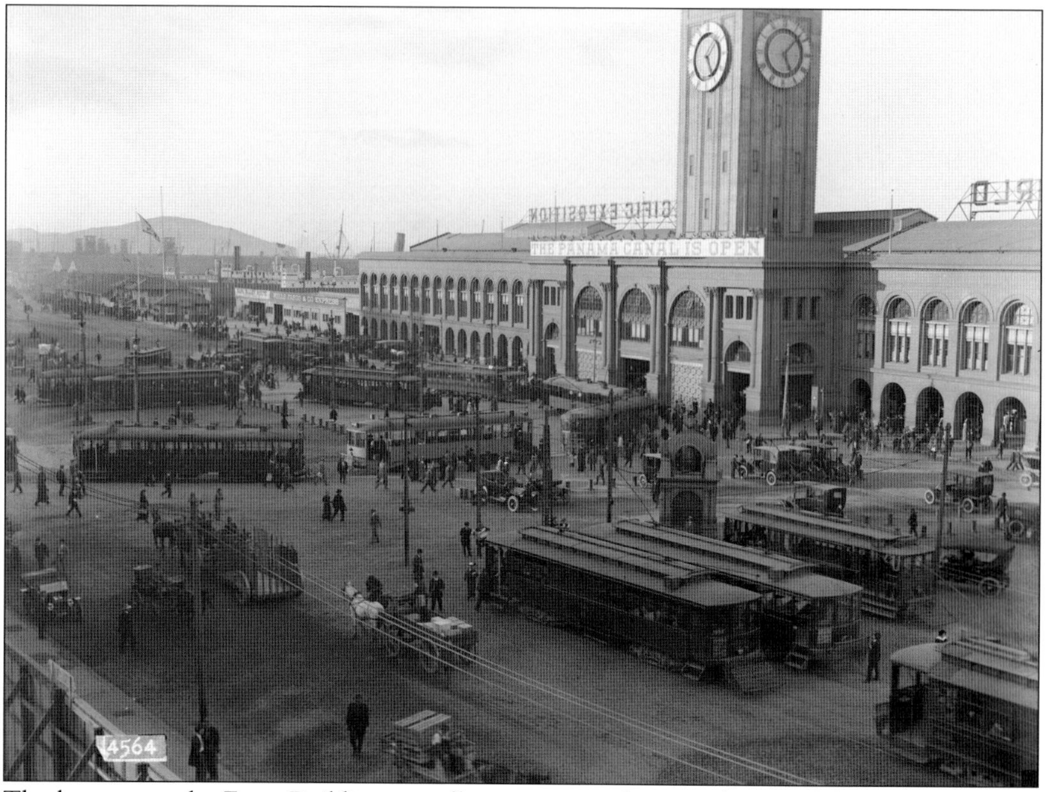

The banner on the Ferry Building proudly announces the completion of the Panama Canal. San Francisco was readying itself for its signature world's fair, the Panama-Pacific International Exposition. The event was not only to celebrate the completion of an engineering marvel, the Panama Canal, but also to prove to the world that San Francisco had more than recovered from the earthquake and fire of 1906. When the fair opened in February 1915, a 550-foot lighted sign on the bay side of the building read, "California Welcomes the World." The sign on the side of the building read, "Panama-Pacific Exposition," which can be partially seen in the image below. (Above, photograph by John Henry Mentz, SFMTA Photo Archive; below, author's collection.)

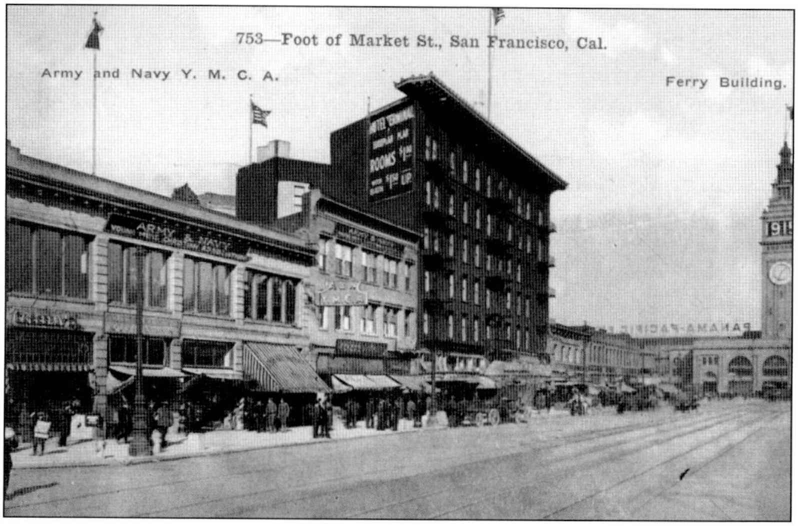

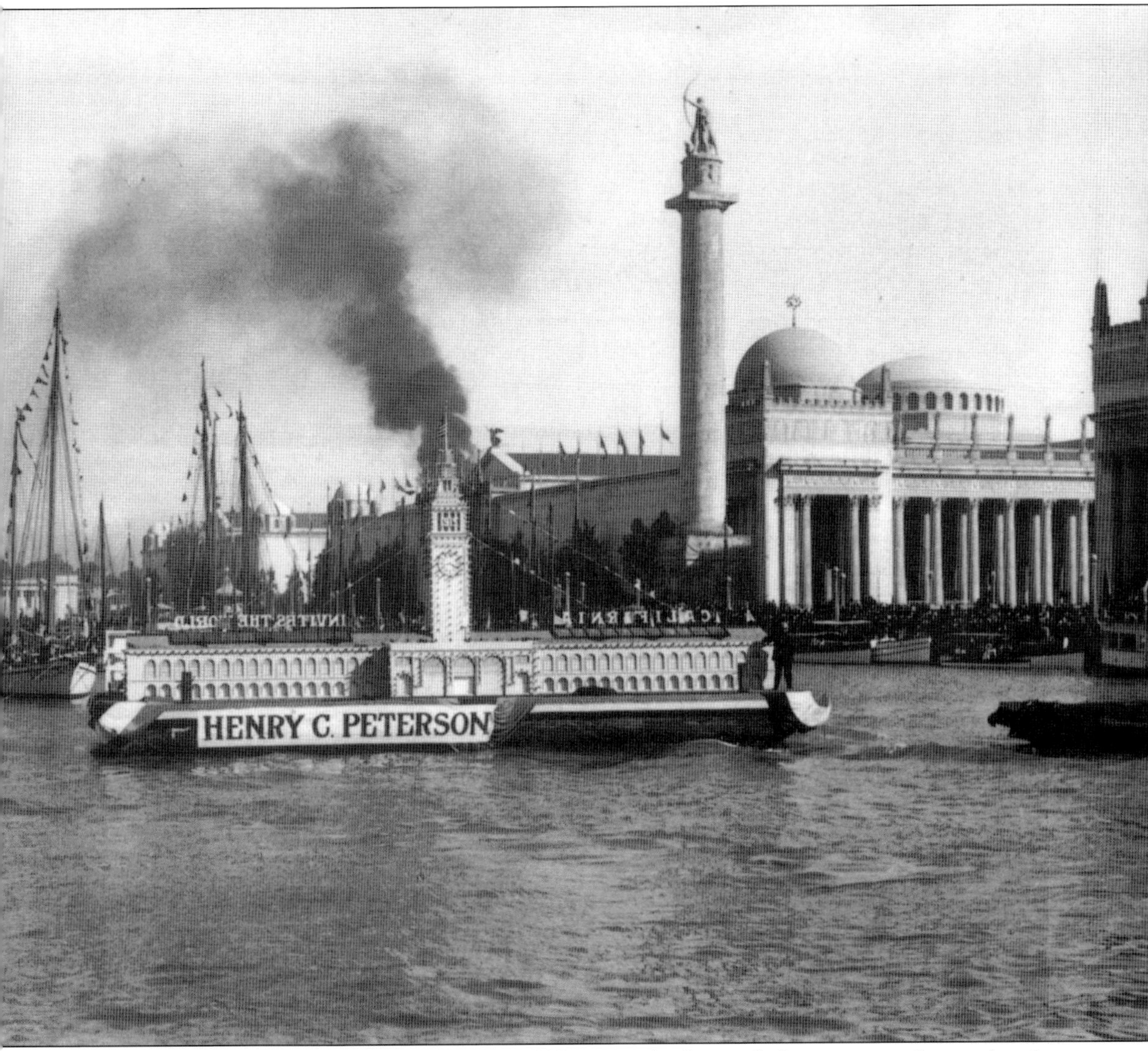

This 60-foot scale model of the Ferry Building, all lit up with electric lights on its arches and with an American flag flying proudly on top of the tower, was towed by a barge to the PPIE on October 23, 1915, Harbor Day, and again on November 2, San Francisco Day. Crowds applauded as it approached. The 30-foot banner promoting Henry C. Peterson was an ad for the businessman who donated the tow. After almost nine months, the fair closed on December 4, 1915, with a total of 18,876,438 visitors, which far exceeded expectations. "About $45 million went into the economy of the state, and around $12 million was spent inside the exposition, which is about $565 million in 2012 dollars," says architectural historian Laura Ackley, author of *San Francisco's Jewel City: The Panama-Pacific International Exposition of 1915*. (San Francisco Port Commission.)

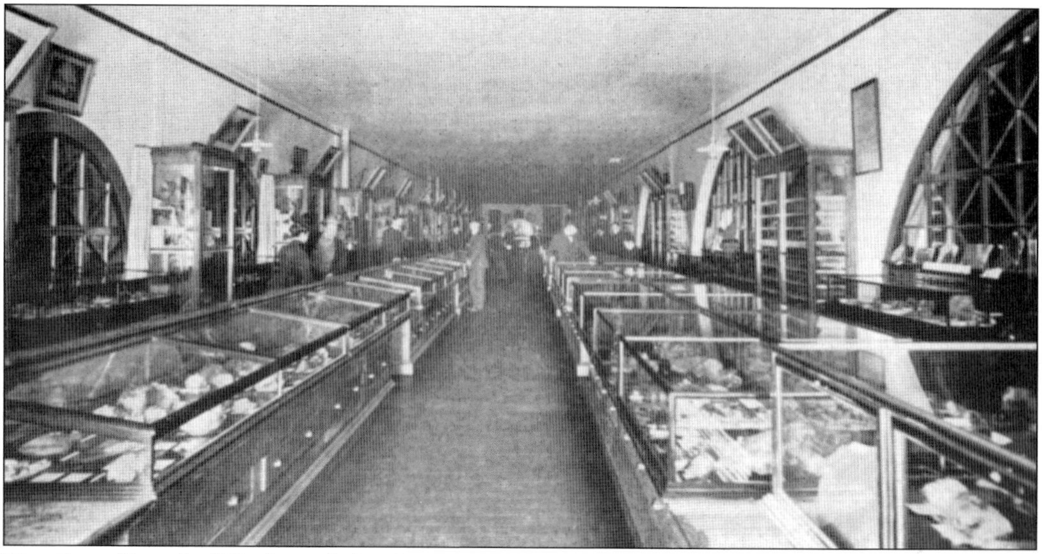

The State Board of Trade and the State Mining Bureau occupied the third floor of the Ferry Building, with exhibits of California agricultural and mining industries. A railway brochure promoting San Francisco tourism notes the exhibits were "well worth the attention of anyone interested in mining, or the romance which always goes with the effort to dig fortunes from the earth." (Internet Archive Book Images.)

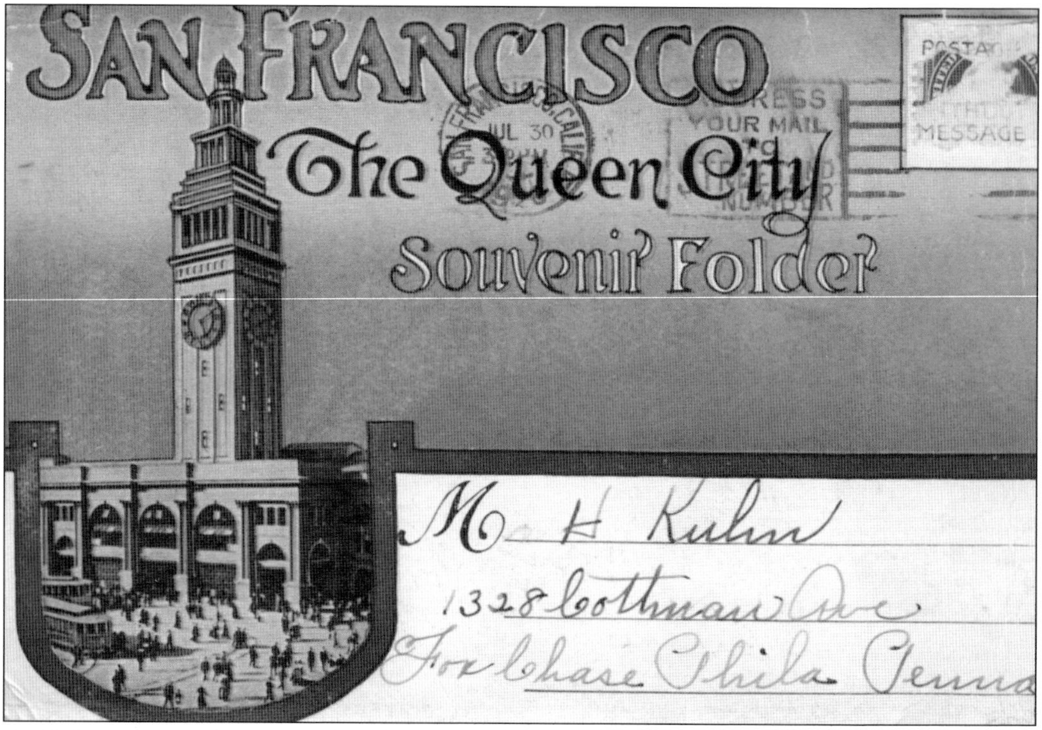

A 1923 souvenir postcard packet showcases the Ferry Building as the star attraction of "San Francisco, The Queen City." Inside, other attractions such as downtown street flower vendors, city hall at Civic Center, and the San Francisco skyline are presented on hand-tinted photographs for visitors to collect or to send to relatives and friends back home. (Author's collection.)

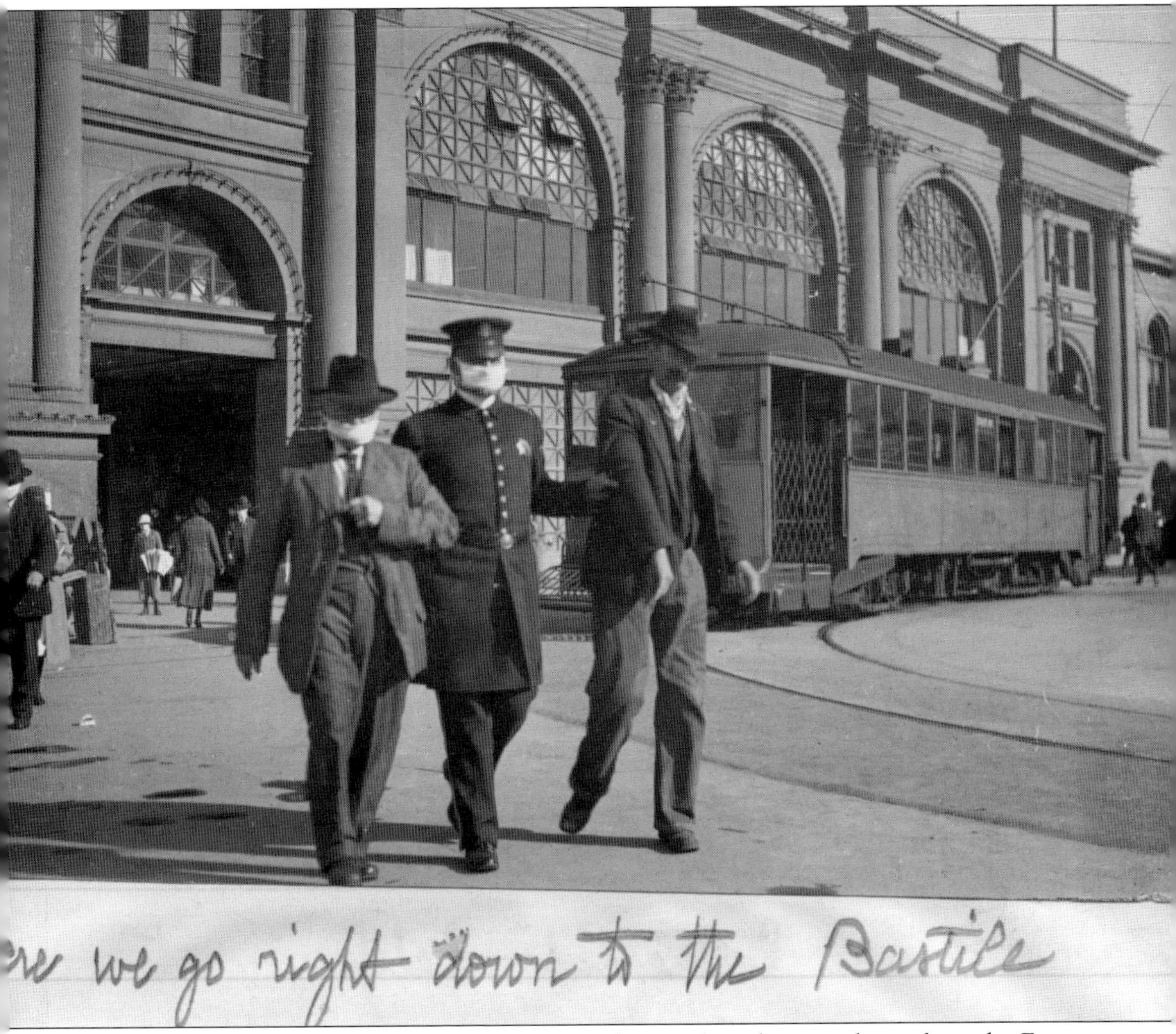

A policeman with a mask escorts two men, one with a mask and one without, from the Ferry Building. The flu epidemic of 1918–1919 hit San Francisco hard in mid-October 1918, and by late October, there were nearly 20,000 cases and over 1,000 deaths. On October 25, every visitor and resident was required to wear a mask in public or when with two or more people. On October 27, police arrested 110 people for failing to either wear or keep their masks properly adjusted. Commuters on the ferries were caught with masks dangling from their chins so they could enjoy a morning pipe on the ferry. Sirens on November 21 let San Franciscans know that they could remove their masks, but it took a few more months for the epidemic to abate. In the end, the final tally was 3,500 fatalities. (Photograph by Hamilton Henry Dobbin, California History Room, California State Library, Sacramento, California.)

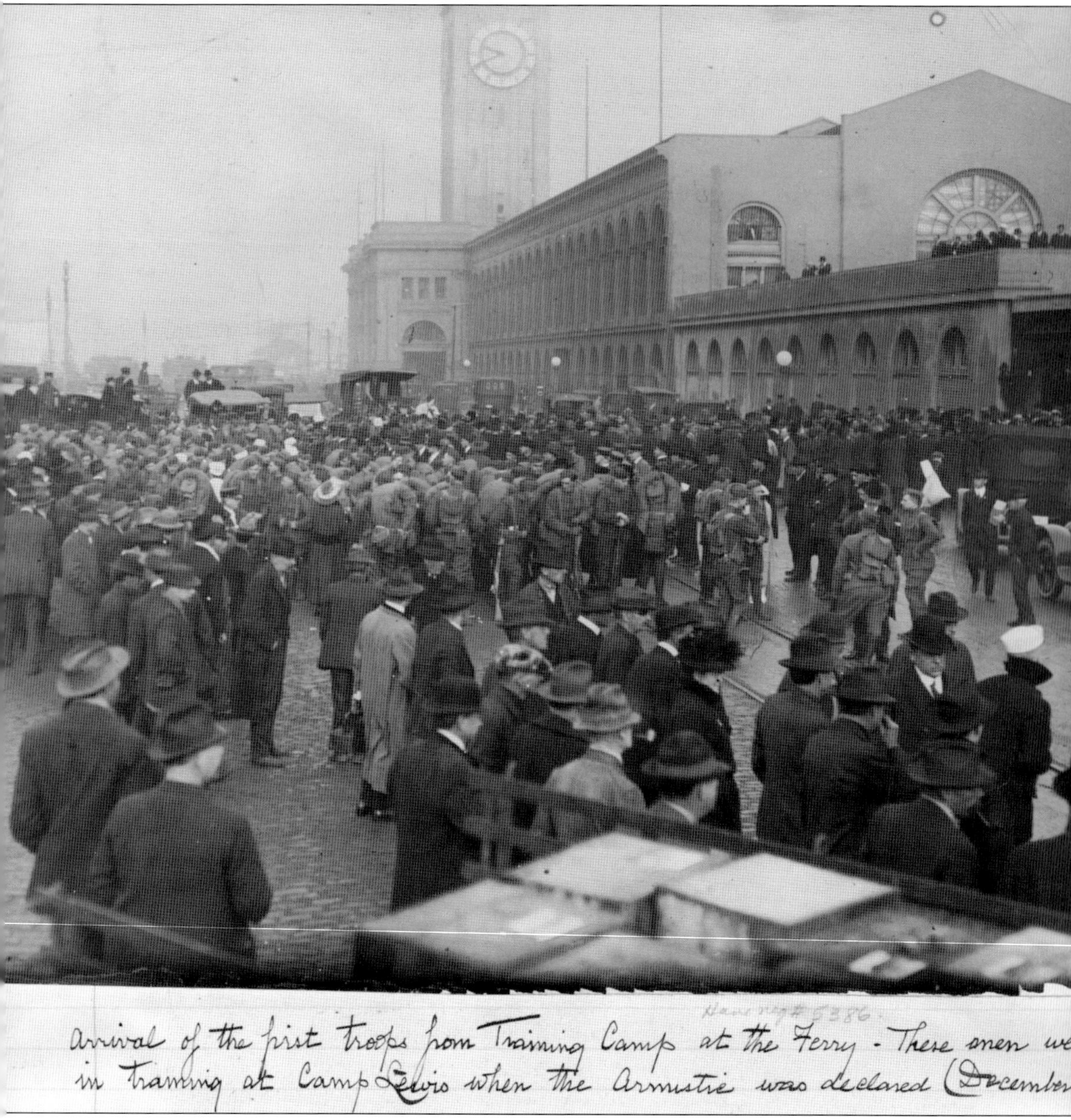

In December 1918, troops arrive from training camp at the Ferry Building, and a crowd lines the street and the rooftops to greet them. The armistice between the Allies and Germany was signed on November 11, 1918, so these men who had been in training at Camp Lewis were able to head home. Camp Lewis (now Fort Lewis) was established in 1917 and located south of Tacoma, Washington. Named after Meriwether Lewis of the Lewis and Clark expedition, the camp was the site of tremendous activity as men mobilized and trained for war service during World War I. Just a year and a half earlier, on July 22, 1916, at the Preparedness Day parade, the largest parade ever in San Francisco, 10 bystanders were killed, and 40 more wounded by a bomb concealed in a suitcase on Steuart Street, near the Ferry Building. (Photograph by Hamilton Henry Dobbin; California History Room, California State Library, Sacramento, California.)

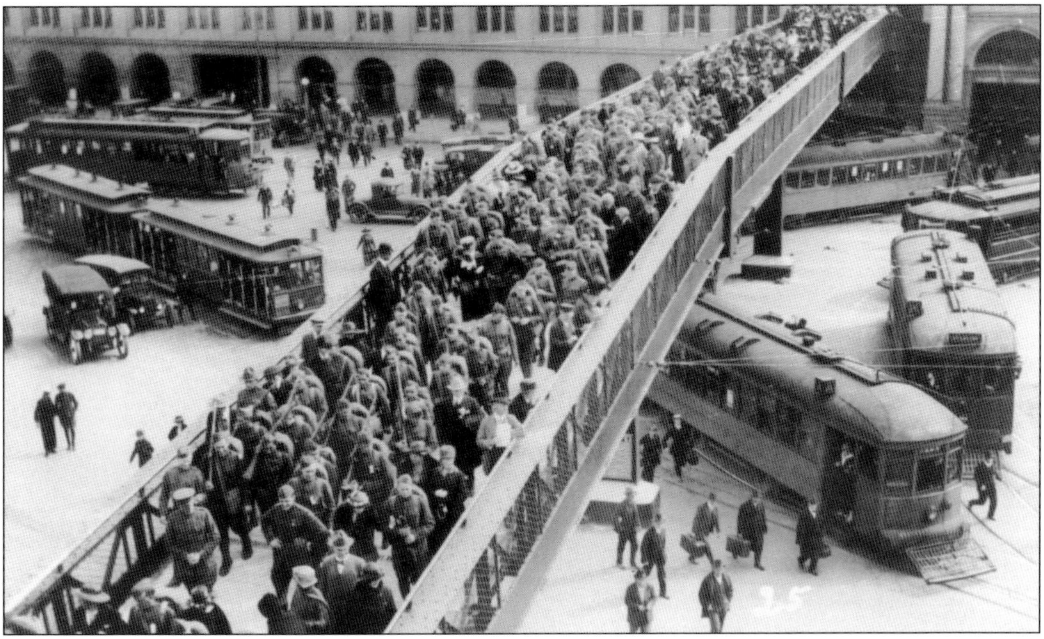

In April 1919, San Francisco rejoiced when members of the 363rd and 347th Divisions, "San Francisco's own," came home from World War I. Here, they cross the pedestrian footbridge from the Ferry Building, having passed through the nave with its welcome banner, seen below. The day of their arrival was declared a holiday, and the city turned out to welcome them. The military authorities agreed to allow the people of San Francisco to greet the regiments on their arrival. During the parade on Market Street, massive crowds cheering the troops stopped the parade. Maj. Gen. John F. Morrison, commanding the Western Department of the Army, is quoted in the April 11, 1919, *San Francisco Chronicle*: "I shall make no objections to wreaths of laurel, to ribbons, or flowers, or anything else, and I am sure the commanding officers of the detachments will make no objections either." (Above, Western Railway Museum Archives; below, SFMNHP, p77-011-247.)

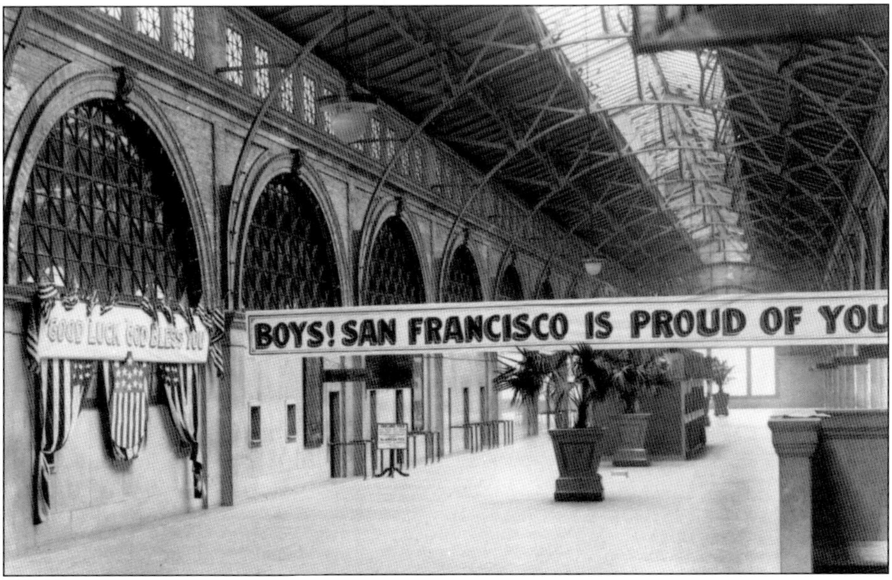

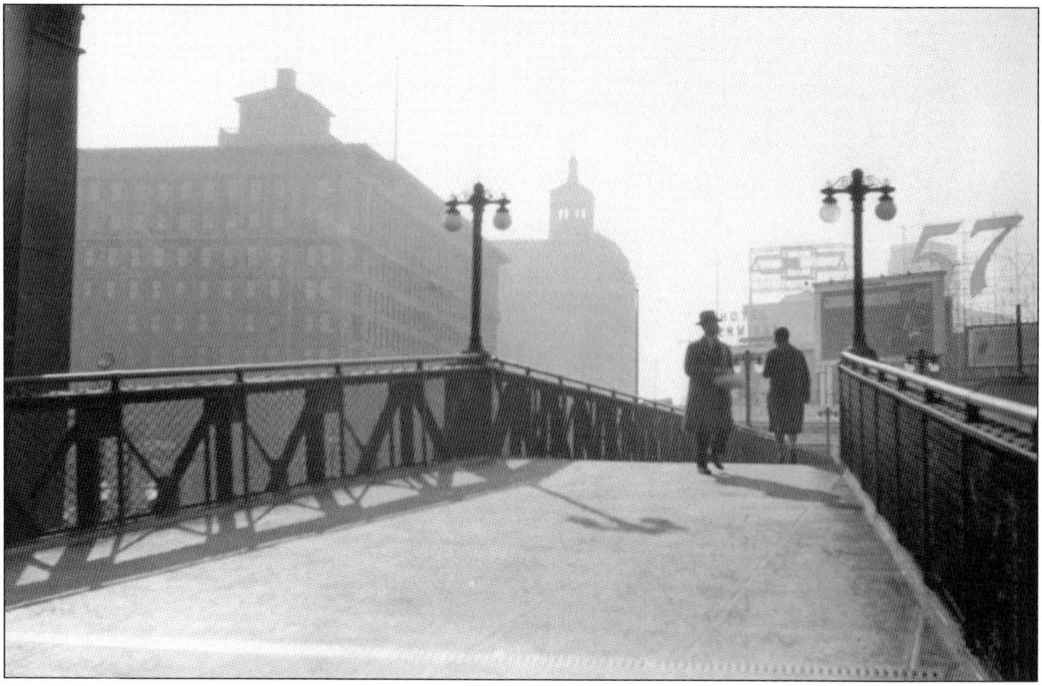

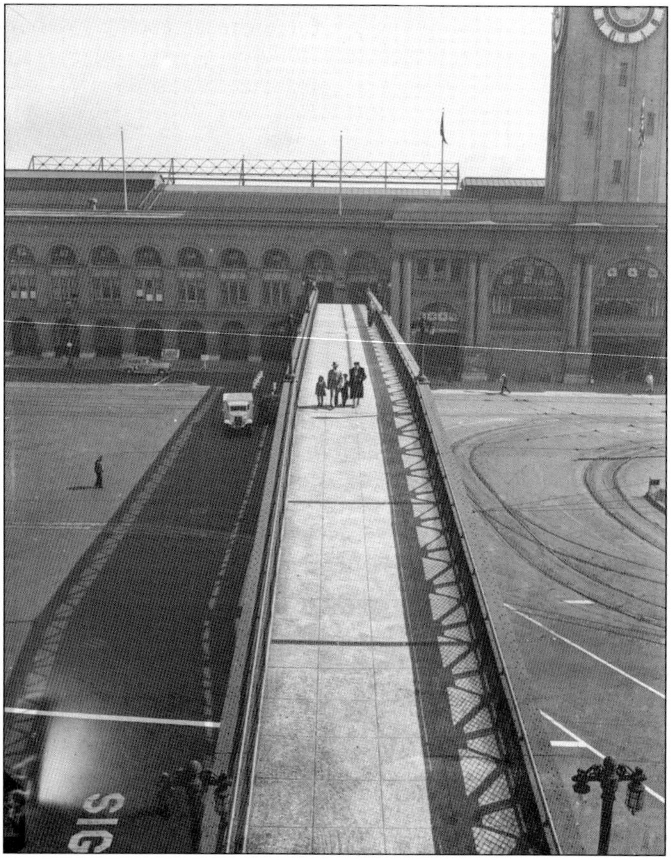

Although there had been talk of a need for a pedestrian bridge (or "viaduct") to the Ferry Building since the 1890s, it was not approved until 1915 and was completed in 1917. Twenty-two years before its completion, an article in the *San Francisco Chronicle* (March 15, 1895) reports, "The absolute necessity of protecting pedestrians from recklessly driven teams and the maze of deadly cable and electric cars at the foot of Market Street upon the completion of the new ferry building was the subject of a brief but earnest discussion by the State Board of Harbor Commissioners yesterday." During World War II, the bridge was deconstructed to supply scrap metal. (Above, California History Room, California State Library, Sacramento, California; left, OpenSFHistory/wnp32.0089.)

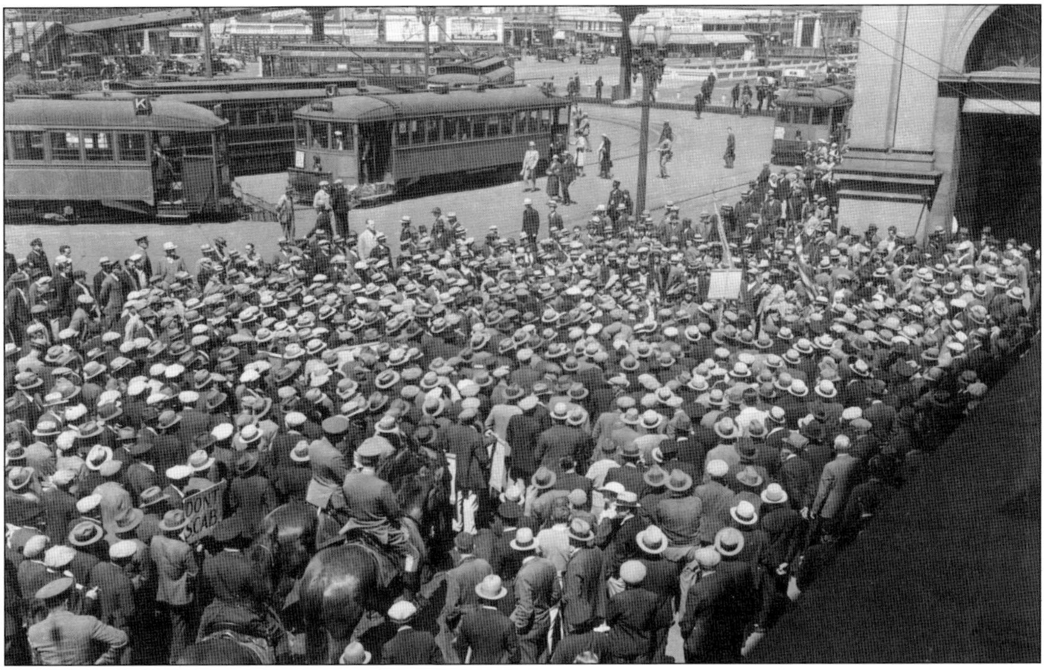

In 1934, the West Coast Longshoremen's Strike lasted 83 days, starting in May, when longshoremen in every West Coast port walked out, paralyzing all shipping up and down the Pacific coast. In the photograph above, longshoremen gather in front of the Ferry Building. Strikebreakers were brought in, violence erupted, and soldiers kept watch along the Embarcadero, as seen below. On Bloody Thursday, July 5, 1934, police shot tear gas canisters into the crowd, then followed with a charge by mounted police. San Francisco police ended up killing two strikers. Four days later, tens of thousands of strikers and sympathizers marched up Market Street for a mass funeral. The workers' general strike effectively shut down both San Francisco and Oakland in the East Bay. (Above, Western Railway Museum Archives; below, OpenSFHistory/wnp32.0032.)

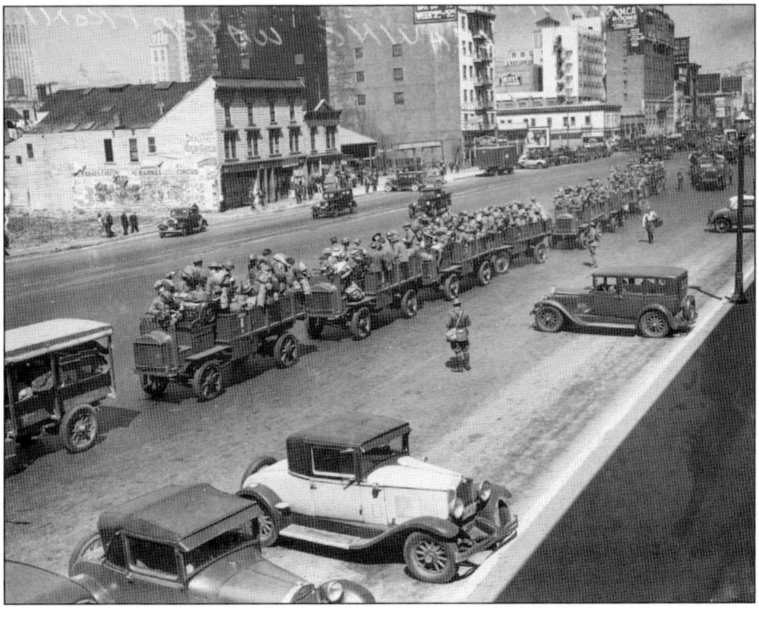

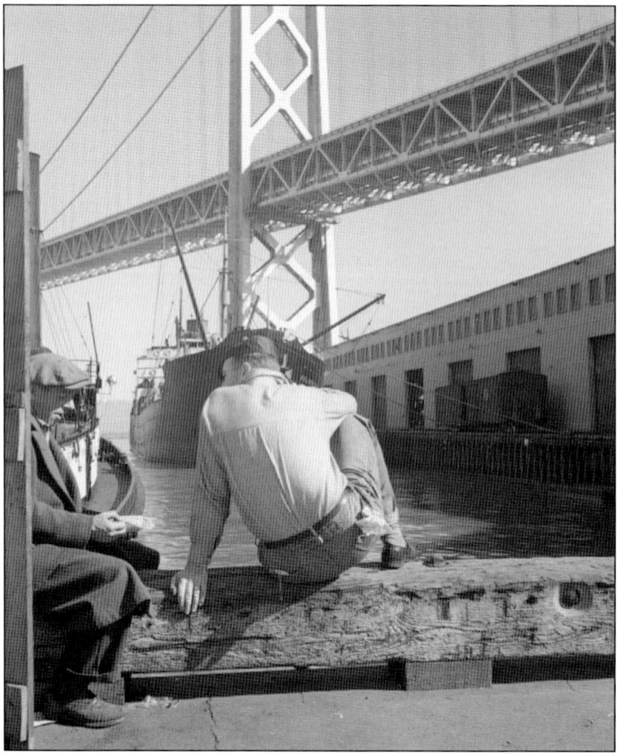

Longshoremen were essential for loading and unloading ships' cargo. They worked long hours, but work was often irregular, and working conditions were tough. In the early 1900s, employers hired dockworkers on an hourly or daily basis. With the Great Depression of the 1930s, the situation got so bad that over half of the longshoremen on the Pacific coast were on relief. It was the strike of 1934 that led to the establishment of the union that would eventually become the International Longshore and Warehouse Union (ILWU). The 1937 image at left shows two longshoremen having lunch under the Bay Bridge, near the Ferry Building. In the photograph below, noted photographer Dorothea Lange, who worked for the Farm Security Administration, captured the dockworkers' despair during a strike. (Both, Library of Congress.)

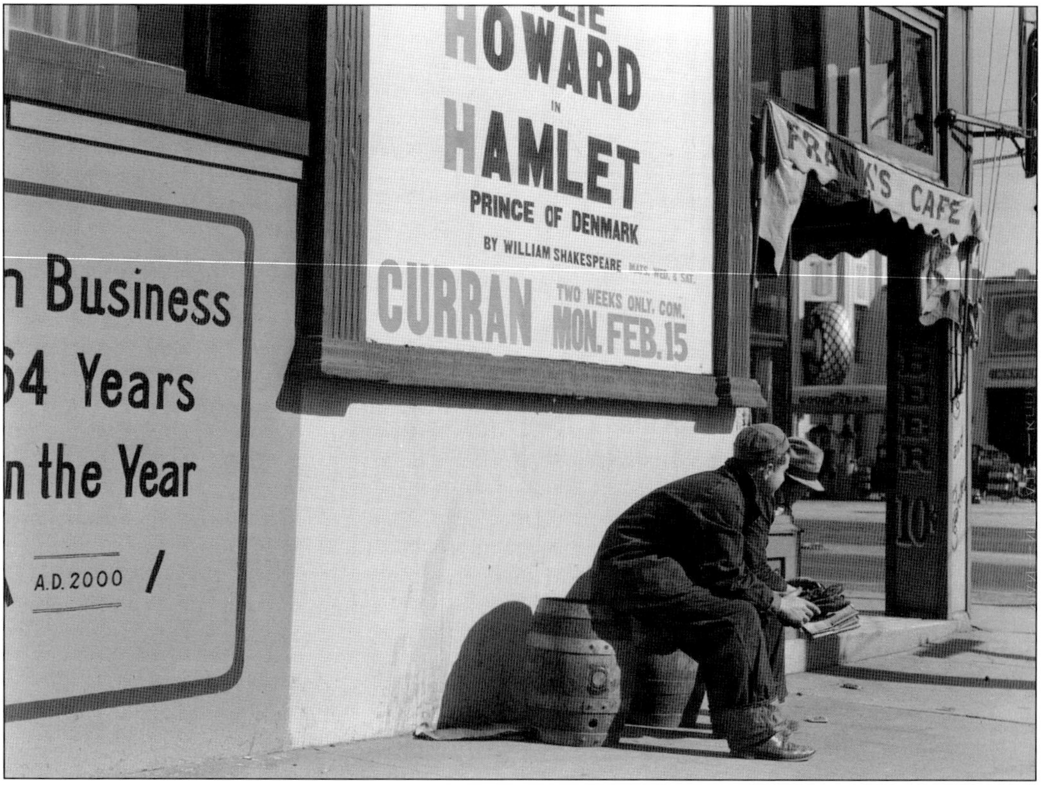

Five

A Major Transportation Hub

The history of mass transit in San Francisco is complex, to say the least. The city's geographic position, with water on three sides and San Mateo County to the south, meant that in the era of transcontinental train travel, journeys began or ended across the bay in Oakland, and passengers departed or arrived in San Francisco by ferryboat from the Ferry Building. Once they arrived, they needed to get to other areas of the city. Horse-drawn streetcars first appeared in 1851, and then were replaced by steam, cable, electric, and in later years, motor buses and trolley coaches. In the era before mass ownership of automobiles, entrepreneurial land developers operated private ventures to provide access to new residential neighborhoods.

Cable cars, first introduced in 1873, operated throughout the city for over 30 years until the arrival of electric streetcars around 1900. Electric streetcars' high capital costs hampered their growth and cable cars continued to dominate up to the 1906 earthquake and fire. Many of the independent and competing systems consolidated into the first Market Street Railway Company in 1893, and then all but three of the remaining independents consolidated into the United Railroads in 1902. The public was not happy with URR, a monopolistic enterprise with callous labor practices, so voters approved bond measures to create a municipal streetcar line in 1909.

However, it took three years until the San Francisco Municipal Railway (commonly called the "Muni") inaugurated streetcar service in 1912, and URR continued as a much larger operation. San Francisco finally acquired the Market Street Railway (renamed in 1921) in 1944. In the years after World War II, bus service and electric trolley coaches replaced streetcar lines. The Ferry Building, in its prime position as transit terminal, was witness to all these changes as overhead electric lines replaced cable car tracks and, eventually, the dominance of the automobile brought major changes.

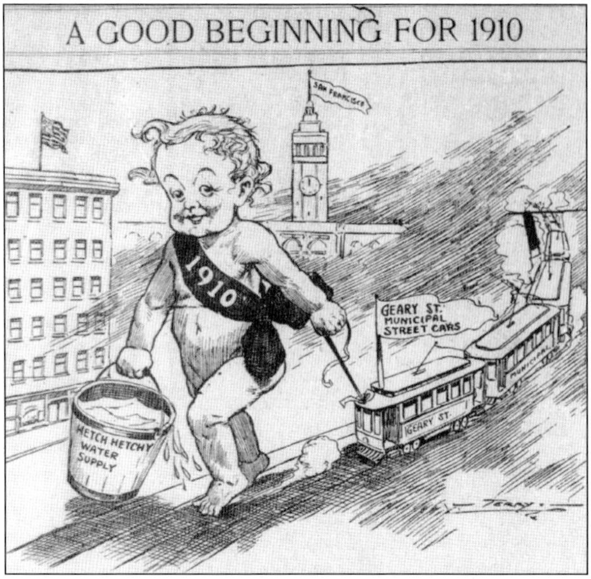

This cartoon from the *San Francisco Call* on January 1, 1910 celebrates the passing of a bond issue to construct a municipal streetcar line on Geary and Market Streets, from the Ferry Building to the ocean. It also celebrated a Hetch Hetchy water system bond. There was a lot of public support for the measures and backlash against the privately owned URR. (Library of Congress.)

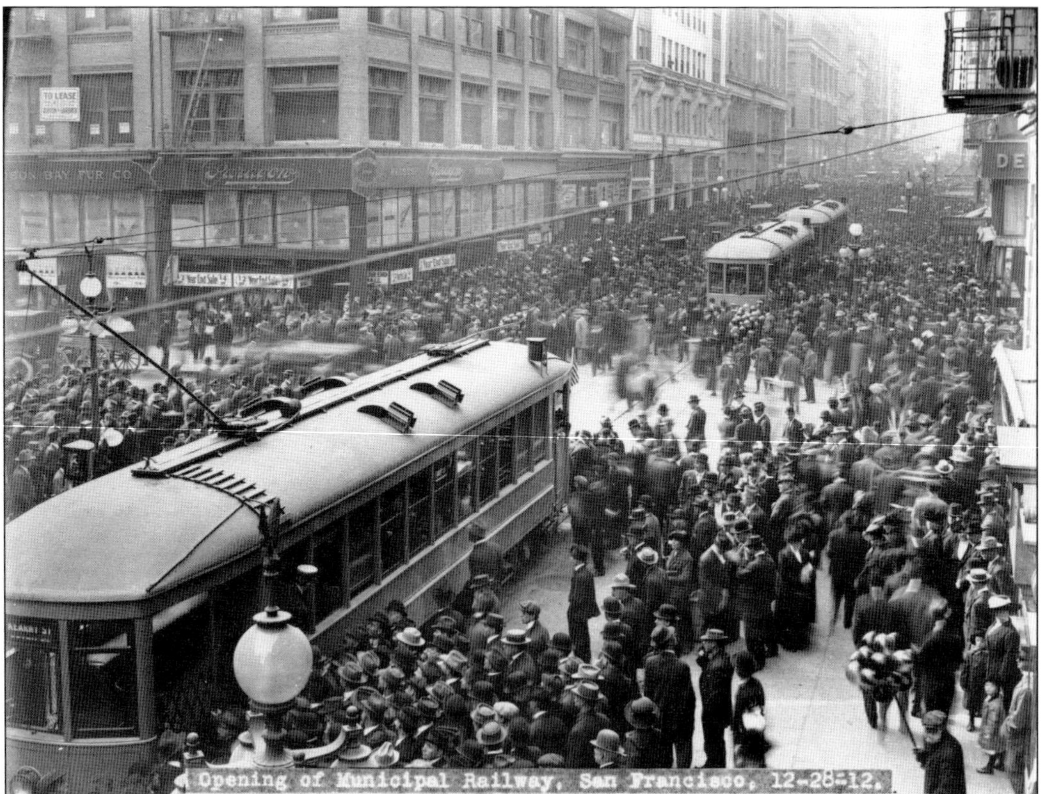

Throngs turned out for opening day of the San Francisco Municipal Transportation Agency in 1912. Not surprisingly, the privately owned URR had campaigned against it, claiming that a city-operated streetcar line would be a financial drain on the city. Over 42,000 voters turned out for the election, making it the largest turnout for any special or primary election in San Francisco up to that time. (Photograph by John Henry Mentz, SFMTA Photo Archive.)

The ferries that left the Ferry Building connected passengers to rail lines in the East Bay. Southern Pacific had a network of tracks that would take vacationers to the mountains, down the coast, and into inland areas. These advertisements from 1909 and 1910 beckon travelers to enjoy their vacations via the railroad. The business magnates known as the Big Four—Charles Crocker, Mark Hopkins, Collis Huntington, and Leland Stanford—established the Southern Pacific railroad system in 1861, and by 1900, Southern Pacific was a major railroad system incorporating many smaller companies. A dominant force in California politics in the late 19th and early 20th centuries, the company's trains traveled throughout the West and Southwest, serving 15 states and the Pacific and Gulf coasts. During the 10-year period from 1900 to 1910, Southern Pacific added a total of 1,870 miles of railroad to its system. (Both, Library of Congress.)

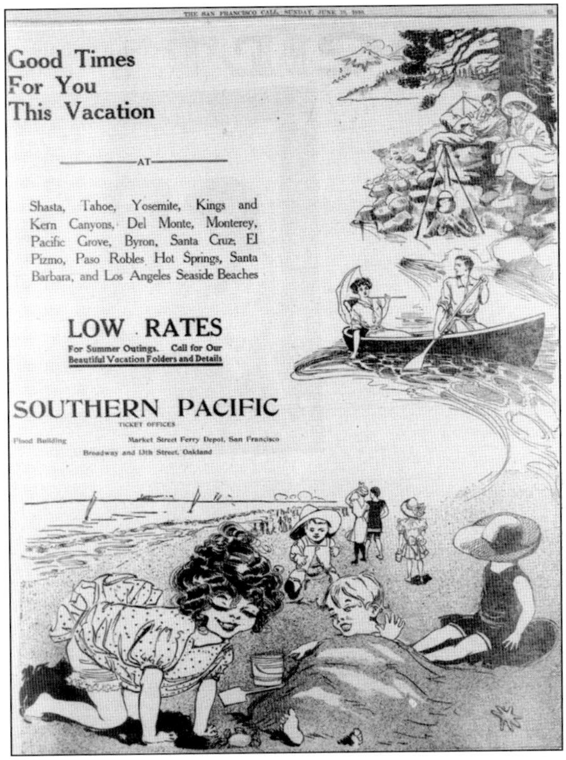

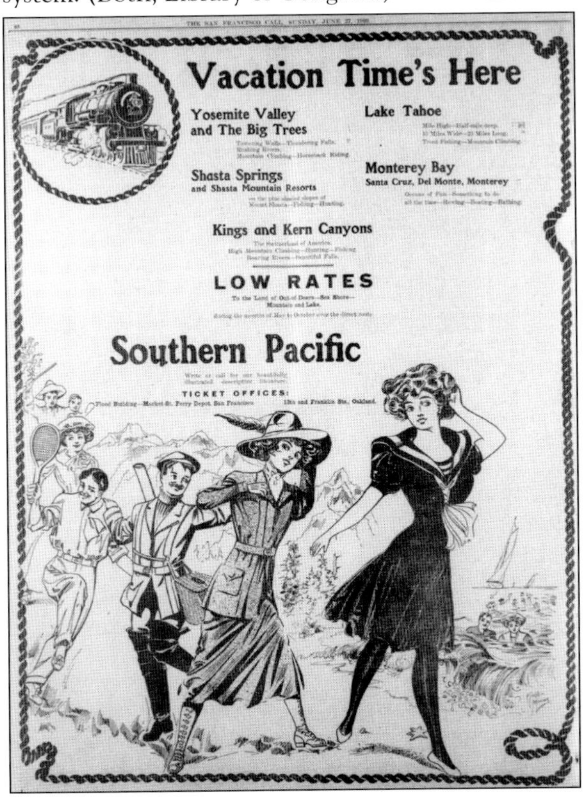

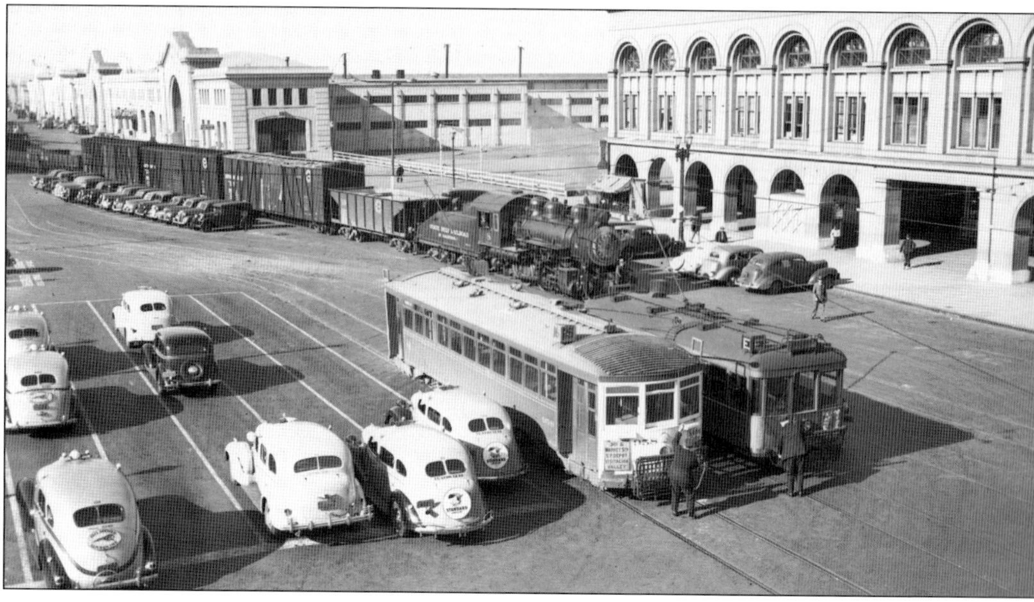

These images illustrate the various modes of transportation that shared the Embarcadero in front of the Ferry Building. Above, cabs line up next to Car 958 of Line 16, which is next to a Muni E-line car. Finally, a State Belt Railroad train is on the tracks closest to the Ferry Building, hauling freight. Below, a State Belt engine pushes boxcars south, underneath the pedestrian footbridge. The belt line began in the 1880s to move freight from ships docked in San Francisco for shipment by rail. Its tracks extended all along the Embarcadero from south of Market Street to Fort Mason and the Presidio. (Both, Western Railway Museum Archives.)

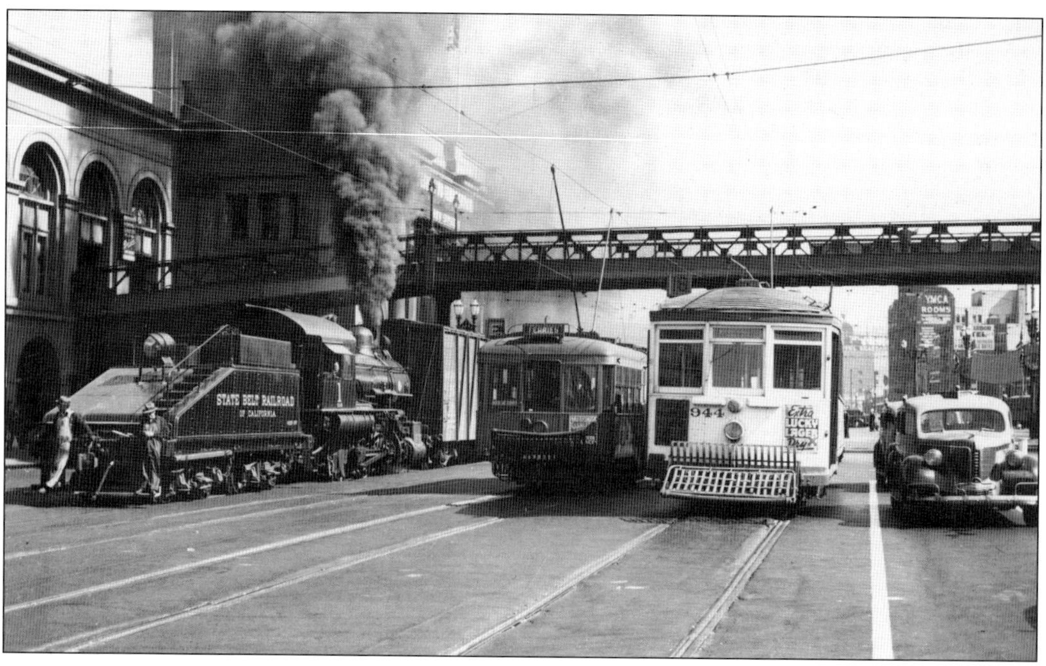

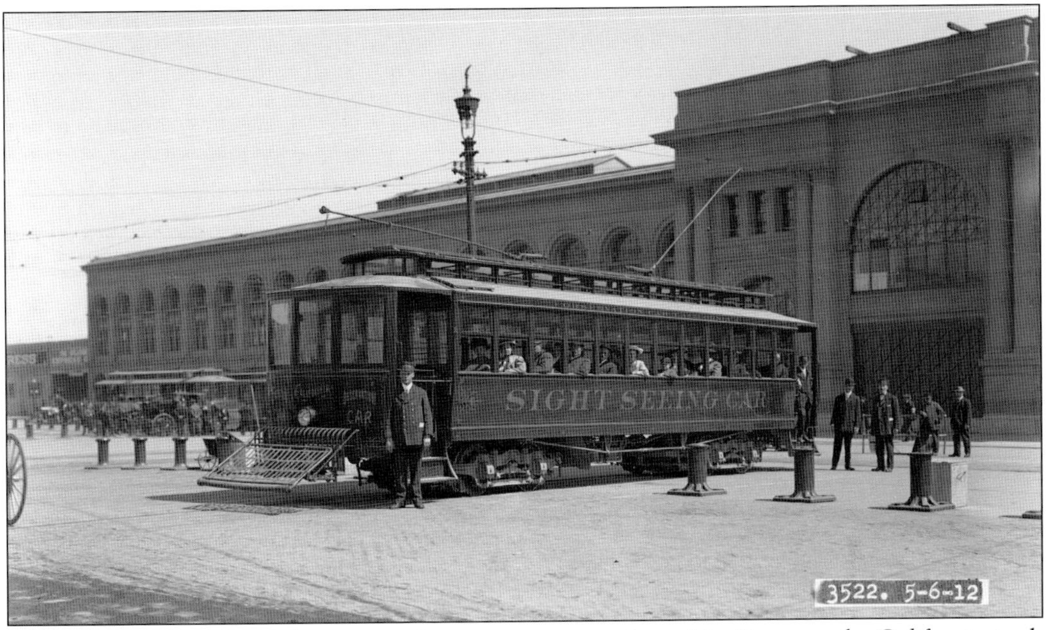

In the early part of the 20th century, observation cars, such as this 48-seater, the *California*, took sightseers from the Ferry Building to San Francisco attractions such as Golden Gate Park, the Cliff House, Lands' End, and Mission Dolores. The fare for a 20-mile, four-hour trip was 25¢. (Photograph by John Henry Mentz, SFMTA Photo Archive.)

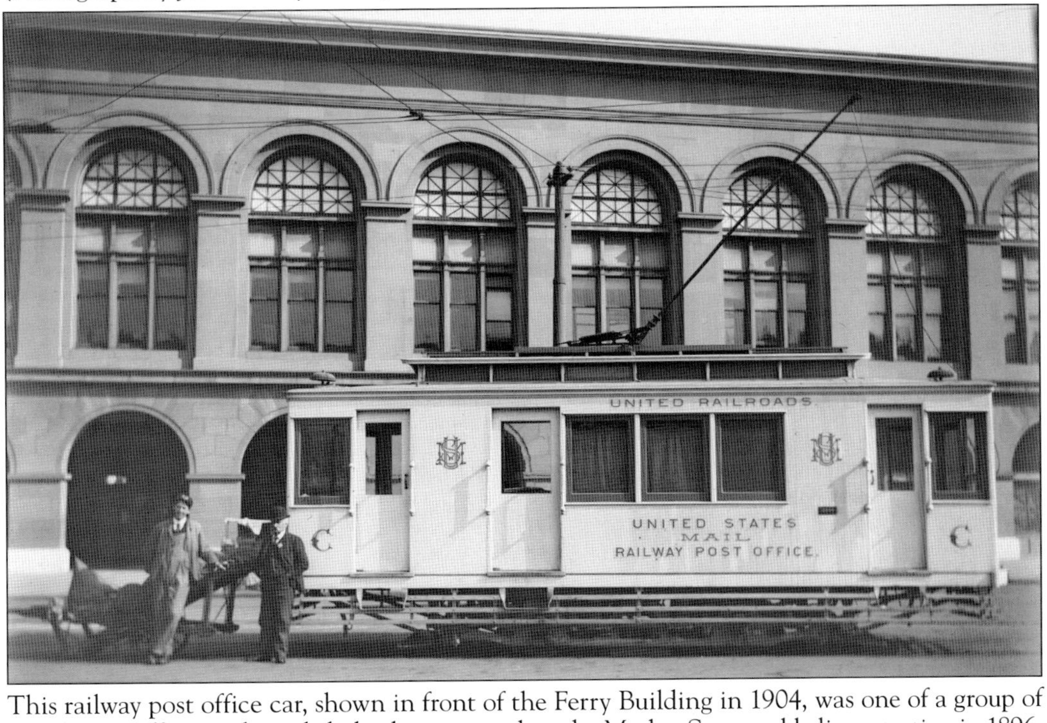

This railway post office car, shown in front of the Ferry Building in 1904, was one of a group of mobile post offices with mail clerks that operated on the Market Street cable lines starting in 1896. Painted white with gold lettering, they were equipped with mail slots and facilities for sorting and canceling mail. (Photograph by John Henry Mentz, SFMTA Photo Archive.)

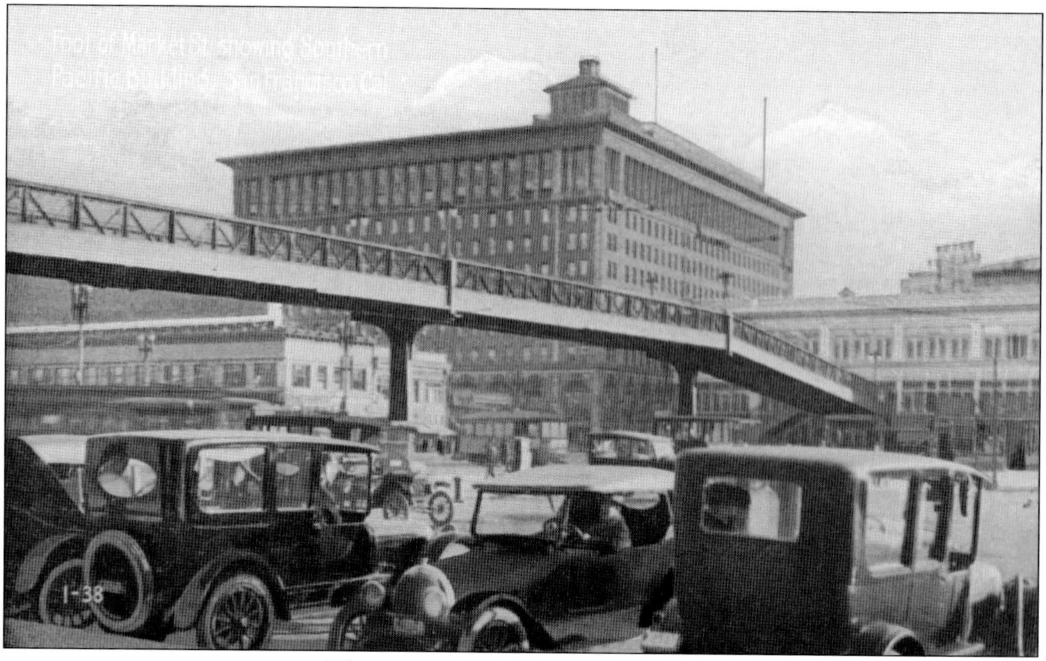

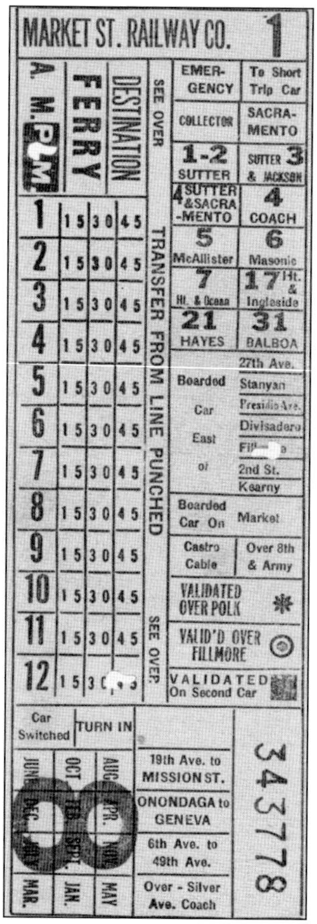

The monumental Southern Pacific Building at 1 Market Street looms over a rather calm scene of cars parked at the Ferry Building, with the pedestrian bridge arching across the Embarcadero. Built in 1916, and designed by Walter Danforth Bliss and William Baker Faville of the architecture firm Bliss and Faville, the Southern Pacific Building was one of the earliest corporate headquarters in San Francisco. (Author's collection.)

Market Street Railway transfers like this one are very familiar to San Franciscans. On the back, this 1928 transfer advertises, "See the whole city. Ride all day Sunday. A pass costs $.25." The punches on the transfer show that the rider boarded east of Fillmore Street at 12:45 p.m., and that the streetcar went all the way to the ferries. (Author's collection.)

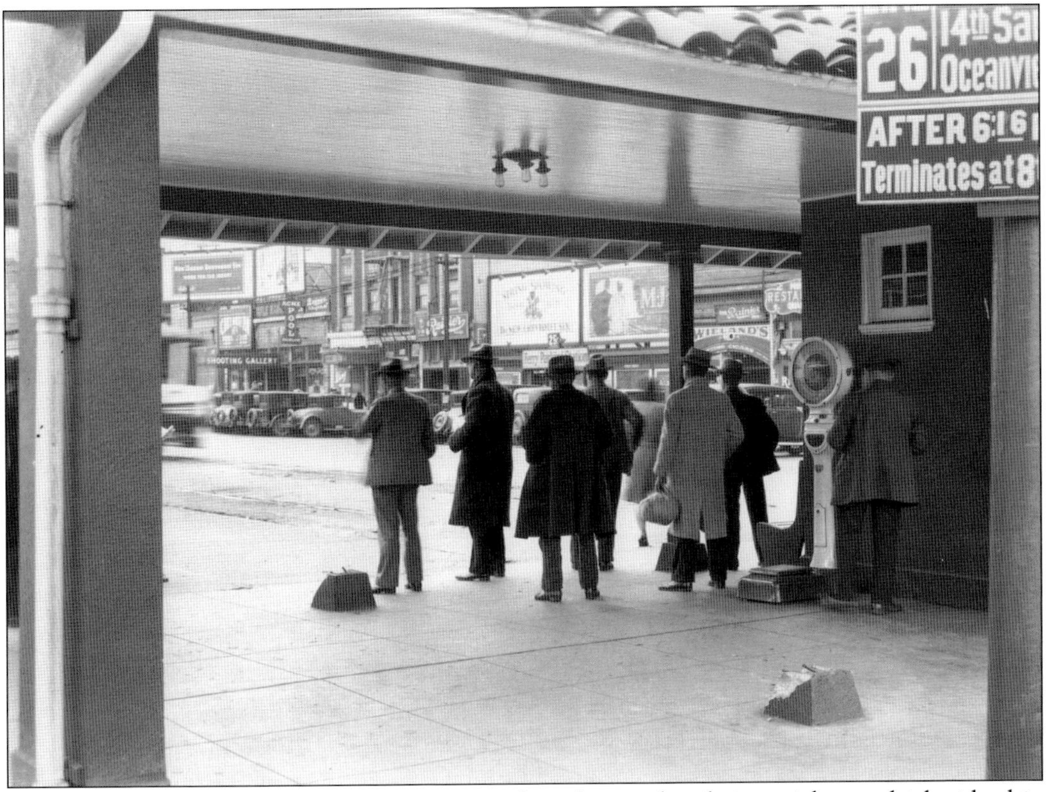

In the 1920s and 1930s, San Francisco was a densely populated city, with very high ridership levels for public transportation. As Tom Matoff describes it in *FoundSF*, "In the mid-1920s [there were] about 275 million revenue rides annually for Muni, the Market Street Railway, and the still-independent California Street Cable Railroad Company combined." Streetcars that picked riders like these up at the Ferry Building linked them to their offices, department stores, theaters, and other downtown attractions. Developers needed transportation options so that they could attract home buyers to outlying areas of the city. Between 1914 and 1927, for example, the construction of the Stockton Street, Twin Peaks, and Sunset streetcar tunnels opened areas for development that had been limited by their topography. (Above, Port of San Francisco; below, OpenSFHistory/wnp28.0205.)

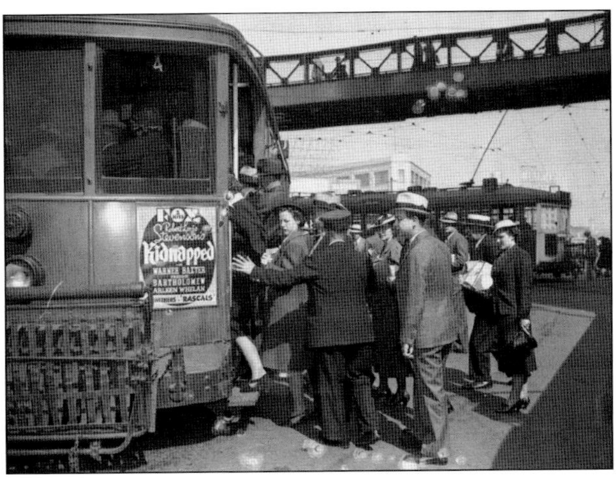

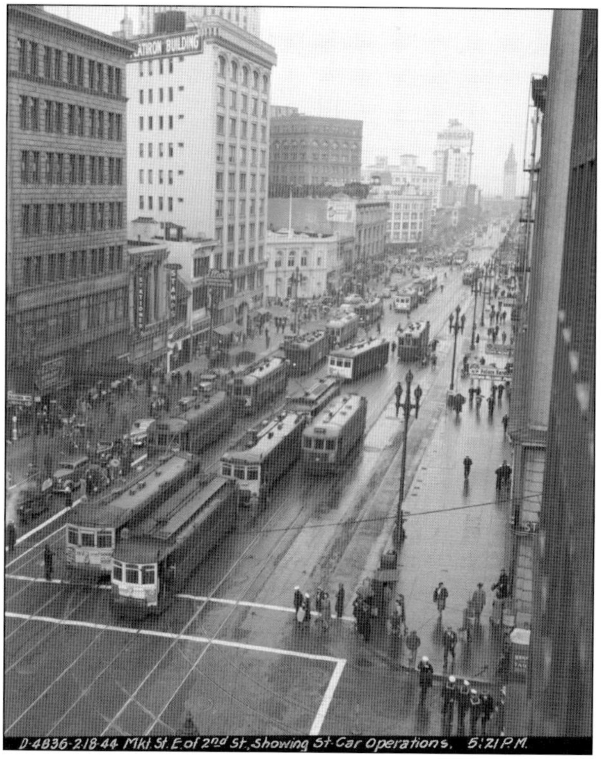

Market Street was a busy place, with streetcars going to and from the Ferry Building. After 1913 and until 1949, there were two transit companies sharing four sets of streetcar tracks on Market Street. Four streetcars could make quite a clamor; locals called it "the roar of four." The city-owned Municipal Railway, with its cars mostly painted gray, had the outside tracks. The private Market Street Railway, with its green-and-white cars, had the inside tracks. It was not the safest arrangement—there were only 23.5 inches between the moving streetcars. (Left, photograph by George Fanning, SFMTA Photo Archive; below, Western Railway Museum Archives.)

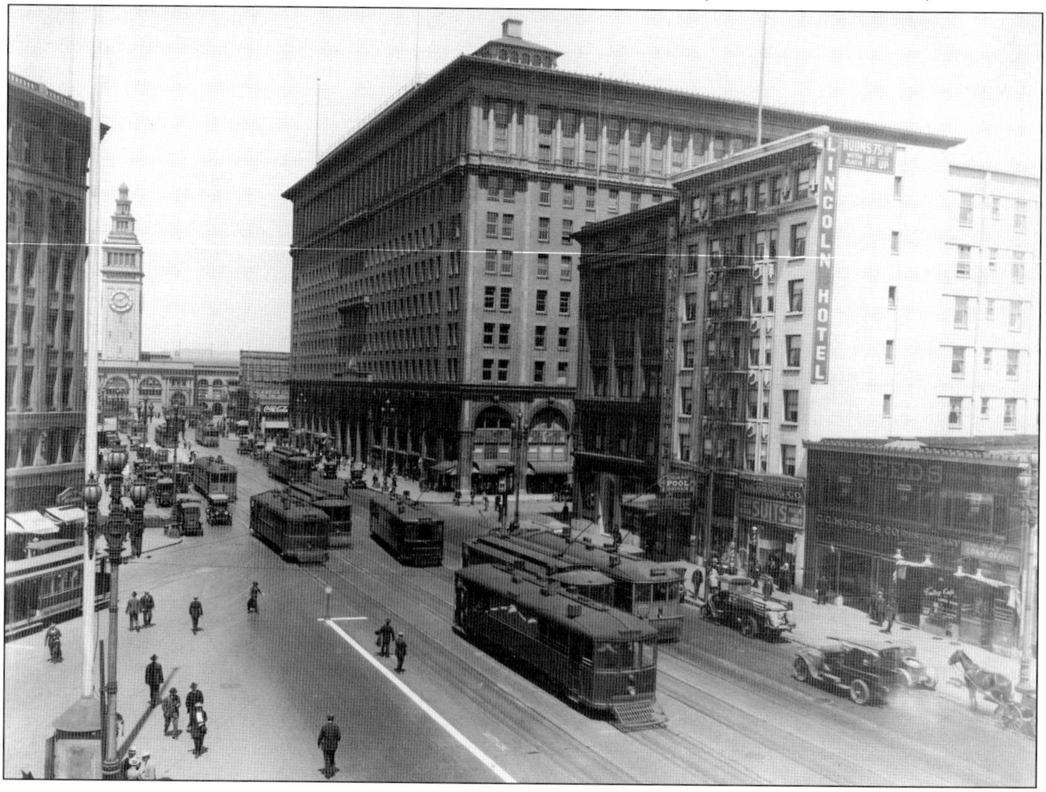

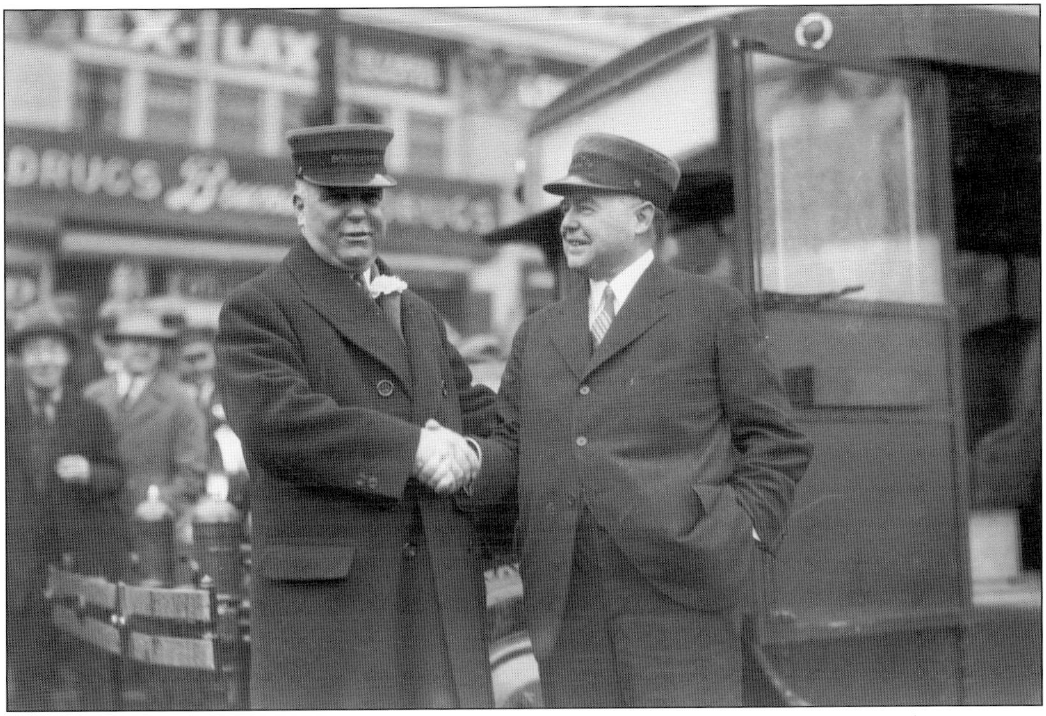

Mayor James "Sunny Jim" Rolph greets the conductor of the new Embarcadero bus line in 1927. Known as gregarious, outgoing, and always smiling, Rolph would pick up pedestrians while on his way to work at city hall and drive them to their destinations. Rolph was mayor of San Francisco from 1912 until 1931, when he became governor. (Photograph by Horace Chaffee, SFMTA Photo Archive.)

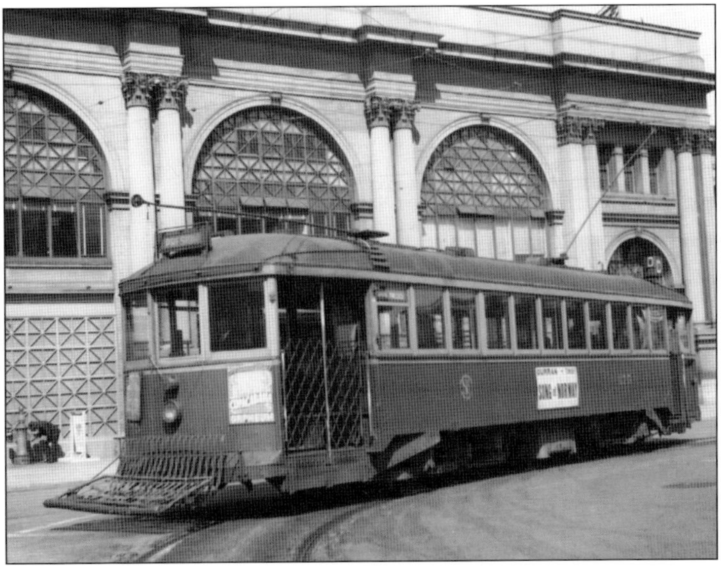

This streetcar in front of the Ferry Building in 1946 has the San Francisco Municipal Railway logo on its side. Even though San Francisco Municipal Railway was established in 1912, it was not until May 1944, after previously defeating the proposal six times, that voters finally elected to purchase the operative properties of the Market Street Railway (formerly URR). This firmly established Muni as the "people's railway." (Harre W. Demoro.)

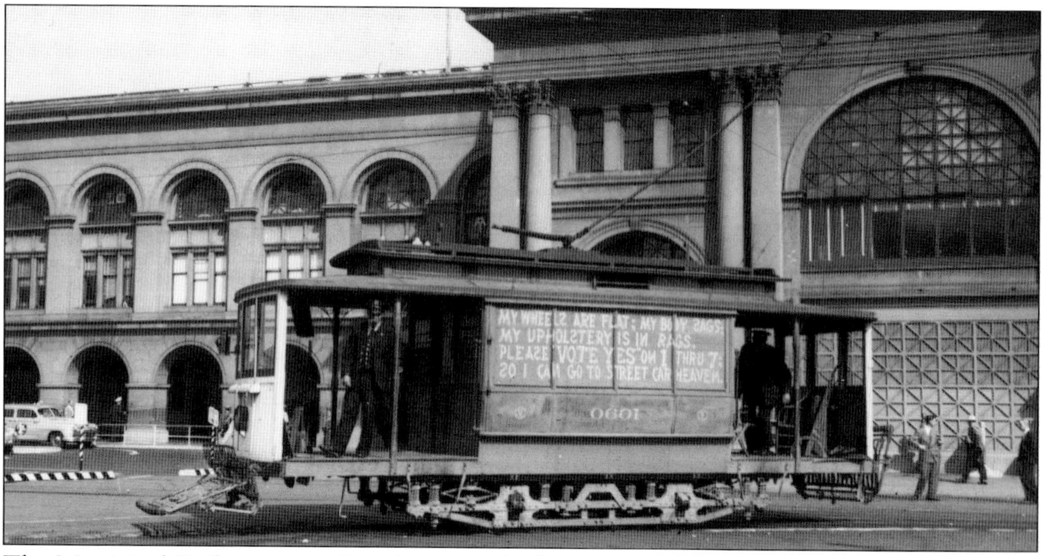

The Municipal Railway campaigned vigorously for passage of the 1947 Modernization Bonds. The sign on this Muni Street Railway streetcar declares, "My wheels are flat; my body sags; my upholstery is in rags. Please Vote Yes on 1 thru 7, so I can go to streetcar heaven." It traveled up and down Market Street to promote a "yes" vote on the bonds. The measure passed. (Western Railway Museum Archives.)

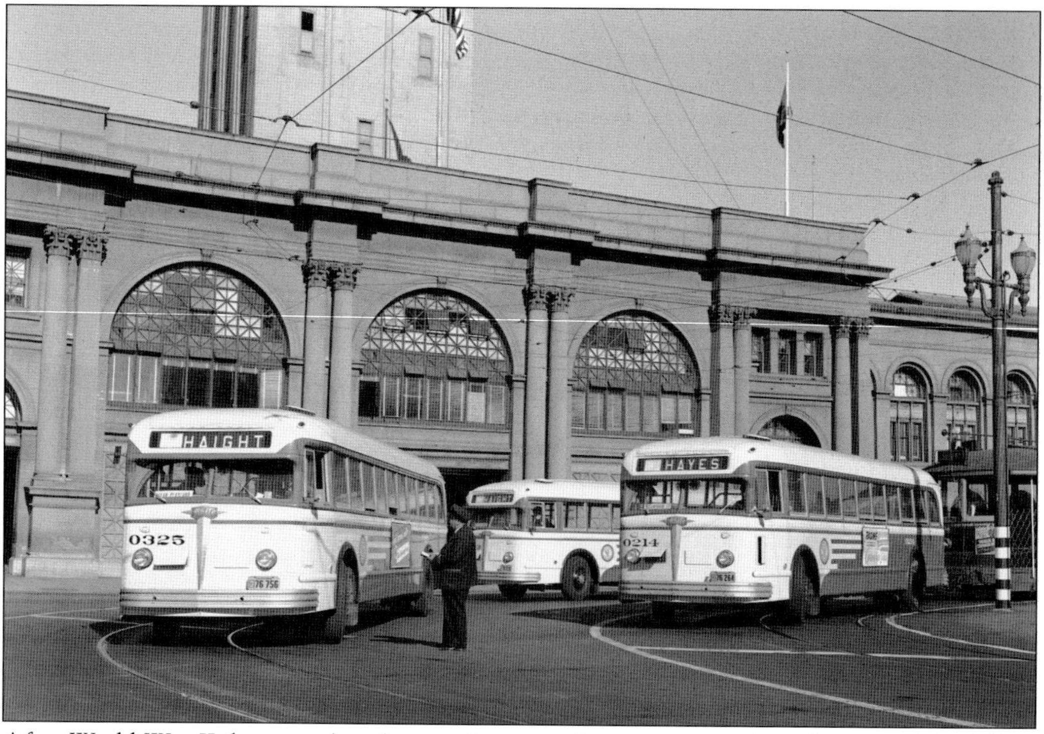

After World War II, buses replaced more than two dozen streetcar lines. Here, in 1948, three White Brand motor coaches—the 21 Hayes Bus Line and two 7 Haight Line buses—line up outside the Ferry Building while an inspector checks them out. (Photograph by Marshall Moxom, SFMTA Photo Archive.)

Six

Ferries Cross the Bay

In their heyday, ferries were a way of life for many San Francisco and Bay Area residents, and once they were gone, there was a sense of loss for this cherished tradition. As columnist Herb Caen observes in the January 5, 1964, *San Francisco Chronicle*,

> During the century of ferryboats, the San Franciscan was very much a part of his watery heritage. Blast of whistle and slap of paddlewheel, sunlight dappling the swells, the breathless excitement of crossing in heavy fog . . . these were all his for only a few pennies. . . . The bay became your personal world. You knew 'Pegleg Pete,' the one-legged seagull. You applauded 'the Caruso of the Ferries,' the boatman who sang operatic arias while he worked. . . . Ferryboats were filled with the dignity of the era and the excitement of approaching the city on its own terms.

Before the opening of the San Francisco–Oakland Bay Bridge in 1936 and the Golden Gate Bridge in 1937, ferryboats went from every major bay port to San Francisco and to places in between. The ride from the Ferry Building to Vallejo, 30 miles, was the longest, and the fast Monticello Line ferryboats could make the trip in an hour and 45 minutes. Oakland to the Ferry Building took 18 minutes. The aptly named "Six-Minute Ferry" was the shortest ride, traveling from Morrow Cove in Vallejo to Crockett, across the Carquinez Straits.

The ferry was a place to hang out with friends, kindle romances, read the paper, get one's shoes shined, or just watch the San Francisco skyline as one departed or arrived. On July 22, 1912, in Ferry Tales, a column that ran regularly in the *San Francisco Call* about ferry life and commuters, the author writes about the various regulars who rode the ferries: "The 'Sunshine club' meets on the southeast corner of the upper deck of whatever Key Route boat leaves the Emeryville pier at a few minutes after 8 o'clock every morning . . . the 'Rudder club' on the deck below hides itself in a cloud of tobacco smoke and frivols away the 15 minutes that span its daily existence in plotting future discomfort for some absent member."

Once the bridges were built, ridership decreased and the various ferry lines dropped off one by one. In 1958, ferry service ended altogether when Southern Pacific ended its main line passenger ferry service from San Francisco to Oakland. It was not until 1970 that commuters could once again enjoy a relaxing ride across the bay.

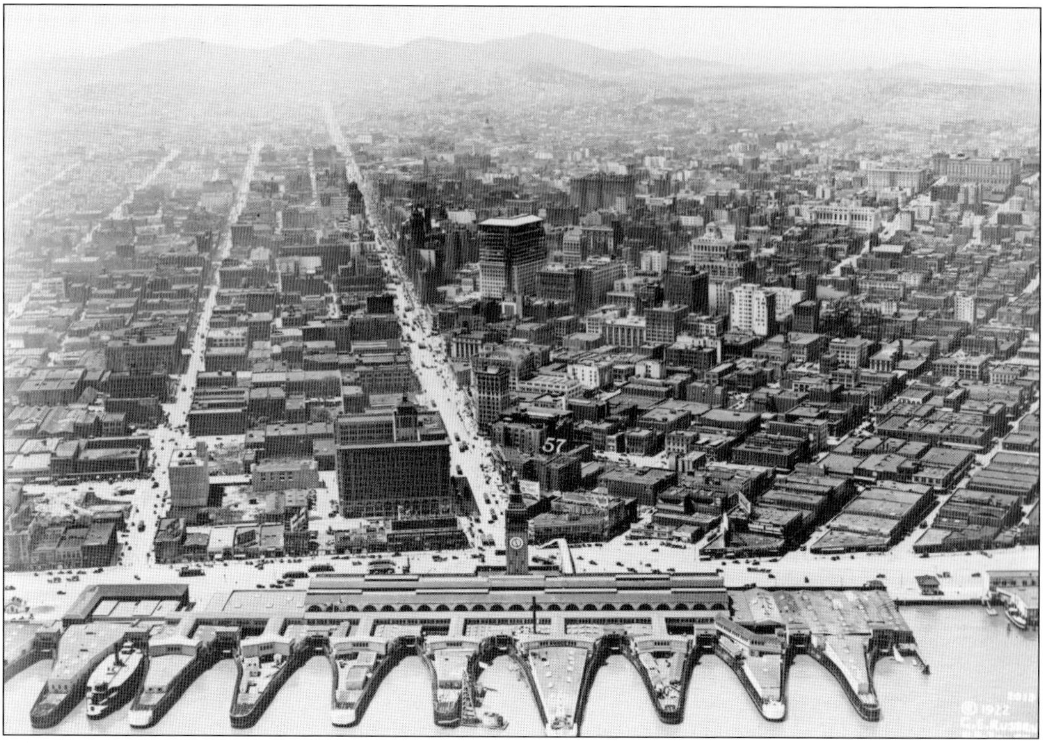

These aerial views (above taken in 1922, and below in 1930) show the Ferry Building and its slips, the specialized docks for ferries. By 1927, more people owned cars, and of the 10 ferry slips, Southern Pacific used slips 9 and 10 at the southern end of the building for its automobile ferries to the East Bay. (It took 18 minutes to travel to Alameda or Oakland.) Ferries to Marin and Vallejo (the longest ride at 30 minutes) left from the north end of the building or from the Hyde Street Pier. (Above, Library of Congress; below, San Francisco History Center, San Francisco Public Library.)

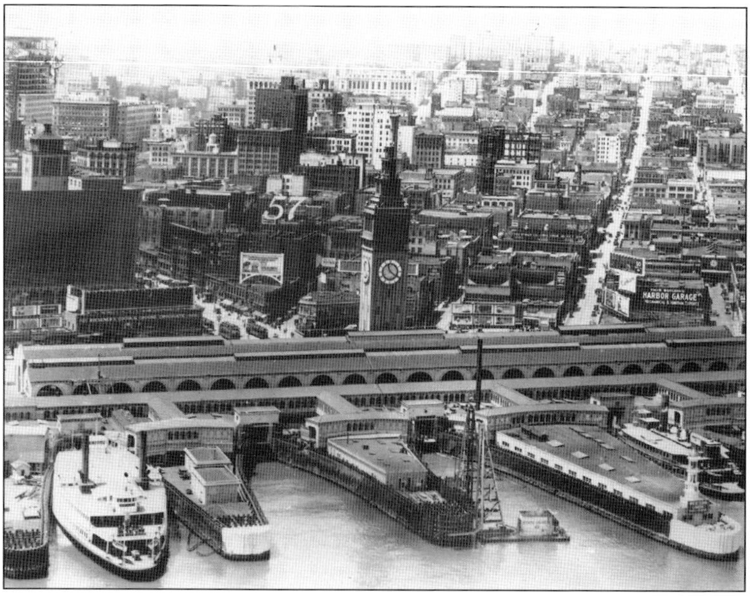

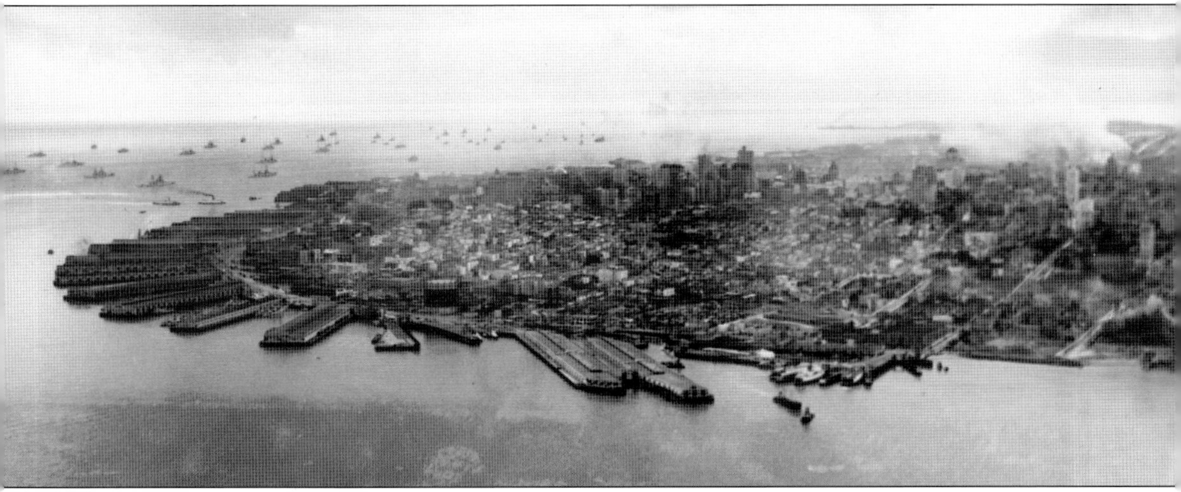

Fr. Pedro Font, a Franciscan padre who was part of the Spanish expedition who explored the land around San Francisco Bay from 1769 to 1776, might have been looking at this aerial view of the San Francisco Bay shoreline when he wrote in his diary in 1776, "The Port of San Francisco is a marvel of nature and may well be called the harbor of harbors, and I think that if it could be well settled like Europe, there would not be anything more beautiful in all the world—for it has the best advantages for founding in it a most beautiful city with all the conveniences desired by land as well as by sea—with that harbor so remarkable and so spacious in which may be established shipyards, docks and anything that may be wished for." (San Diego Air and Space Museum Archives.)

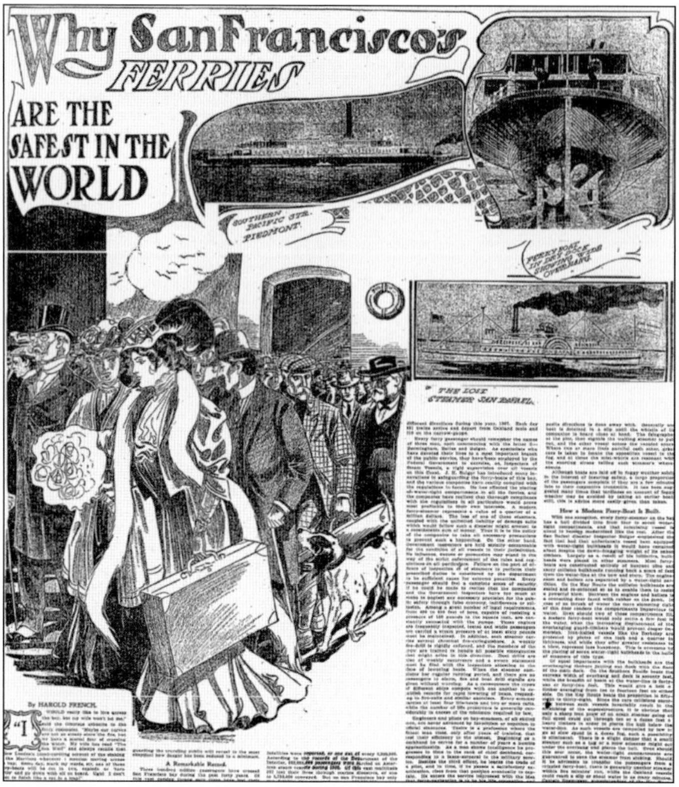

Why San Francisco's FERRIES ARE THE SAFEST IN THE WORLD

By HAROLD FRENCH.

In "Why San Francisco's Ferries are the Safest in the World" in the *San Francisco Chronicle* on May 5, 1907, the author declares, "For nearly forty years, in fog and storm, sunshine and darkness, more than a score of ferryboats have churned the yellowish-green waters of San Francisco Bay, making an aggregate of half a million trips up to this date and established a record that is without parallel on all the seven seas." (Library of Congress.)

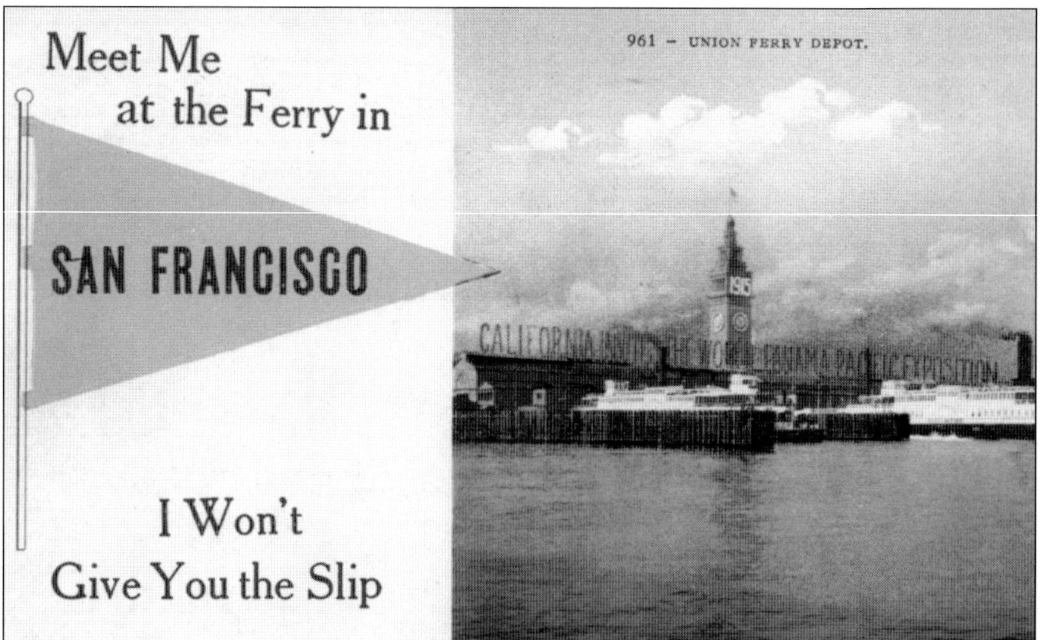

This c. 1915 postcard features the Ferry Building adorned with the Panama-Pacific International Exposition banner. "Meet Me at the Ferry in San Francisco, I Won't Give You the Slip" playfully invites travelers to visit the city—via ferry, of course. (Author's collection.)

The first auto ferry, the *Melrose,* was launched in 1909. Its lower deck was specifically intended for automobiles, with its upper deck for passengers. By the 1920s, Southern Pacific offered four auto ferry routes across San Francisco Bay. This schedule, provided by Crocker First National Bank, shows how frequently the ferries traveled to the Oakland Pier and Oakland Harbor (foot of Broadway). Other Southern Pacific routes included San Francisco–Richmond Pier and San Francisco–Alameda Pier. A Southern Pacific travel brochure declares that the company "operates the finest fleet of auto ferries in the world in point of safety, comfort, reliability, cleanliness, and excellence of travel appointments and refinements." (Both, author's collection.)

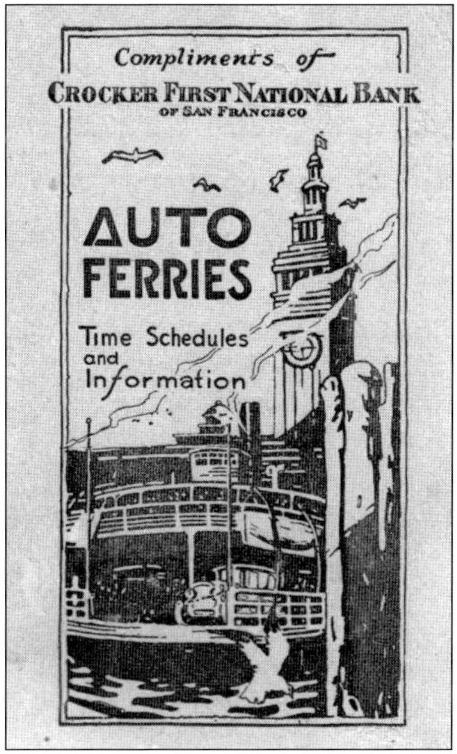

11-8 4 11-8

Southern Pacific Company

SAN FRANCISCO-OAKLAND

Oakland Pier

Leave San Francisco Foot of Mission Street			Leave Oakland Pier		
6.00	**12.42**	**6.18**	6.15	**12.48**	**6.24**
6.30	**12.54**	**6.30**	6.30	**1.00**	**6.36**
6.45	**1.06**	**6.42**	6.45	**1.12**	**6.48**
7.00	**1.18**	**6.54**	7.00	**1.24**	**7.00**
7.15	**1.30**	**7.00**	7.15	**1.36**	**7.12**
7.30	**1.42**	**7.15**	7.30	**1.48**	**7.24**
7.45	**1.54**	**7.30**	7.45	**2.00**	**7.36**
8.00	**2.06**	**7.45**	8.00	**2.12**	**7.50**
8.15	**2.18**	**8.00**	8.15	**2.24**	**8.10**
8.30	**2.30**	**8.20**	8.30	**2.36**	**8.30**
8.45	**2.42**	**8.40**	8.45	**2.48**	**8.50**
9.00	**2.54**	**9.00**	9.00	**3.00**	**9.10**
9.15	**3.06**	**9.20**	9.15	**3.12**	**9.30**
9.30	**3.18**	**9.40**	9.30	**3.24**	**9.50**
9.45	**3.30**	**10.00**	9.45	**3.36**	**10.10**
10.00	**3.42**	**10.20**	10.00	**3.48**	**10.30**
10.15	**3.54**	**10.40**	10.15	**4.00**	**10.50**
10.30	**4.06**	**11.00**	10.30	**4.12**	**11.10**
10.45	**4.18**	**11.20**	10.45	**4.24**	**11.30**
10.54	**4.30**	**11.40**	11.00	**4.36**	**11.50**
11.06	**4.42**	12.00	11.12	**4.48**	
11.18	**4.54**	12.20	11.24	**5.00**	12.10
11.30	**5.06**	12.40	11.36	**5.12**	12.30
11.42	**5.18**	1.00	11.48	**5.24**	1.30
11.54	**5.30**	2.00	**12.00**	**5.36**	2.30
12.06	**5.42**	3.00	**12.12**	**5.48**	3.30
12.18	**5.54**	4.00	**12.24**	**6.00**	4.30
12.30	**6.06**	5.00	**12.36**	**6.12**	5.30

Light face figures A. M.; dark face figures P. M.

Additional Service during rush hours Saturdays, Sundays and Holidays

Rate—Automobile, each way............ $ [illegible]

Passengers in automobiles, each way...... [illegible]

Motorcycles, each way............ [illegible]

CROCKER FIRST NATIONAL BANK of San Francisco

11-8 5 11-8

Southern Pacific Company

SAN FRANCISCO–OAKLAND

Broadway

Daily Except Sundays and Holidays

Leave San Francisco Foot of Mission Street			Leave Oakland		
7.45	**12.50**	**5.45**	7.00	**12.10**	**5.00**
9.15	**2.45**		8.30	**2.00**	
10.45	**4.15**		10.00	**3.30**	

Rate—Automobile, each way............ $ .60

Passengers, each way............ .05

Motorcycles, each way............ .25

SAN FRANCISCO--ALAMEDA

Leave San Francisco Foot of Mission Street			Leave Alameda		
6.30	**12.00**	**5.30**	6.00	**12.00**	**6.00**
7.00	**12.30**	**6.00**	6.30	**12.30**	**6.30**
7.30	**1.00**	**6.30**	7.00	**1.00**	**7.00**
8.00	**1.30**	**7.00**	7.30	**1.30**	**7.30**
8.30	**2.00**	**7.30**	8.00	**2.00**	**8.00**
9.00	**2.30**	**8.00**	8.30	**2.30**	**8.30**
9.30	**3.00**	**8.30**	9.00	**3.00**	**9.00**
10.00	**3.30**	**9.00**	9.30	**3.30**	**10.00**
10.30	**4.00**	**9.30**	10.00	**4.00**	**11.00**
11.00	**4.30**	**10.30**	10.30	**4.30**	12.00
11.30	**5.00**	**11.30**	11.00	**5.00**	
		12.30	11.30	**5.30**	

Light face figures A. M.; dark face figures P. M.

Rate—Automobile, each way............ $ .60

Passengers, each way............ .05

Motorcycles, each way............ .25

CROCKER FIRST NATIONAL BANK of San Francisco

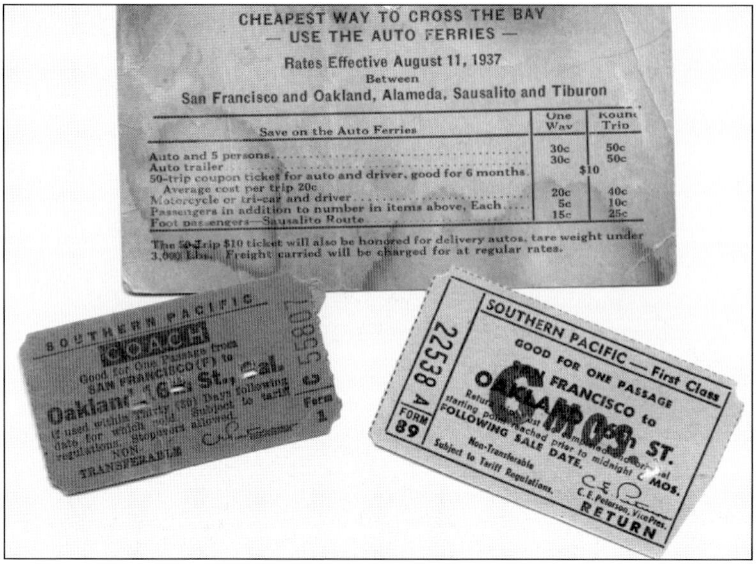

Ferry tickets for passage on the Oakland-bound Southern Pacific ferries would get passengers across the bay to meet their trains. These ferries would go to the Oakland Mole at the foot of Seventh Street, where electric or steam trains would be waiting. One could also take the auto ferry to the East Bay or Marin. One-way fare for an auto and five persons in 1937 was 30¢. (Author's collection.)

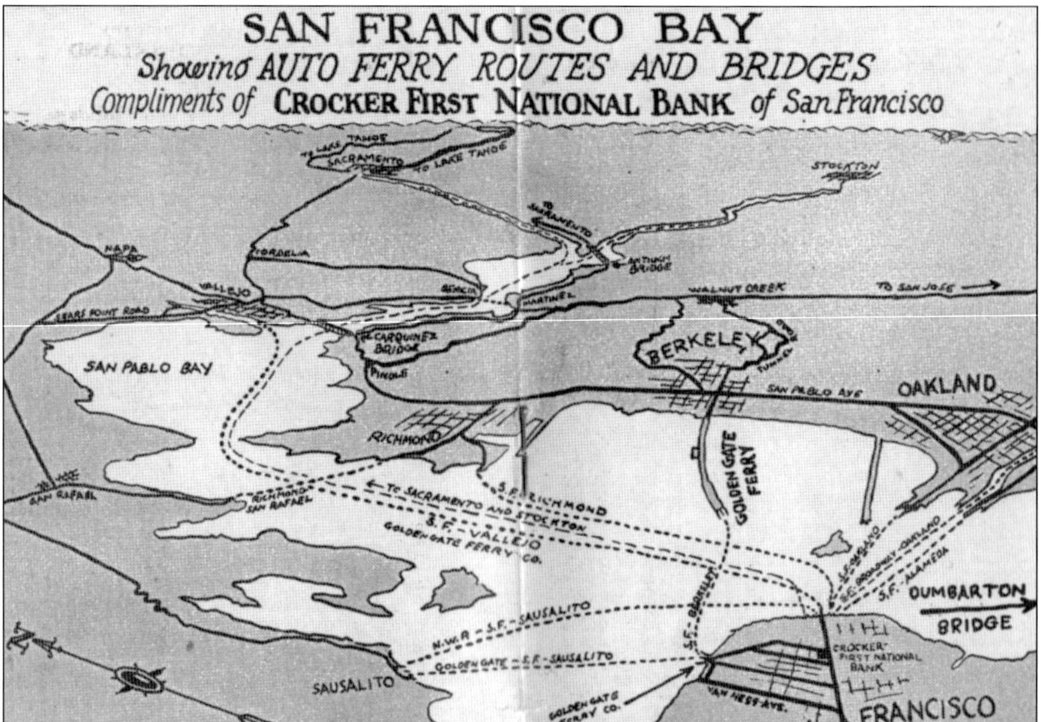

This hand-drawn map from 1927 is part of the ferry schedule given out by Crocker First National Bank. It shows the ferry routes such as the Golden Gate Ferry Co., which left from San Francisco's Hyde Street Pier, and all the routes emanating from the Ferry Building to the south. (Author's collection.)

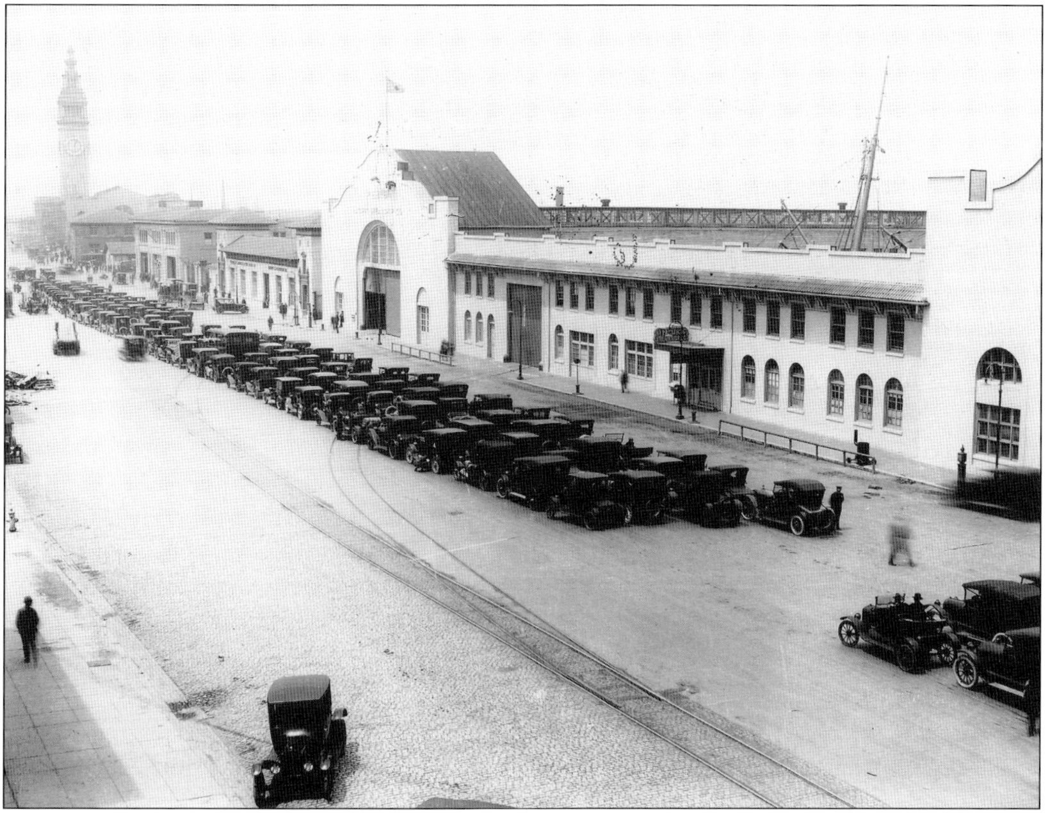

In the 1900s, the rapid increase in the number of cars meant that ferry operators needed to accommodate motorists in the era before bridges spanned the bay. Different ferry companies soon had ferries that could handle auto traffic. Motorists could easily take the ferry to Marin or the East Bay and go on a Sunday drive. Here, motorcars line up on the Embarcadero to wait their turns for the auto ferries. The ferries supposedly followed their published schedules, but actually left when the deckhands had gotten as many cars on board as possible. (Above, San Francisco History Center, San Francisco Public Library; below, OpenSFHistory/wnp30.0215.)

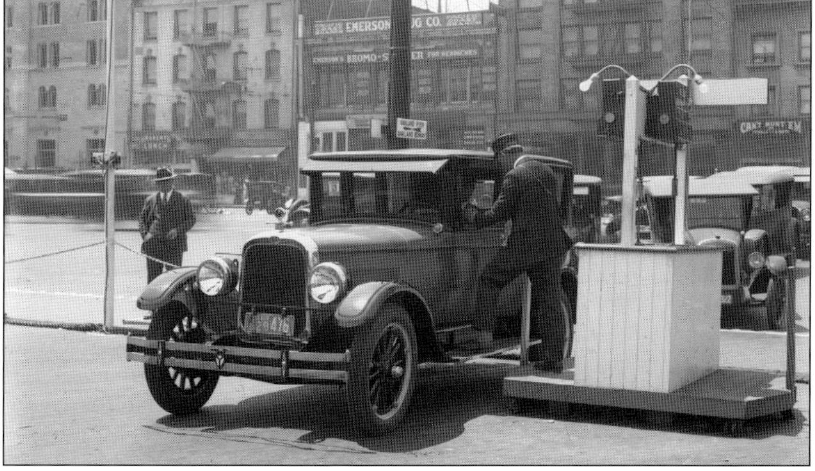

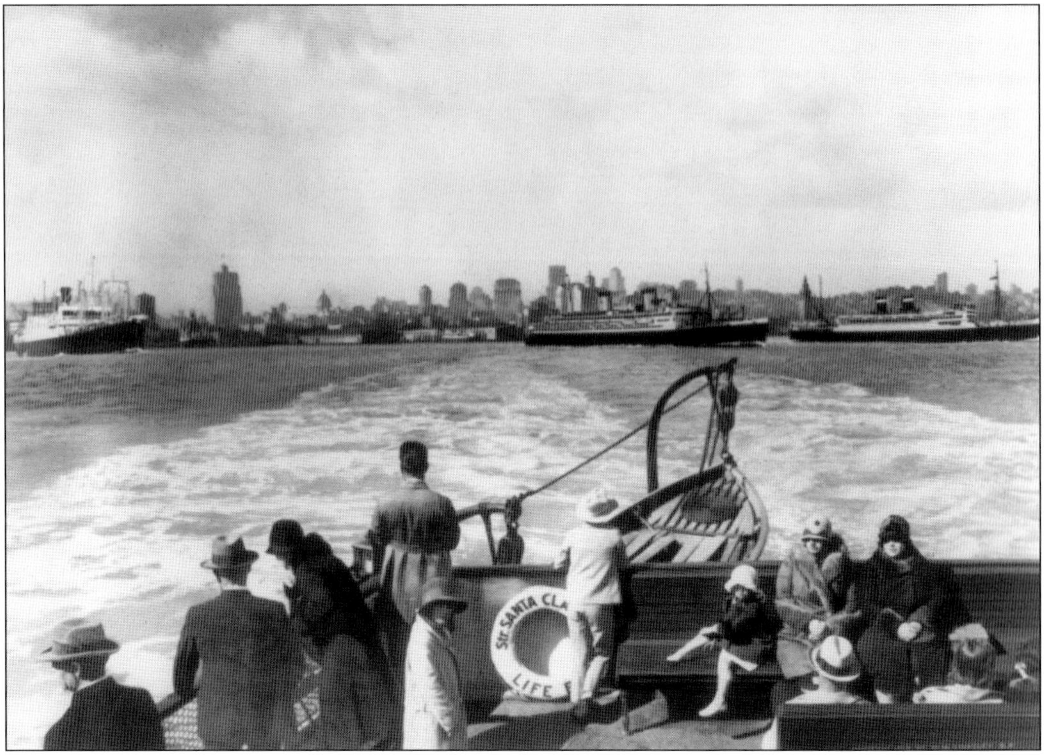

As the *Santa Clara* ferry approaches San Francisco, the city looks magical. The *Santa Clara*, a side-wheel passenger ferry, was built in 1915 and ended operations in 1945. During World War II, it carried shipyard workers from San Francisco to the Marinship shipyard in Sausalito, which built ships required for the war effort. (Library of Congress.)

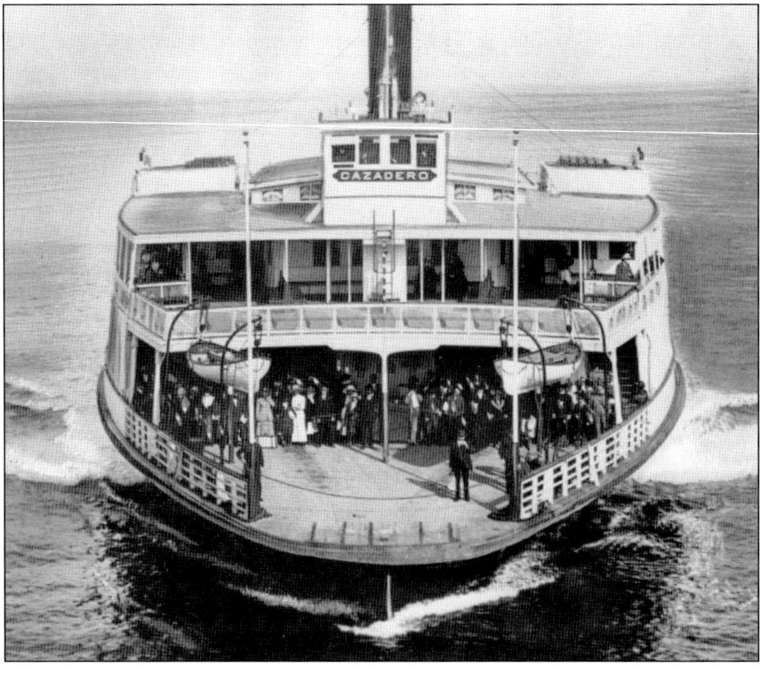

Northwestern Pacific ferryboat *Cazadero* traveled to Sausalito from San Francisco in 30 minutes, reaching a speed of 14 knots. The double-ended side-wheeler's 26-foot paddle wheels could revolve 24 times a minute. Built in 1903, it was converted to a barge in 1941. (SFMNHP.)

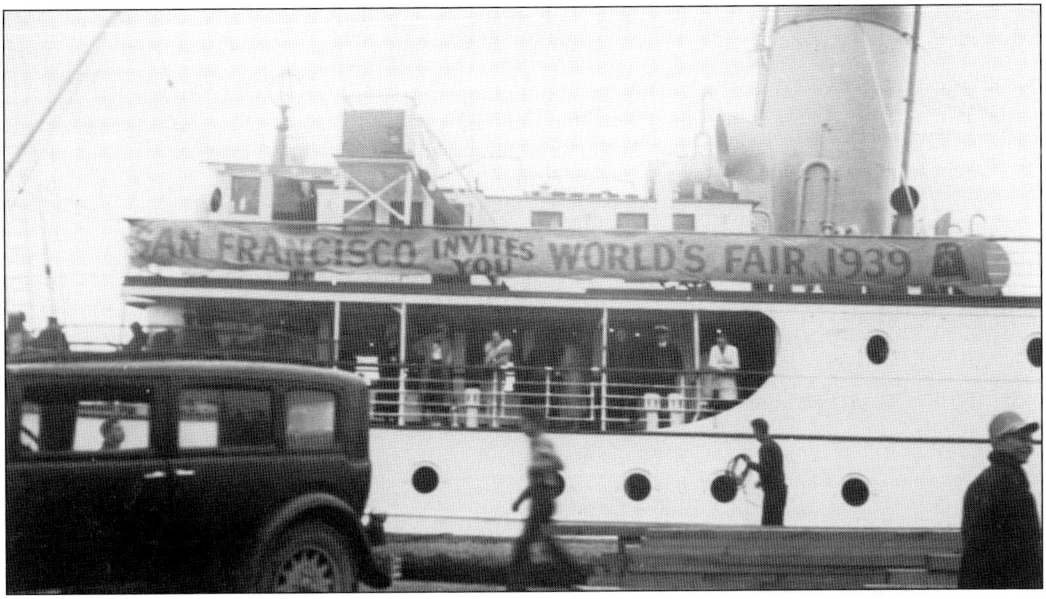

"San Francisco Invites You. World's Fair 1939" declares the banner on the ferry in the photograph above. In the photograph below, crowds head past the souvenir stands on opening day, February 18, to load onto one of the Key System or Southern Pacific ferries, which scheduled additional runs for the duration of the fair. Officially called the Golden Gate International Exposition (1939–1940), the fair was held at San Francisco's Treasure Island, a 400-acre artificial island in San Francisco Bay, built 1936–1937. Fairgoers marveled at the many attractions, including the 400-foot Tower of the Sun. It was San Francisco's last world's fair and the last large-scale public celebration before America's entry into World War II. (Above, author's collection; below, San Francisco History Center, San Francisco Public Library.)

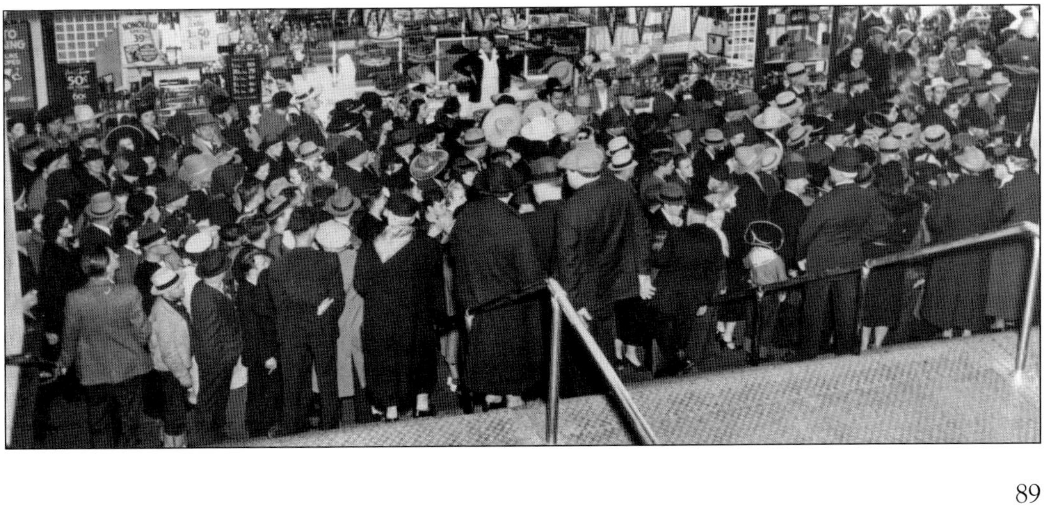

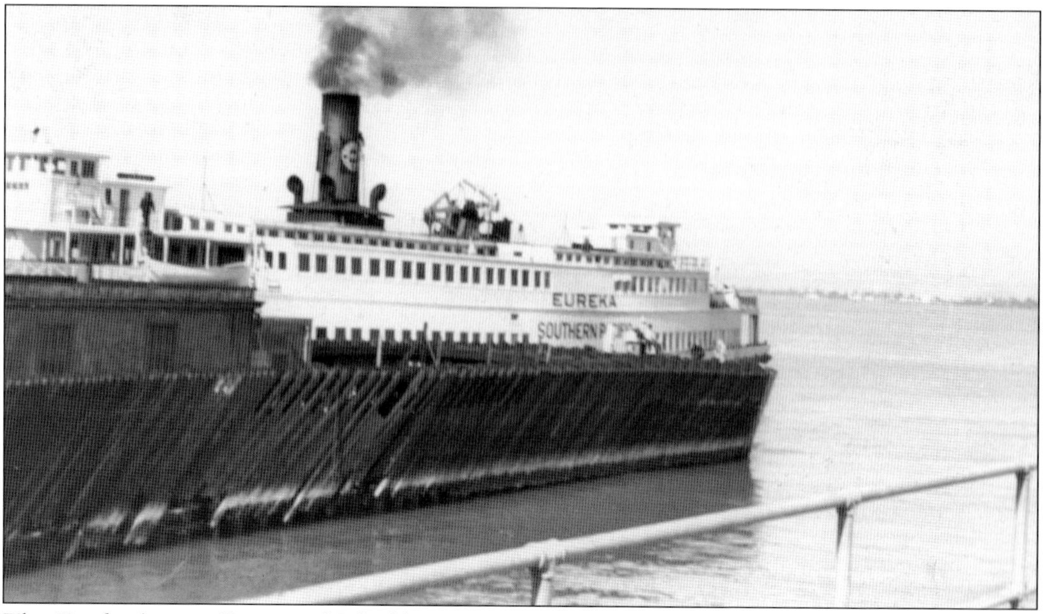

The *Eureka* (originally named *Ukiah)* was a side-wheel paddle steamboat built in 1890. Its first job was to carry commuters during the day between San Francisco and Tiburon, then haul railroad freight cars at night. In 1907, *Ukiah* was rerouted to the Sausalito–Ferry Building route by Northwestern Pacific Railroad, its new owner. *Ukiah* was rebuilt at the Southern Pacific yards in Oakland between 1920 and 1922, and rechristened as the auto/passenger ferry *Eureka*. From 1922 to 1941, *Eureka* carried an average of 2,200 passengers per trip from Sausalito to the Ferry Building in 26 minutes. Six inches short of a football field, it was the largest wooden ferryboat afloat in the world. In the 1950s, *Eureka* connected with Southern Pacific's transcontinental railroad trains at the Oakland Station and took passengers and baggage to San Francisco. Today, *Eureka* is afloat at the San Francisco Maritime National Historical Park. (Both, author's collection.)

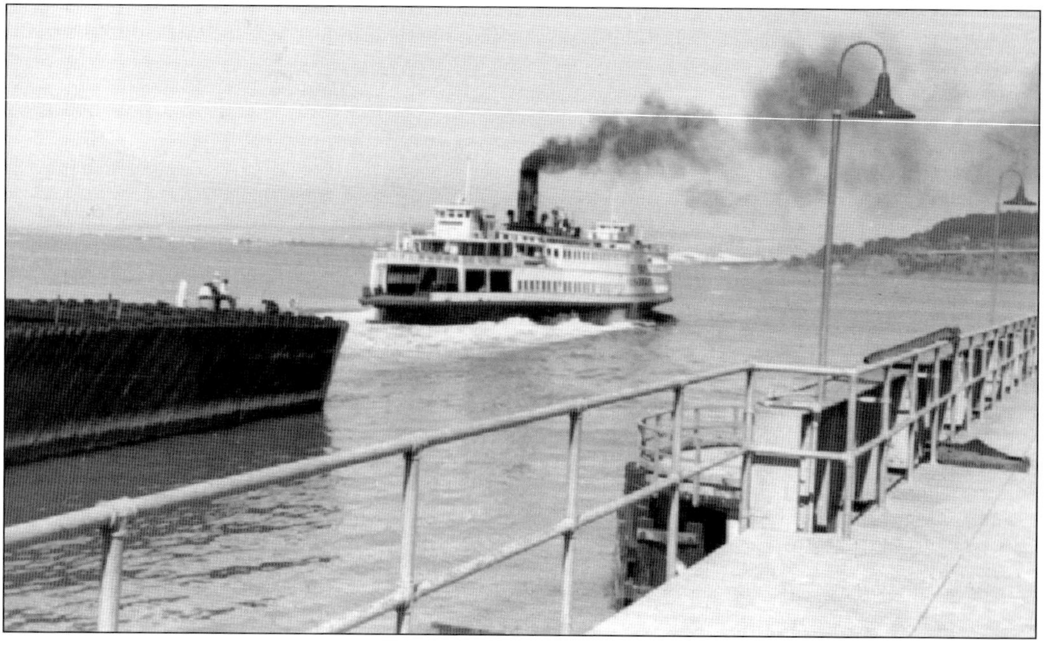

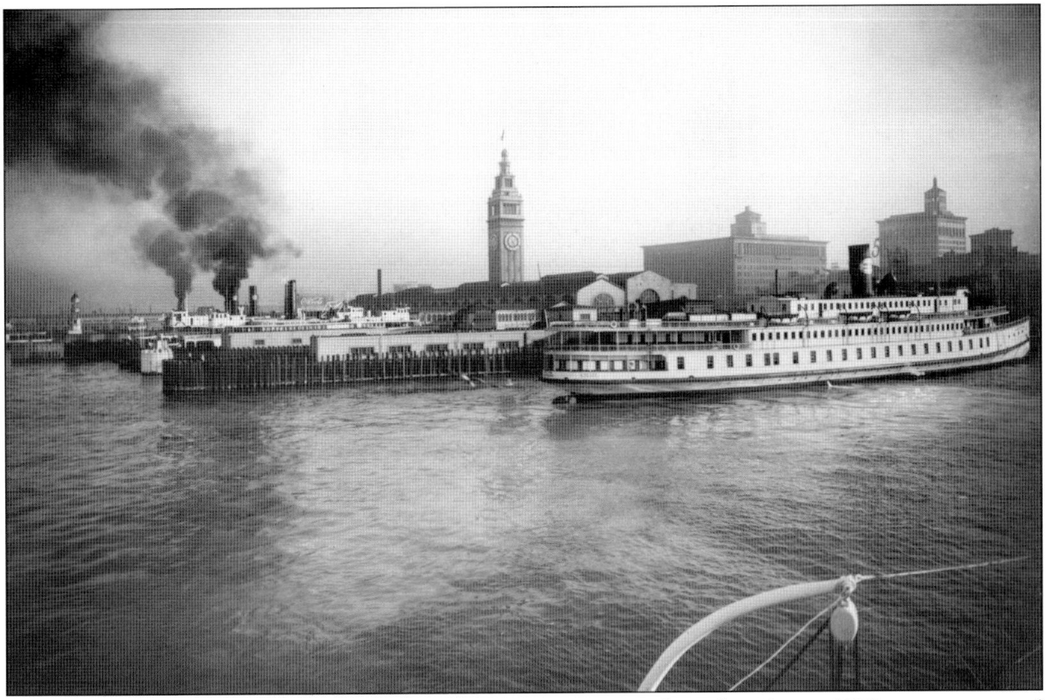

The SS *Asbury Park,* a high-speed coastal steamer pictured in the above 1922 image, started steaming across the waters of San Francisco Bay in 1918. In 1925, the vessel was extensively modified and renamed *City of Sacramento,* crossing San Francisco Bay between San Francisco and Vallejo. In 1927, Southern Pacific–Golden Gate Ferries bought her. In the photograph below, she sails near the San Francisco–Oakland Bay Bridge, which was under construction at the time. (It was completed in 1936). As ferry service declined after the bridges opened, the *City of Sacramento* was sold to a company in Puget Sound in 1941. (Above, SFMNHP A12, 4769; below, Western Railway Museum Archives.)

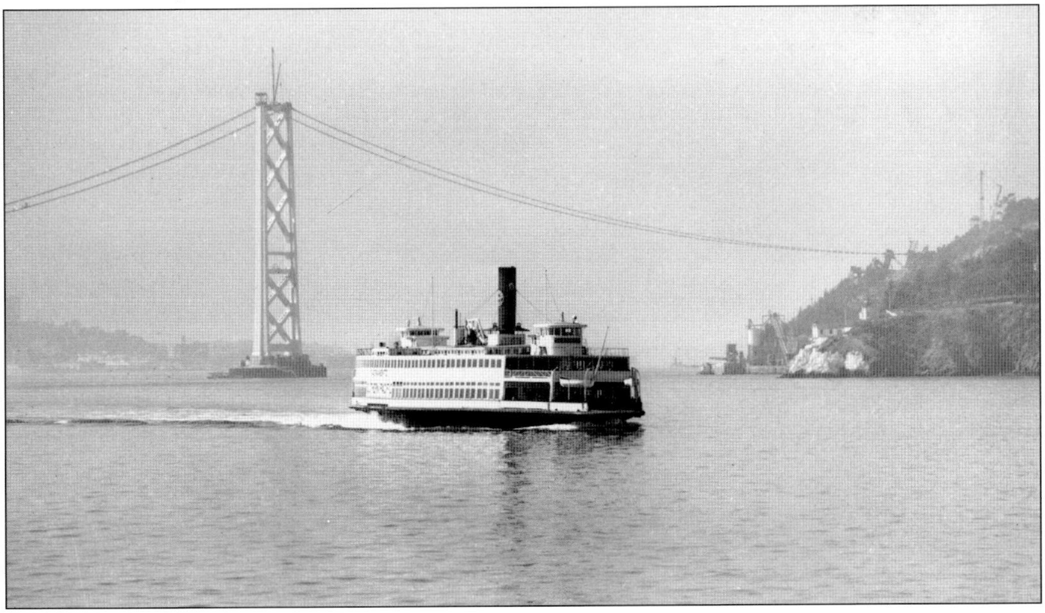

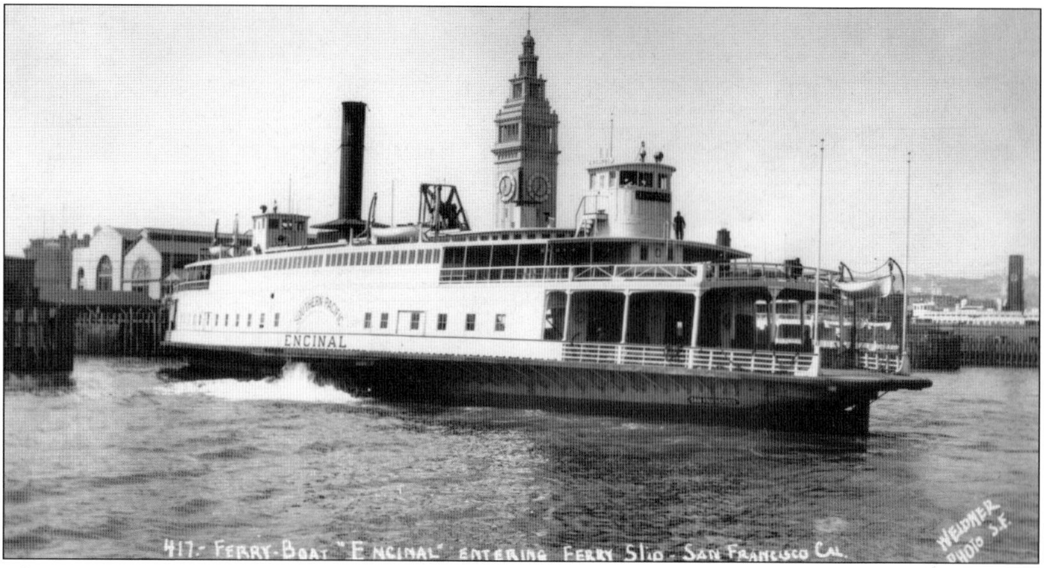

The *Encinal* was a side-wheel passenger ferry that served Alameda in the East Bay. It was put into service in 1888 by the South Pacific Coast Railroad (SPC) and retired in 1930. Southern Pacific subsequently bought SPC, and the *Encinal* worked Oakland's "Creek Route." (SFMNHP p84-081, 9n. Charles Weidner, Charles Smallwood Collection.)

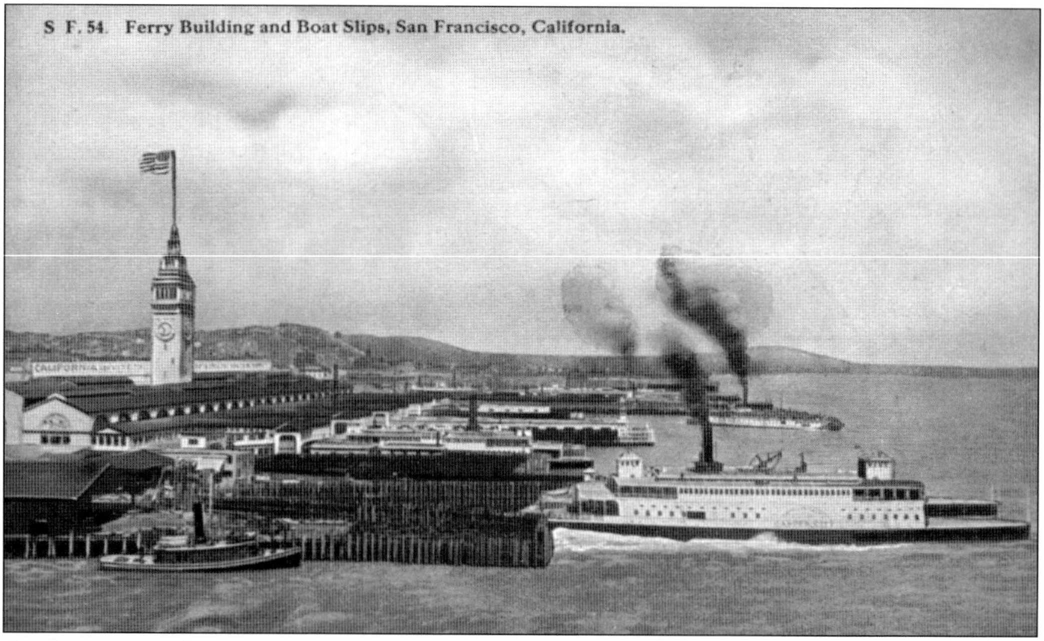

Garden City, a side-wheel passenger ferry built in 1879, carried autos and passengers until her last run in 1929. Here, she is steaming away from the Ferry Building, headed toward the East Bay. In 1921, during a full gale on Christmas morning, she attempted an eastbound bay crossing and ended up drifting into the Key System pier, which was seriously damaged. Twenty-foot-high waves drenched the ferry passengers as they scrambled to safety. (Author's collection.)

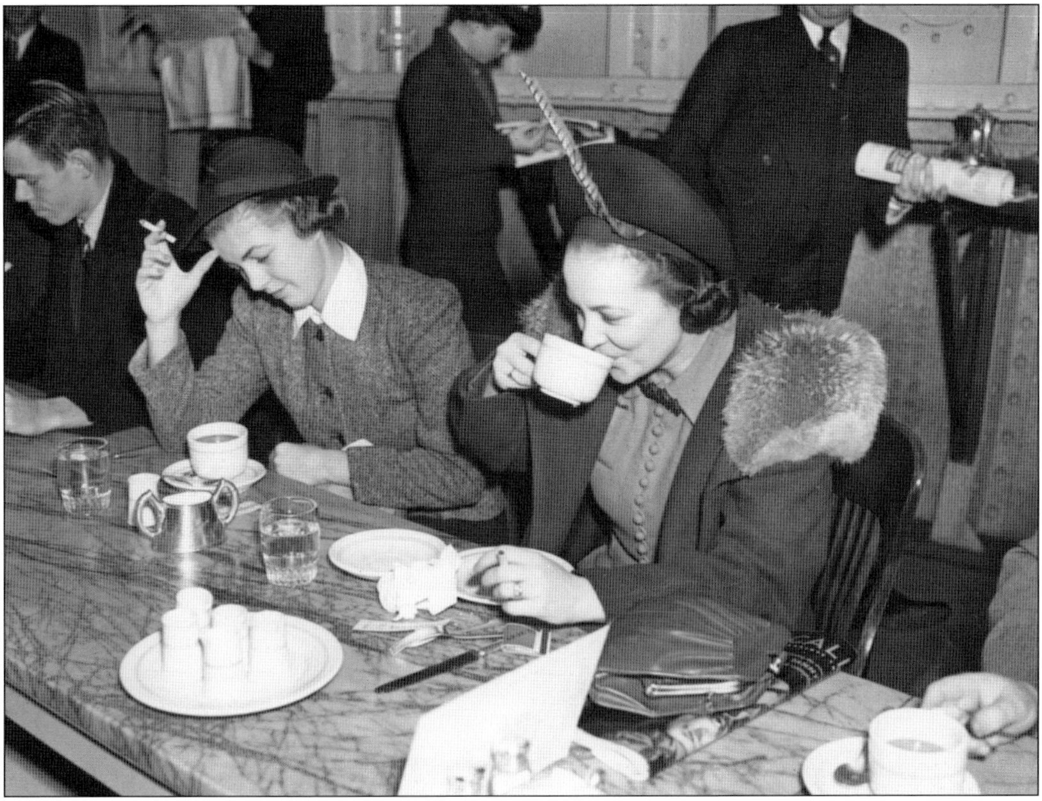

It took 30 minutes or less to cross the bay, and the cafés were crowded. Columnist Herb Caen especially loved "the incomparable corned beef hash on the Oakland ferry (on the way back after a night with Benny Goodman at McFadden's Ballroom)," as published in the *San Francisco Chronicle* on January 25, 1959. A 1938 menu from the *Eureka* features roast beef jardinière (40¢), boiled brisket of beef with Spanish sauce (45¢), and homemade corned beef hash (30¢). (Western Railway Museum Archives.)

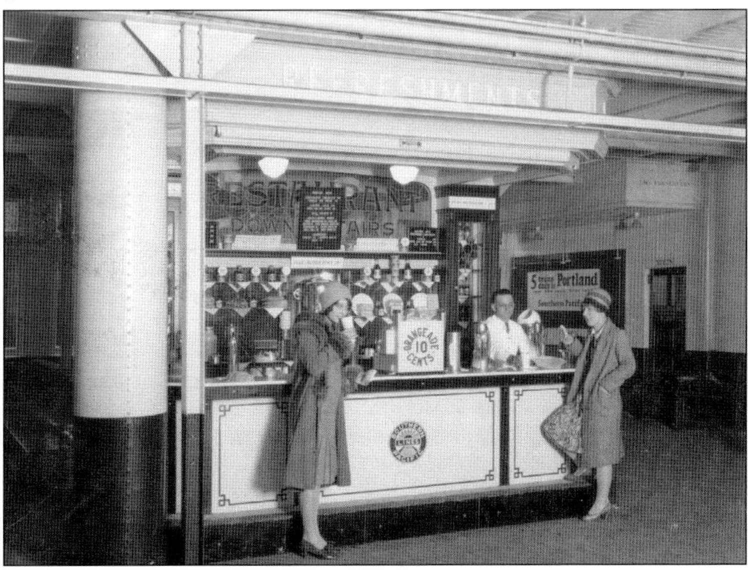

These lovely ladies sip their Orangeade at a ferry's concession. Concessionaires on board sometimes included barbershops, bootblacks, and newsstands that had every magazine one could want, plus comic books, candy bars, cigars, cigarettes, and popcorn (5¢). Passengers could also get souvenirs and guide maps for the city. (Western Railway Museum Archives.)

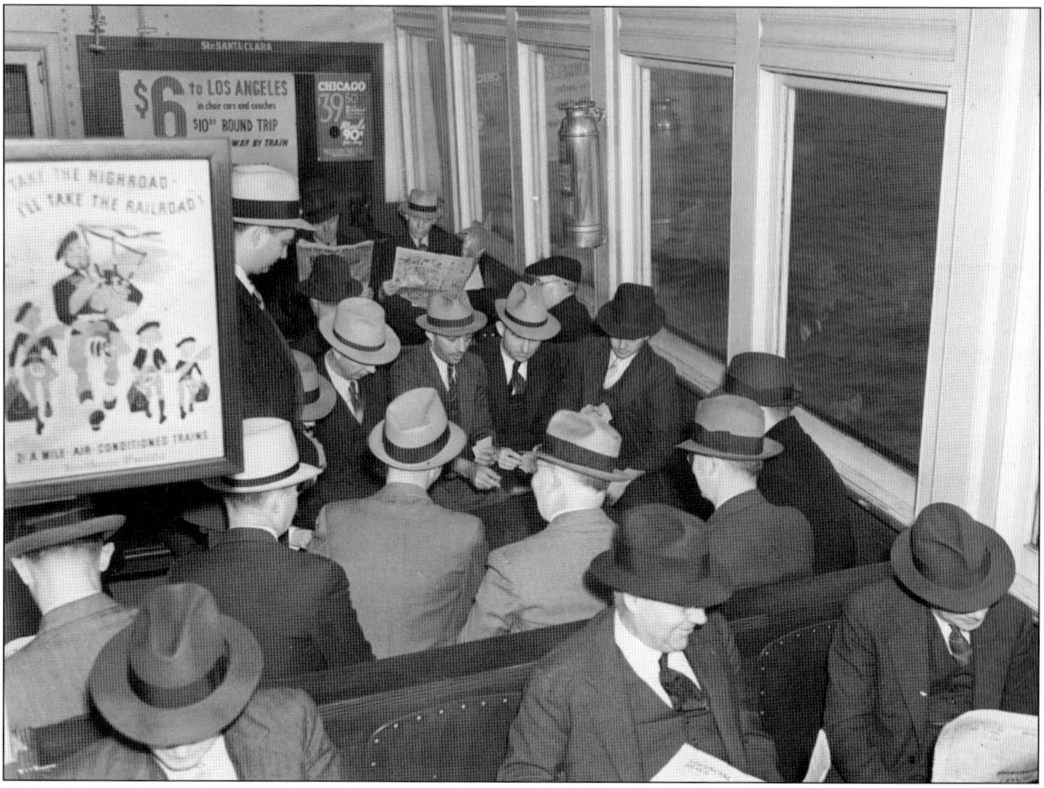

Commuters who traveled back and forth on the bay often formed closely knit groups, and these groups always sat in the same seats. Woe to the newcomer who dared take someone's regular seat. As described on July 22, 1912, in Ferry Tales, the *San Francisco Call* column that ran tidbits about ferry life: "To a large extent the commuter is an individual of regular habits. The same crowd travels at the same hour every day. Congenial souls naturally gravitate together. Hence the commuter clubs." Many of the groups had ongoing card games, like the group in this picture. Players provided their own cards or could buy cards on the ferry, like the one pictured below. Large playing boards provided by the ferry companies were kept in wooden racks on the decks. (Above, Western Railway Museum Archives; below, author's collection.)

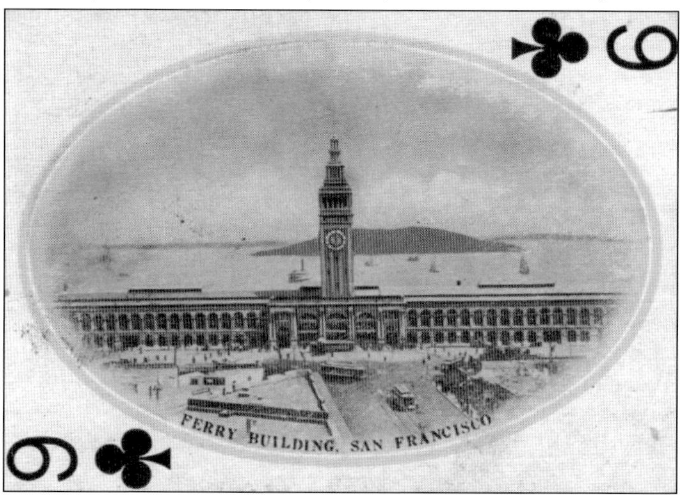

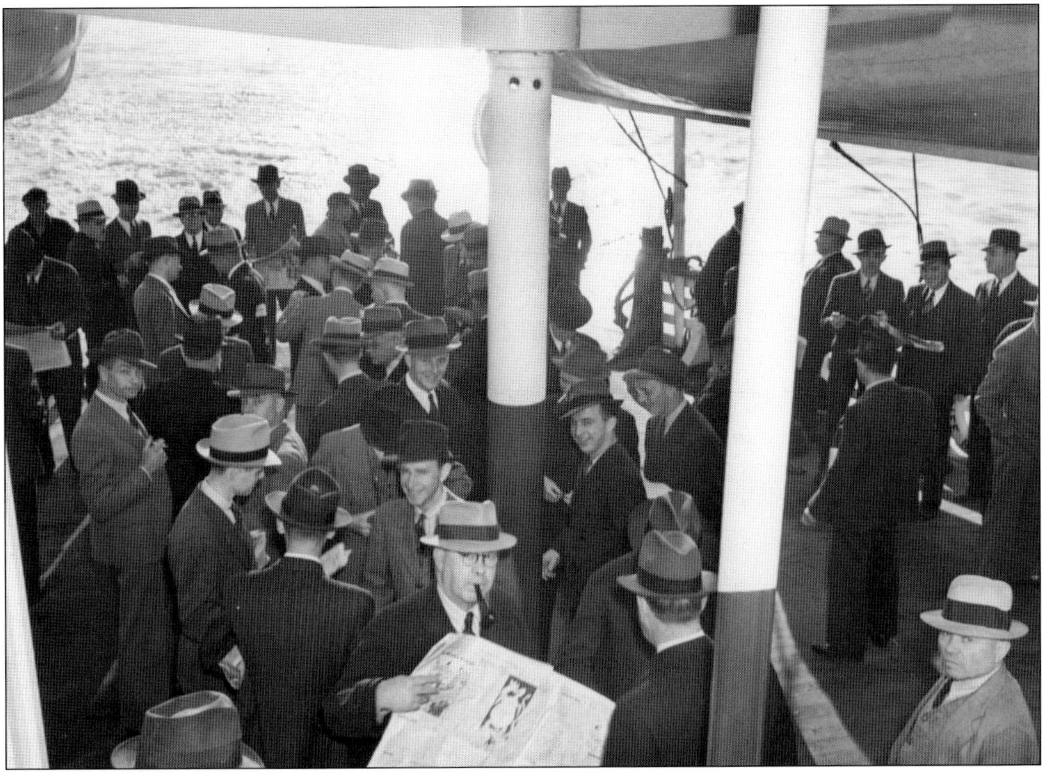

The July 22, 1912, Ferry Tales column notes a clique on the ferry known as the "After Deck Squad (ADS)," like the group pictured above, could "be found any business afternoon on the boat that leaves the ferry at 5:45 for the Alameda mole. To locate the squad all that is necessary is to stand on the afterdeck until the boat gets under way. It will not be long before you hear a chorus of laughter. Walk right over to the scene of the disturbance and in a voice as nearly natural as the somewhat unusual proceeding will permit, utter one of the squad passwords. There are several of these. Here are a few of them: 'Oh George!', 'Jack!', 'Hello, Van!', 'Say, Denny!' Any of these will do." (Above, Western Railway Museum Archives; right, author's collection.)

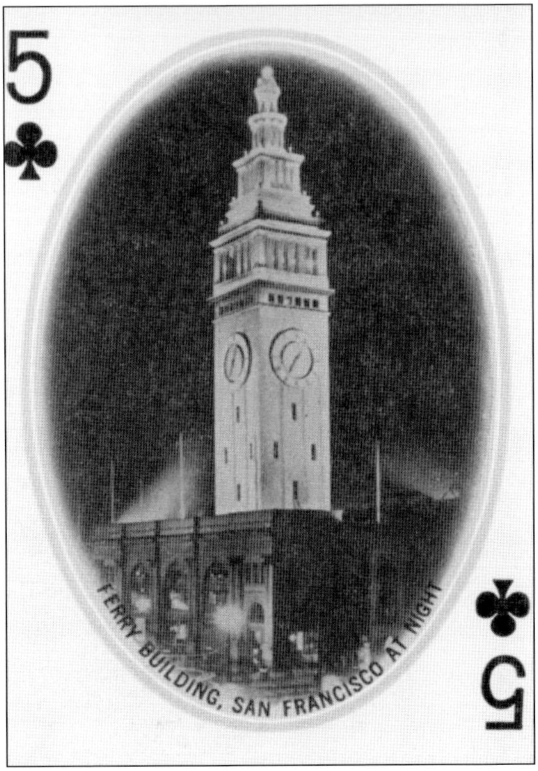

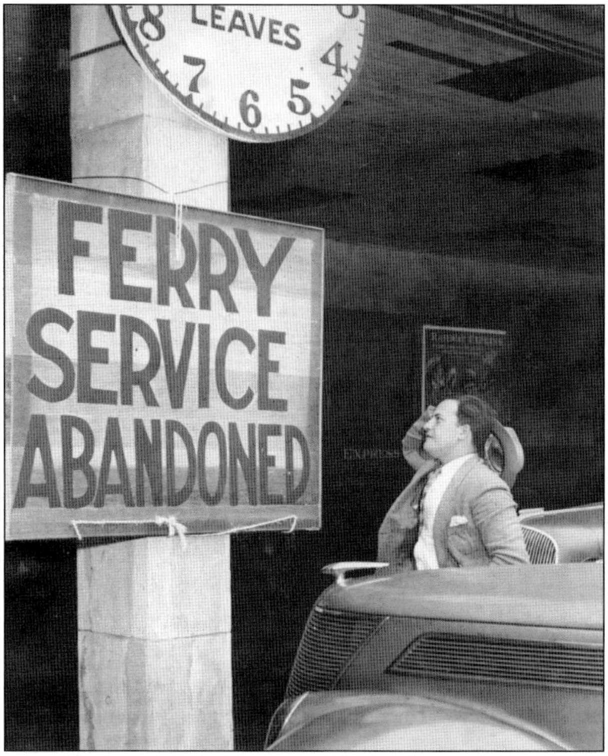

A surprised auto ferry passenger in 1940 confronts a "Ferry Service Abandoned" notice. After the two bridges opened, Southern Pacific reduced its service to three routes: San Francisco to the Oakland Pier, San Francisco to the Alameda Pier, and Hyde Street to Sausalito. By 1940, autos and interurban trains traveled on the bridge, but passenger ferries continued until 1958. (San Francisco History Center, San Francisco Public Library.)

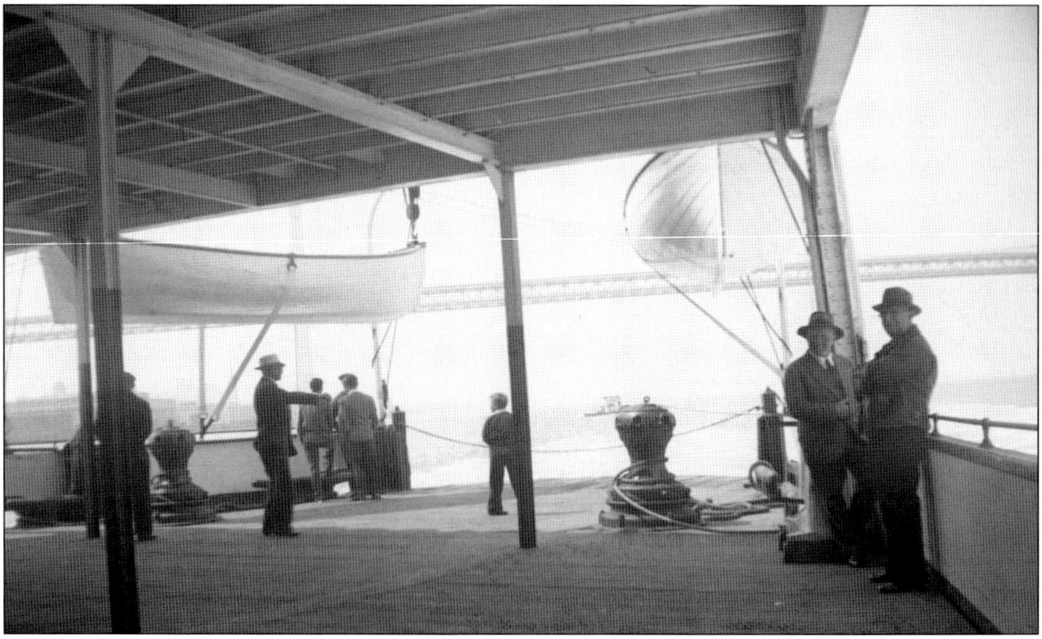

The Bay Bridge looms over this quiet ferry scene, which could illustrate the drop-off in ridership once the bridges were built. Many people regretted the ferries' demise. As columnist Herb Caen wrote in 1964, many years after ferries stopped operating, "Today, thousands of people live at the edge of the bay they've never been on. . . . Ferryboats were close to the foaming heart of the matter—something to love." (Western Railway Museum Archives.)

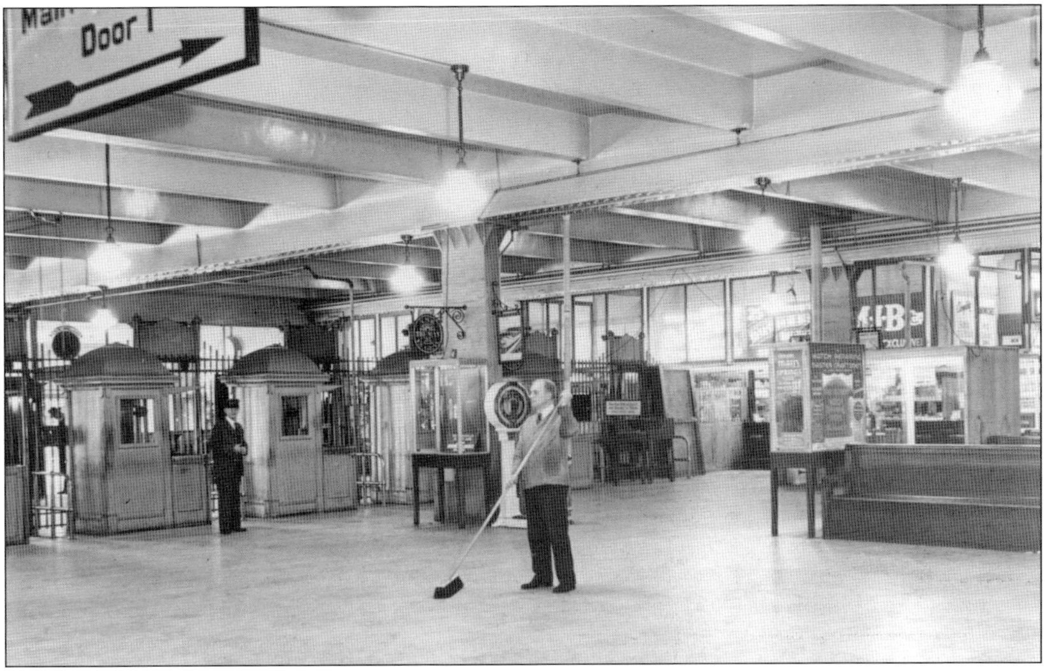

These rather bleak images of nearly empty ferry waiting rooms (the above image was taken in 1940, and the one below in 1958) contrast with the busy, vibrant images from the 1920s and 1930s. The last Southern Pacific ferry ran between Oakland and San Francisco in July 1958. (Above, San Francisco History Center, San Francisco Public Library; below, Western Railway Museum Archives.)

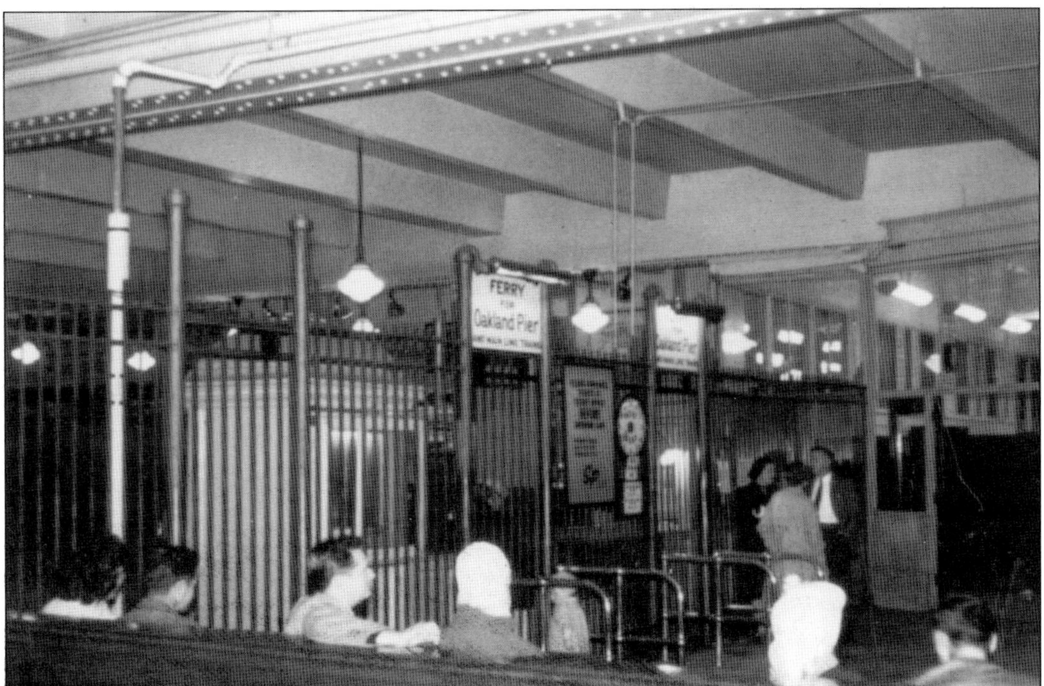

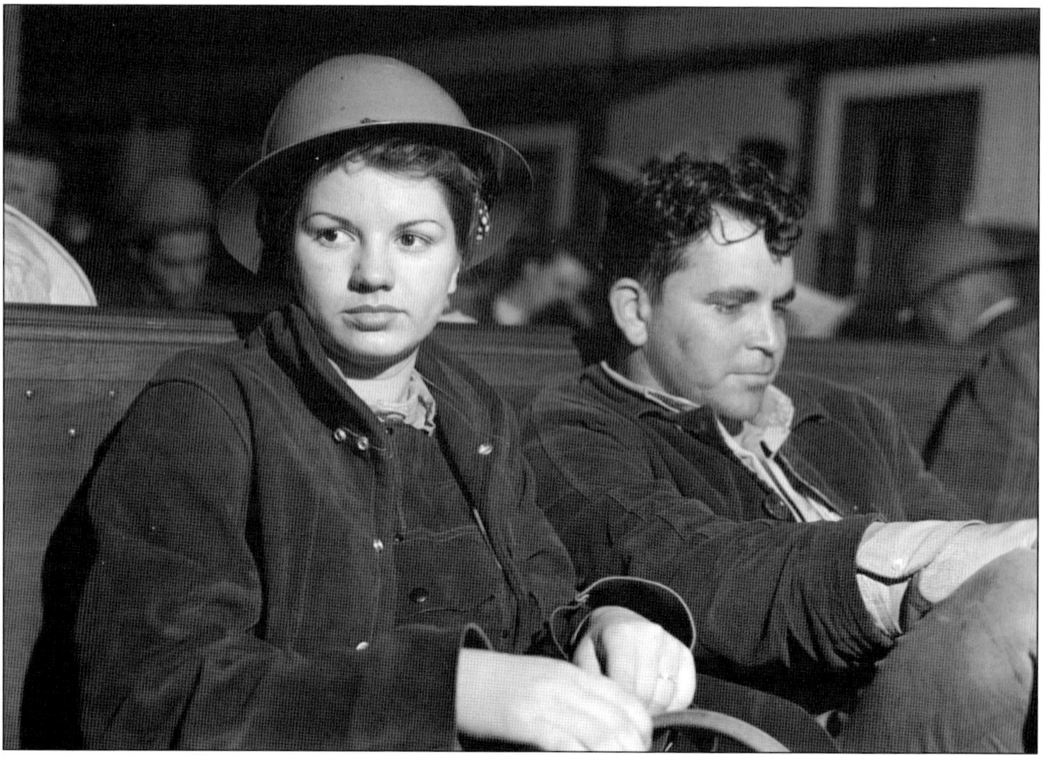

Ann Rosener, hired as a photographer for the Farm Security Administration (later called the Office of War Information), took these striking images of shipyard workers riding the ferries from San Francisco to Marinship (Sausalito) and Richmond Shipyards in 1943. Many of the large passenger ferries stopped running in the late 1930s and early 1940s, so the federal government was able to mobilize them during World War II to transport military personnel and shipyard workers around the bay. In these images, after eight hours of work in a shipyard, these workers may have been grateful for the calm and quiet of the ferry trip back to San Francisco. (Both, Library of Congress.)

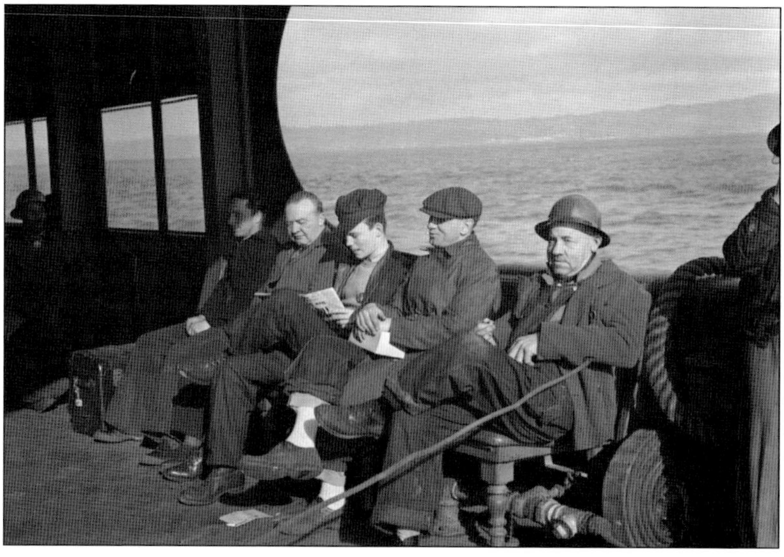

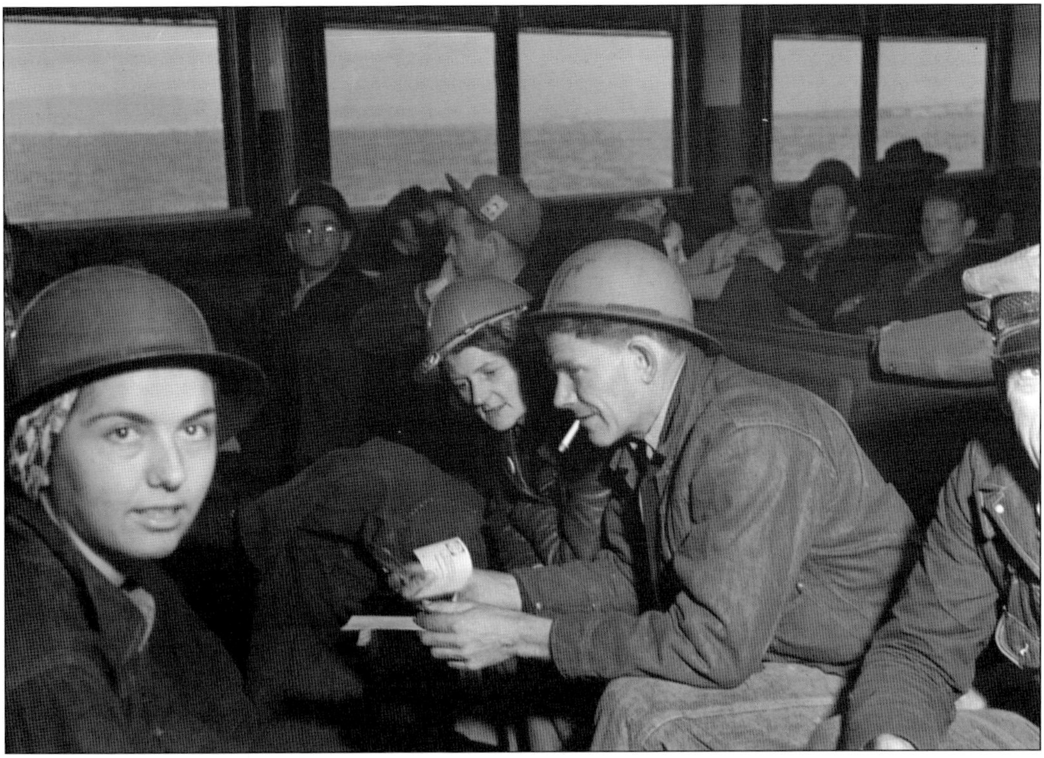

In the above photograph, San Francisco war workers have time for relaxation and discussion on the 45-minute ferry ride to the Richmond Shipbuilding Company yards. In the below photograph, workers disembark, headed for home. One of the themes of Rosener's photograph assignments was "Americans All," images showing citizens making contributions essential to the war effort. Her goal was to show Americans working together to build tanks, ships, and airplanes, with no thought of differences of race or creed. She also photographed women and others filling essential jobs formerly reserved for able-bodied men, who were in the armed forces. (Both, Library of Congress.)

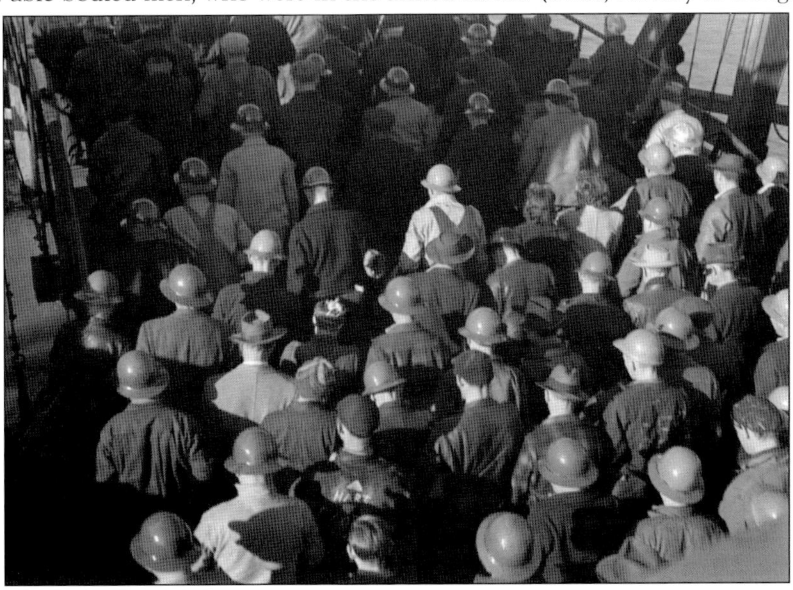

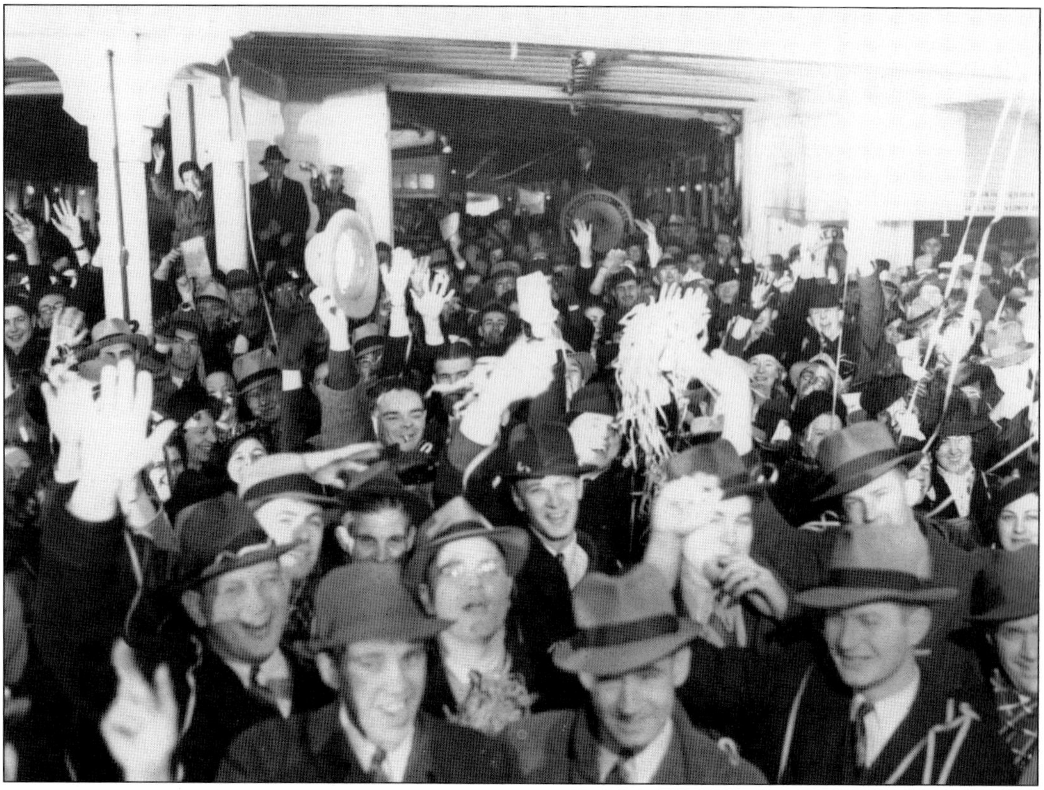

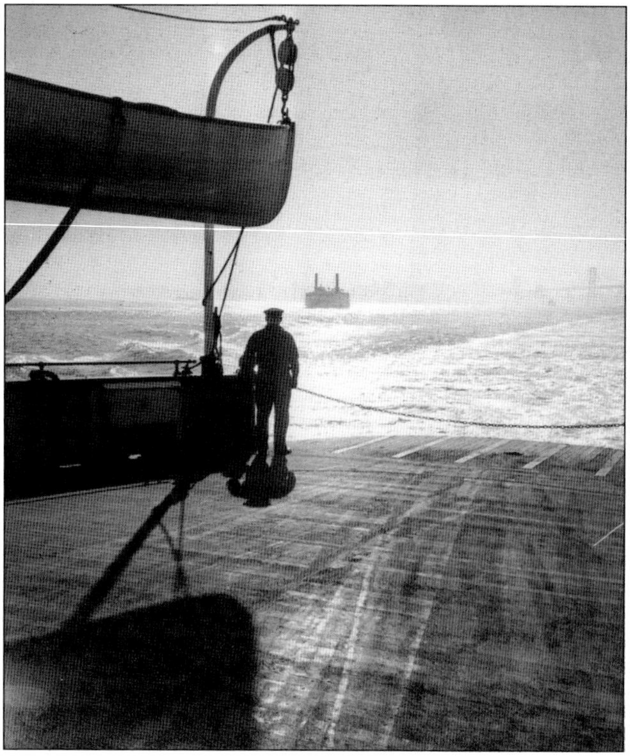

In 1938, the year this photograph was taken, auto ferry service to Sausalito ended, as the Golden Gate Bridge had opened in 1937 and ridership had declined significantly. It is interesting to note that in 1930, just eight years earlier, 43 ferryboats had carried 47 million passengers around the bay. Looks like the regulars wanted to end on a high note, as they throw streamers and cheer. (Western Railway Museum Archives.)

A crew member stands alone on the deck in 1938, an image that brings to mind the words of Clyde Rice, author of *A Heaven in the Eye* (published in 1984): "The deck-hands cast off the lines. Sea gulls on the pilings winced at the whistle's blast. Great paddle wheels began chopping the water to a froth and out of the slip moved the *Eureka*." (Western Railway Museum Archives.)

Seven

Dark Days of Bridges and Freeways

The two bridges built in the 1930s brought dramatic changes to the Bay Area and signaled the end of the Ferry Building's usefulness as a transit center. By 1943, the second-floor waiting rooms, once busy with commuters coming and going to their ferries, were used to house servicemen on leave. The city streetcar terminus was moved to the new Alameda–Contra Costa County terminal shared with the Key System, the transbay railroad that ran on the lower deck of the Bay Bridge. The pedestrian overpass was torn down in 1942. Three ferry slips (6, 7, and 8) were removed by 1949. The Ferry Building was converted from a transit terminal to an office building in the 1950s.

The final blow came in the form of a plan, and partial completion, of a network of freeways, a symbol of postwar enthusiasm for automobiles and building infrastructure. In the 1950s, the thinking was that freeways could relieve traffic, even though every local highway was jammed with traffic within a few years.

State Route 480 was originally planned to include the Embarcadero Freeway, a partly elevated Doyle Drive approach to the Golden Gate Bridge, and a section connecting them. The first section of the double-decker Embarcadero Freeway, which cut the Ferry Building off from the financial district and the rest of the city, opened in 1959.

However, opposition to the freeway plans was fierce, and in 1959, the board of supervisors voted to cancel seven of the remaining 10 planned freeways—including part of the Embarcadero Freeway—after 30,000 people signed a petition. But the damage to the Ferry Building was done. As John King, architecture critic for the *San Francisco Chronicle*, noted on October 17, 2004, "[The Embarcadero Freeway] cut off the downtown from the water that gave birth to it, and it left the iconic Ferry Building—a statuesque survivor of the 1906 earthquake—stranded behind a dark wall of car exhaust and noise. Oppressive does not begin to describe it."

Everything changed on October 17, 1989, at 5:04 p.m., when Mother Nature once again shook the Bay Area, this time with a magnitude 6.9 earthquake. The Embarcadero Freeway was badly damaged, as was the Bay Bridge. However, it gave the Ferry Building an unexpected second chance.

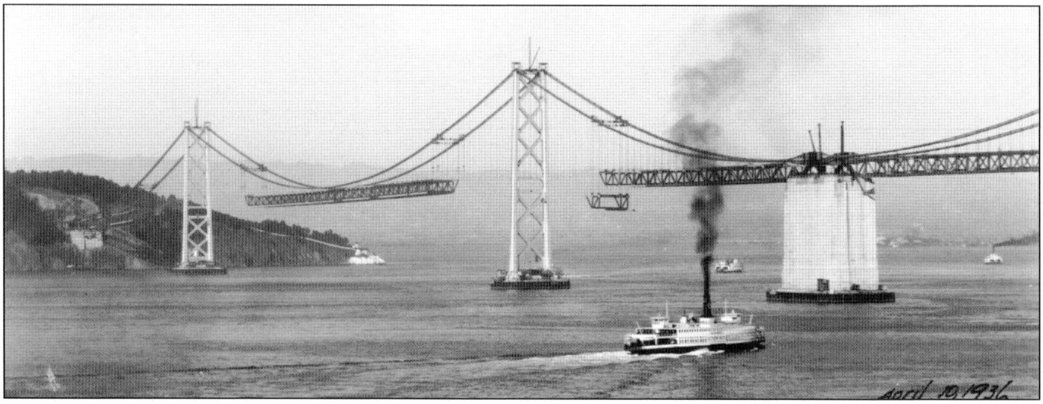

In April 1936, the *Sacramento* ferry travels on its route to Oakland, dwarfed by the nearly finished San Francisco–Oakland Bay Bridge. The bridge, which had been under construction since 1933, would officially open November 12, 1936. It originally carried automobile traffic on its upper deck and trucks and trains on the lower deck. (Western Railway Museum Archives.)

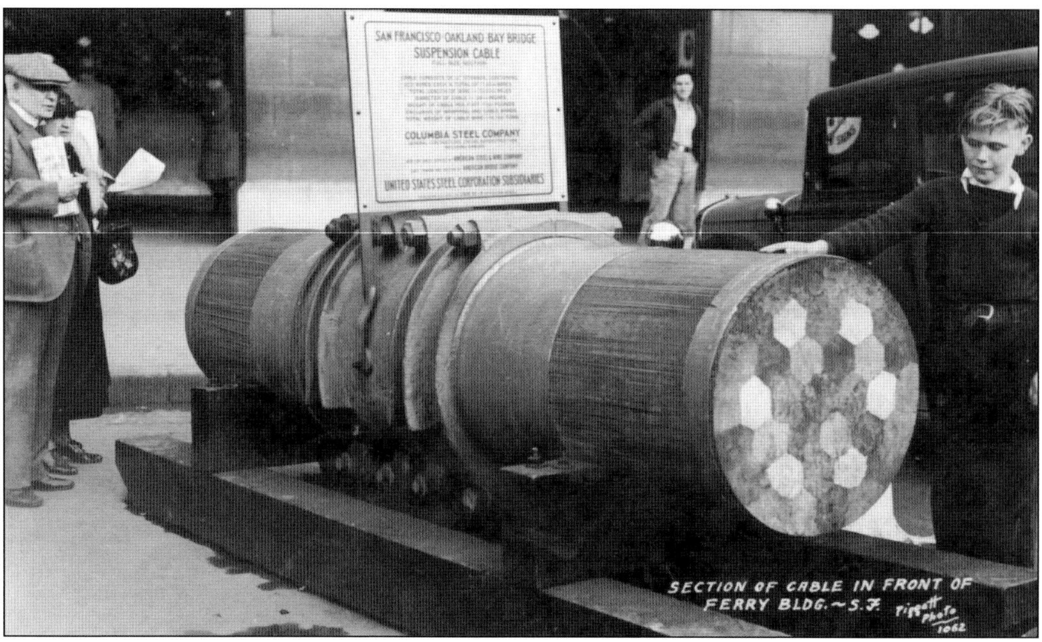

Curious onlookers view a sample of a San Francisco–Oakland Bay Bridge suspension cable displayed in front of the Ferry Building in the mid-1930s. The impressive chunk of cable weighed 1,750 pounds per foot, according to the descriptive placard, and had 37 strands containing 472 wires each. (Author's collection.)

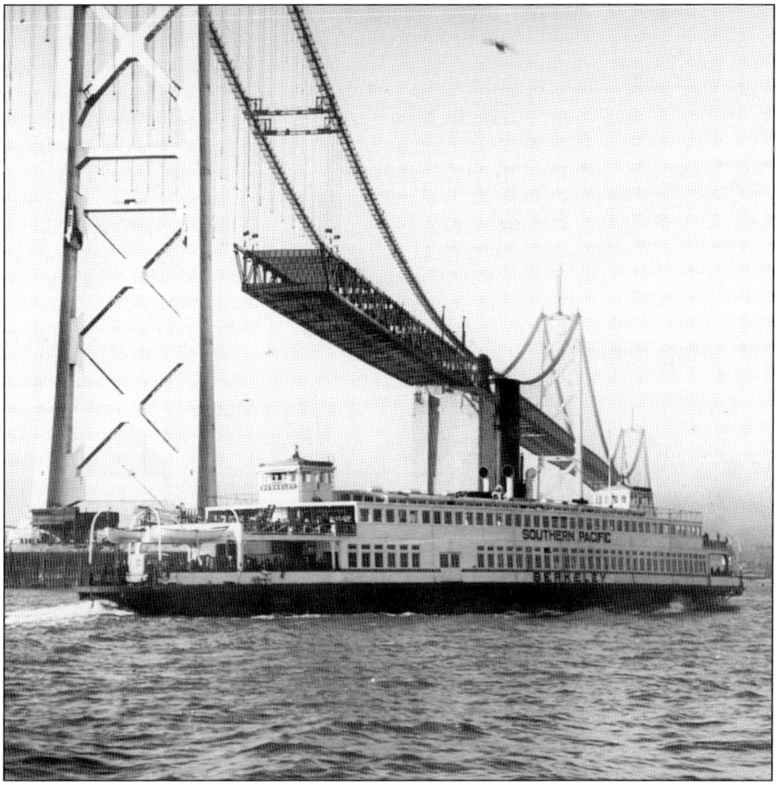

The passenger ferry *Berkeley* sails under the Bay Bridge with its semi-complete roadway. When the ferry was built in 1898, it was the fastest ferry on the bay. The *Berkeley* sailed for Southern Pacific for 60 years, until it was sold in 1959 and became a floating emporium in Sausalito. (Western Railway Museum Archives.)

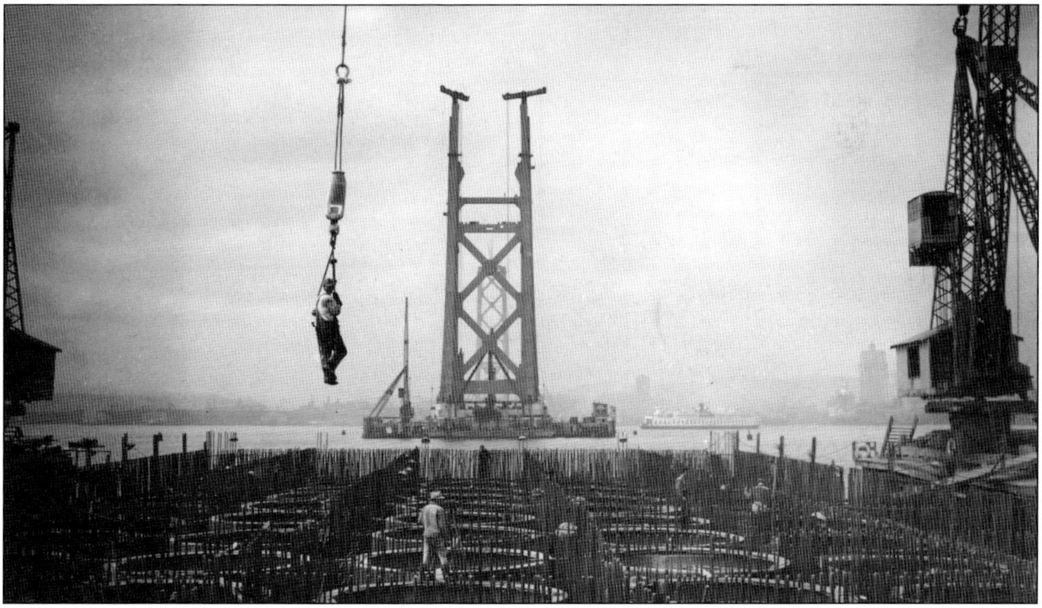

This Standard Oil Company photograph shows a San Francisco–Oakland Bay Bridge construction worker hanging from a rig in 1933 with bridge supports and a ferry and San Francisco in background. Constructing the bridge across the bay was an enormous engineering challenge because of the water's depth and the difficulties of building the foundation. (California History Room, California State Library, Sacramento, California.)

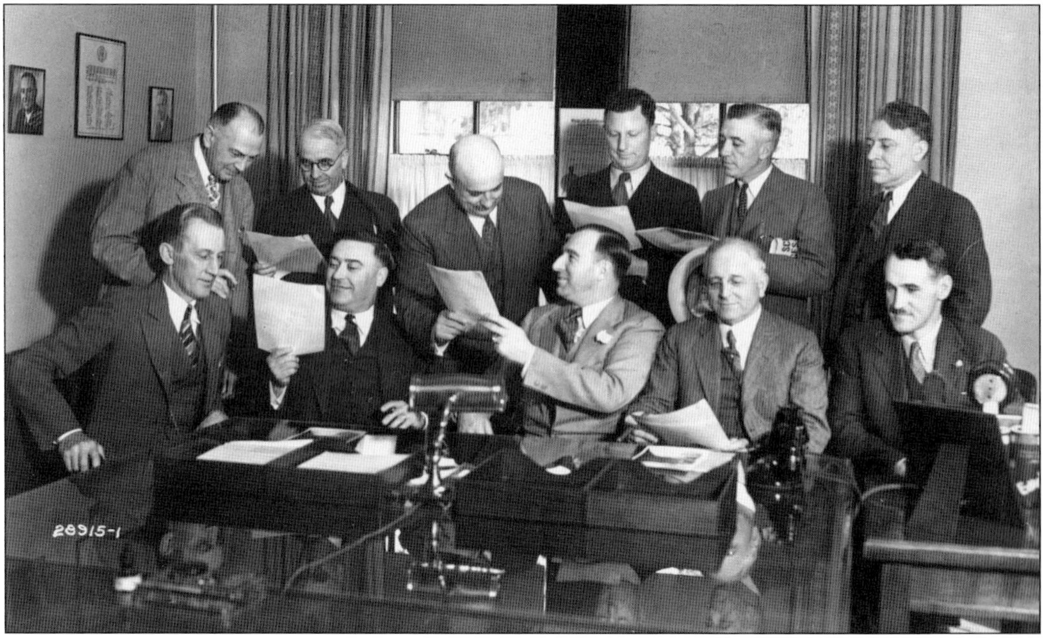

In the above photograph, dated April 1933, San Francisco–Oakland Bay Bridge contract recipients, engineers—including Charles Andrew, the bridge engineer, first row, second from left—planners, and representatives from the various government departments gather, with contracts in hand. Below, Andrew inspects the Bay Bridge while workers keep busy behind him and his colleagues. As a *San Francisco Chronicle* article from November 12, 1936, states, "Distinguished engineers, among them men who had built other bridges, were no less astonished at the courage displayed in tackling the seemingly impossible, and candidly amazed when the task was successfully completed." (Above, Library of Congress; below, California History Room, California State Library, Sacramento, California.)

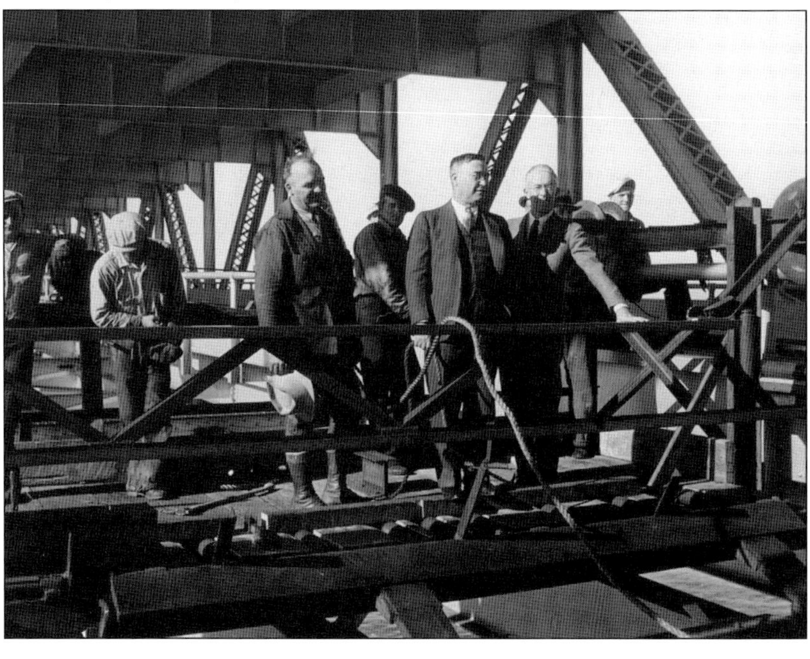

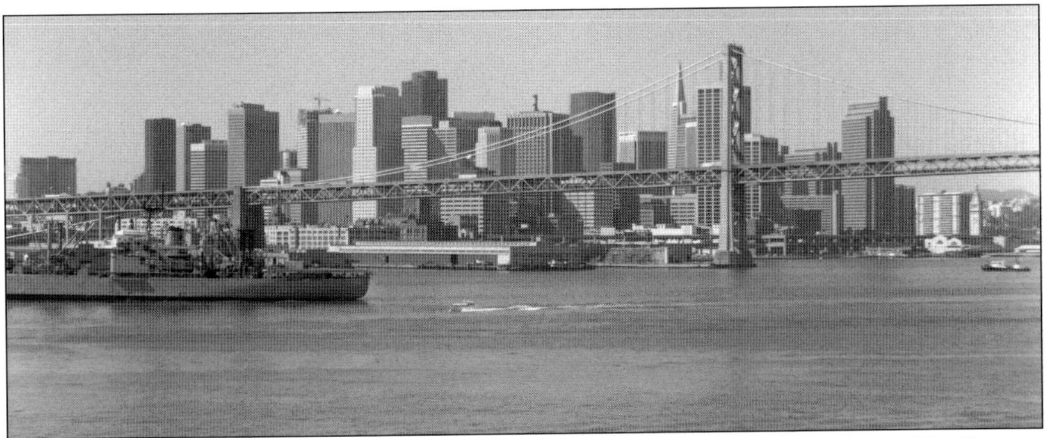

This calm skyline view with the Bay Bridge and the ammunition ship USS *Mauna Kea* floating by belies the incredible challenges faced in constructing the bridge. As a November 12, 1936, article in the *San Francisco Chronicle* declares, "More than once beads of perspiration stood out on the normally composed face of Chief Engineer Charles H. Purcell, members of the consulting board and subordinate engineers." (National Archives.)

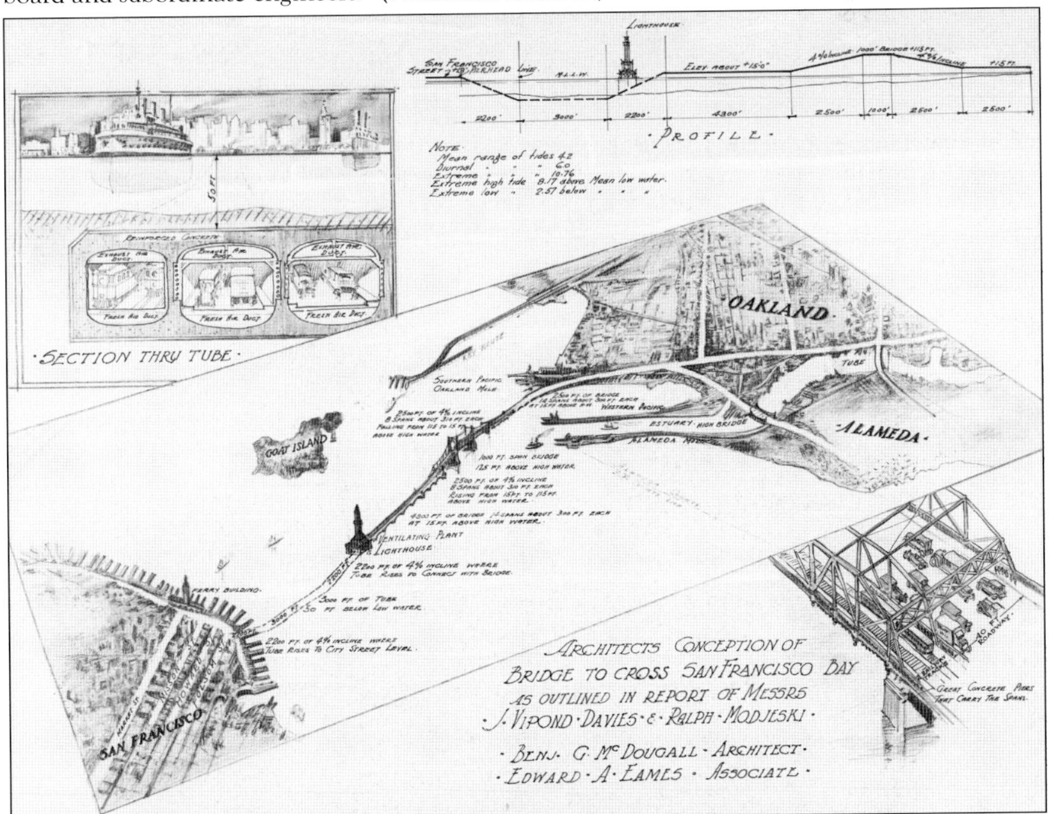

This futuristic conception of a proposed bridge from 1925 by engineers J. Vipond Davies and Ralph Modjeski includes section through tubes on the Oakland side. The engineers were concerned about ventilation issues presented by a combined auto and rail tunnel. It would be another 50 years before the Bay Area Rapid Transit's (BART) transbay tube, a 3.6-mile-long underwater rail tunnel, would be built. (Photograph by George Fanning, SFMTA Photo Archive.)

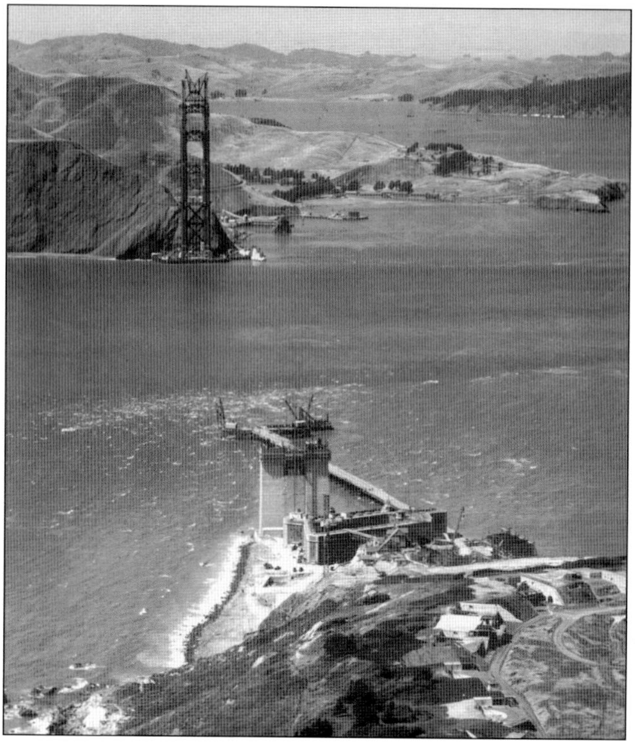

On January 5, 1933, construction began on the Golden Gate Bridge and lasted four and a half years. The bridge cost over $35 million. The bridge opening had a devastating effect on ferry traffic. In the photograph at left, footbridge ropes stretch across the Golden Gate during construction, in September 1935. This is a view of the south (San Francisco) tower of the Golden Gate Bridge, after the north (Marin County) tower had been built. Below, also in 1935, a bridge worker stands atop the north (Marin) tower. Catwalks, used to transport workers and materials, soon replaced the footbridge ropes seen here. (Both photographs by Charles M. Hiller, Anne T. Kent California Room, Marin County Free Library.)

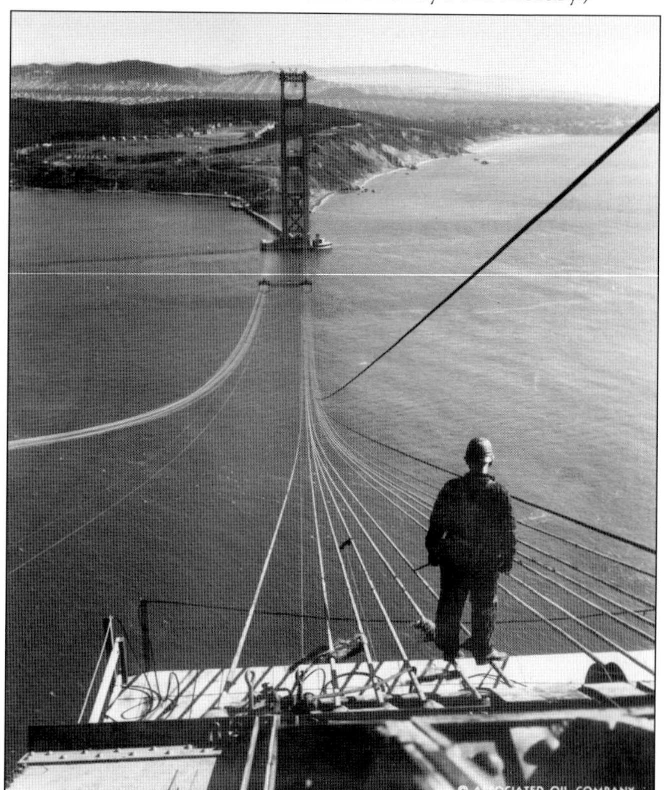

Post–World War II California went on a freeway binge. Gov. Earl Warren led a campaign to modernize the state, and plans were drawn up to crisscross San Francisco with freeways, as shown at right in the 1945 Master Plan for the City and County of San Francisco Major Thoroughfares. In 1953, work began on the Embarcadero Freeway, intended to connect the San Francisco–Oakland Bay Bridge with the Golden Gate Bridge to Marin County. It went directly in front of the Ferry Building, blocking its view from Market Street. The 1950 image below shows a proposed master plan of toll crossings on Yerba Buena Island—four different bridges would have had roadways crossing the island in the middle of San Francisco Bay. (Both, Eric Fischer.)

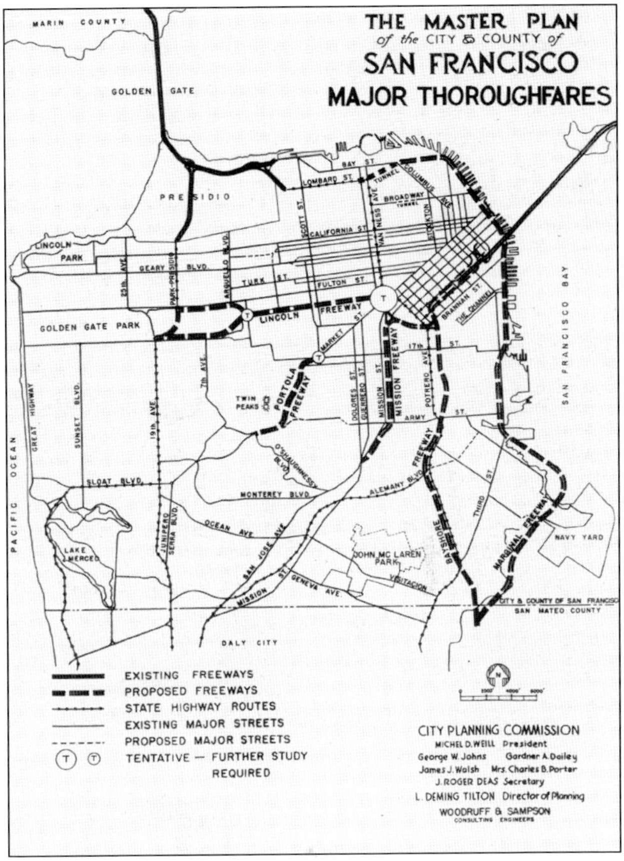

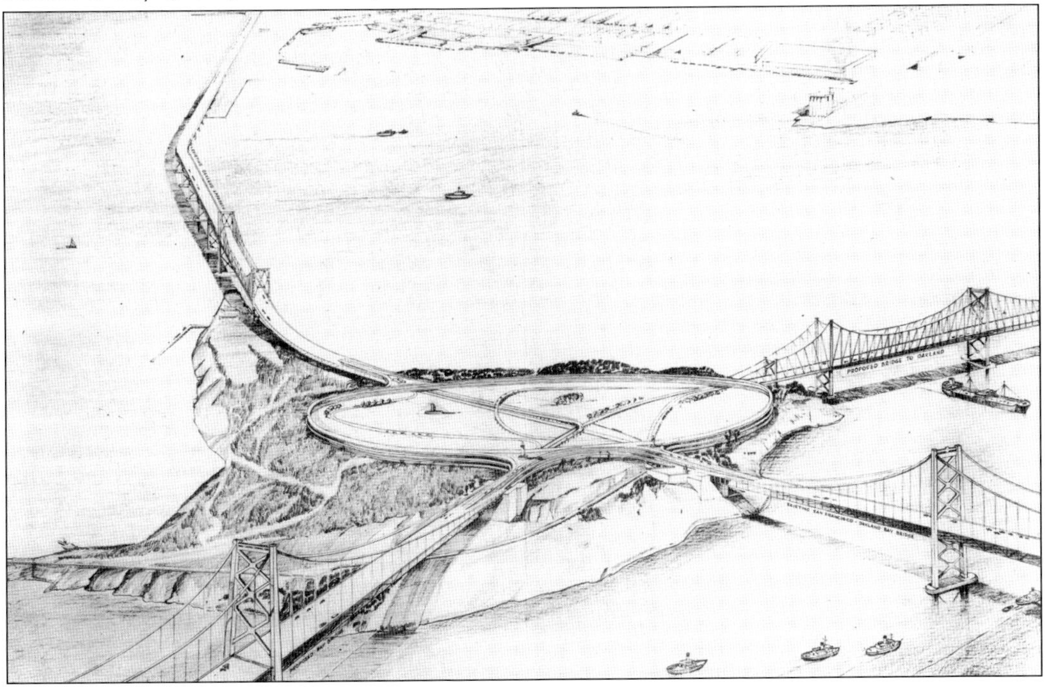

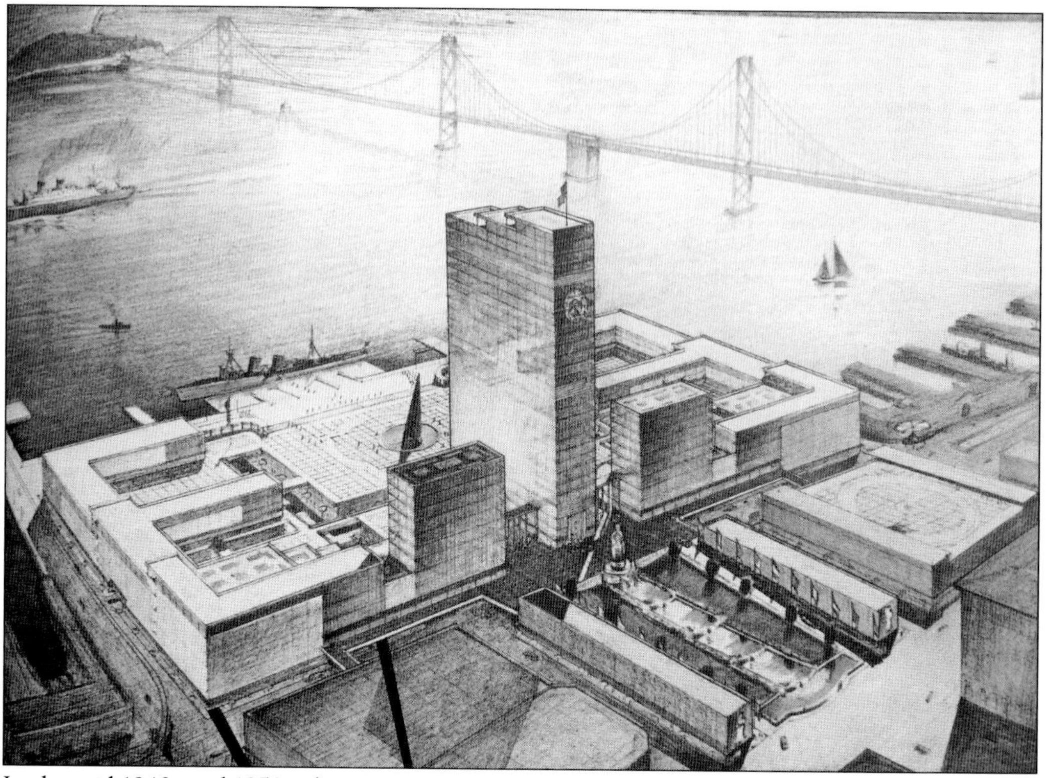

In the mid-1940s and 1950s, there were grand schemes for the declining waterfront. One of these was a proposal for a San Francisco World Trade Center, depicted in these drawings from *San Francisco World Trade Center: Prospectus*, published in 1951. It was envisioned to provide three million square feet of floor space centered on a 30-story tower for "agencies, services, individuals and companies dealing with world commerce," with the result that San Francisco would become a center of world business. The tower would be located on bay fill due east of the Ferry Building (not a great idea in an area prone to earthquakes). As Jasper Rubin notes in *A Negotiated Landscape: The Transformation of San Francisco's Waterfront Since 1950*, "by 1955 support for the revenue bonds that were required to fund the project had evaporated and directed to the plans for the Embarcadero Freeway." (Both, San Francisco Public Library.)

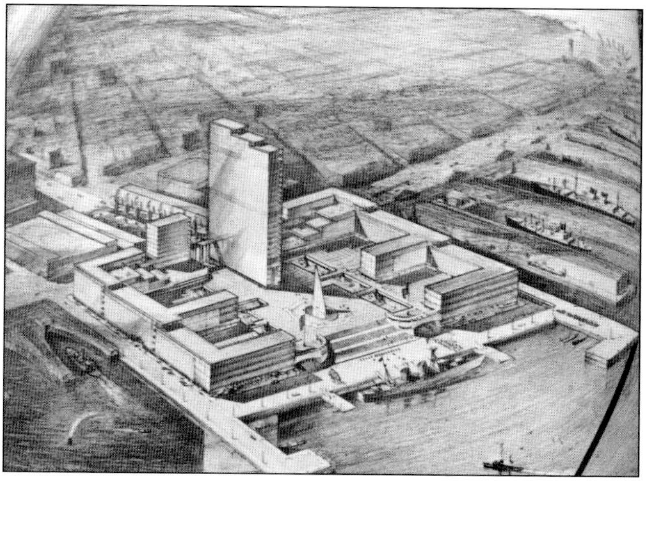

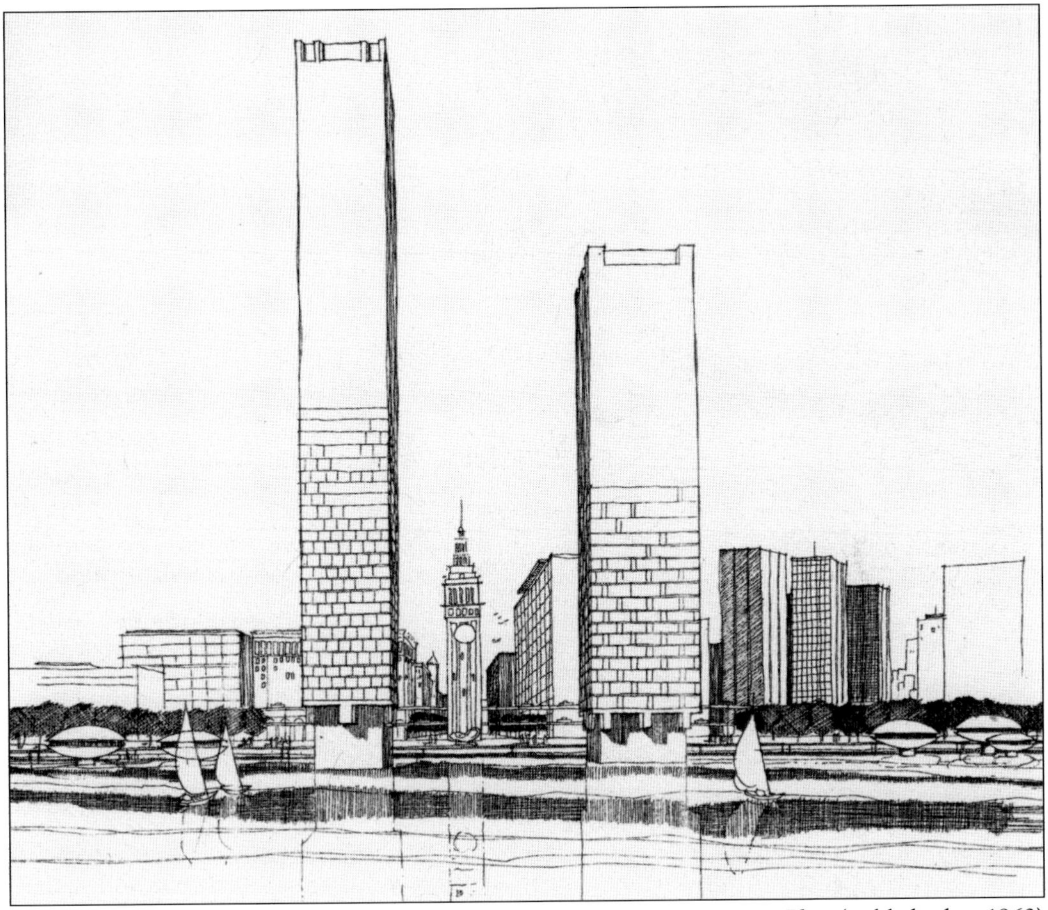

These sketches from the *San Francisco Planning Commission Downtown Plan* (published in 1963) propose high-rises at the foot of Market Street, towering over the Ferry Building. The proposal indicates that the development "would provide a sound economic foundation for the redevelopment of the waterfront." The proposal includes removing the wings of the Ferry Building, just leaving the tower to be at a center of the "Ferry Park." A passenger ship terminal would be to the south, with an international trade center and heliport on the north side. The planners called it an "interim" plan, as eventually they believed that "sometime in the future, when conditions permit, the elevated freeway would be removed," replaced by an underpass. (Both, San Francisco Public Library.)

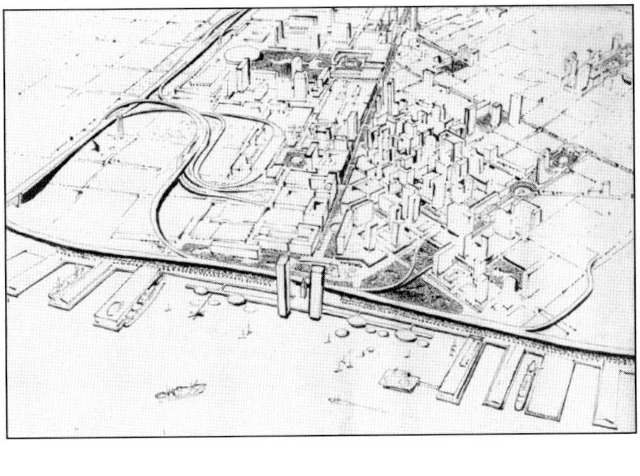

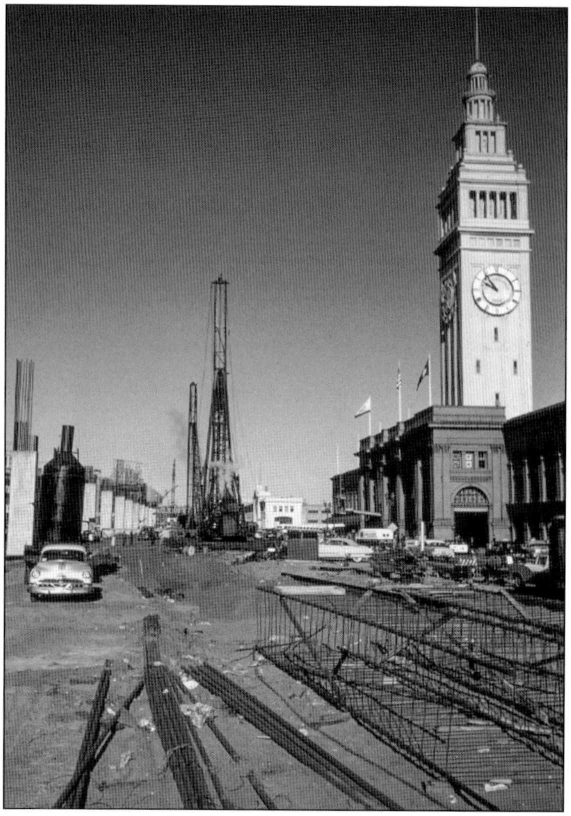

This 1957 image at left shows the Embarcadero Freeway under construction, with the Ferry Building on the right. The first section of the freeway opened in 1959, and construction was soon halted on parts of it after more than 30,000 people signed petitions, forcing the board of supervisors to vote to cancel seven of the 10 planned freeway routes through the city. After the freeway was constructed, the Ferry Building was a mere shadow of what it had been. In the image below, members of Local 410 strike on Market Street, with the freeway and the Ferry Building in the distance. (Left, OpenSFHistory/wnp25.0594; below, California History Room, California State Library, Sacramento, California.)

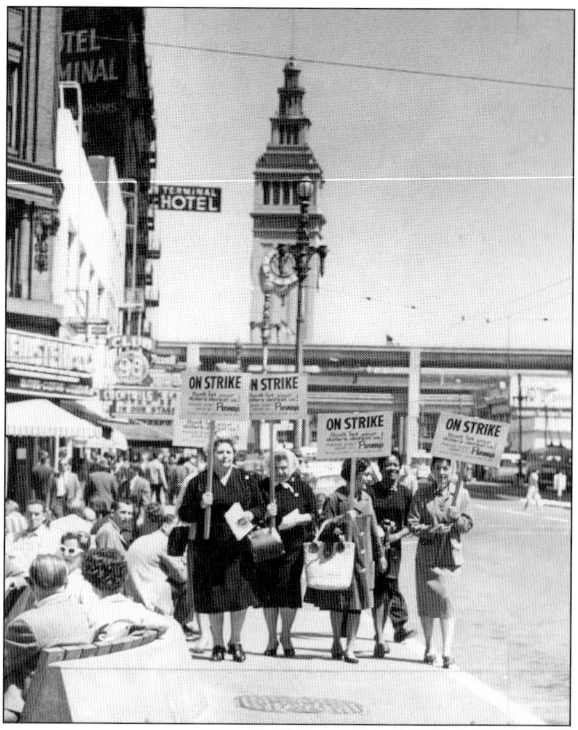

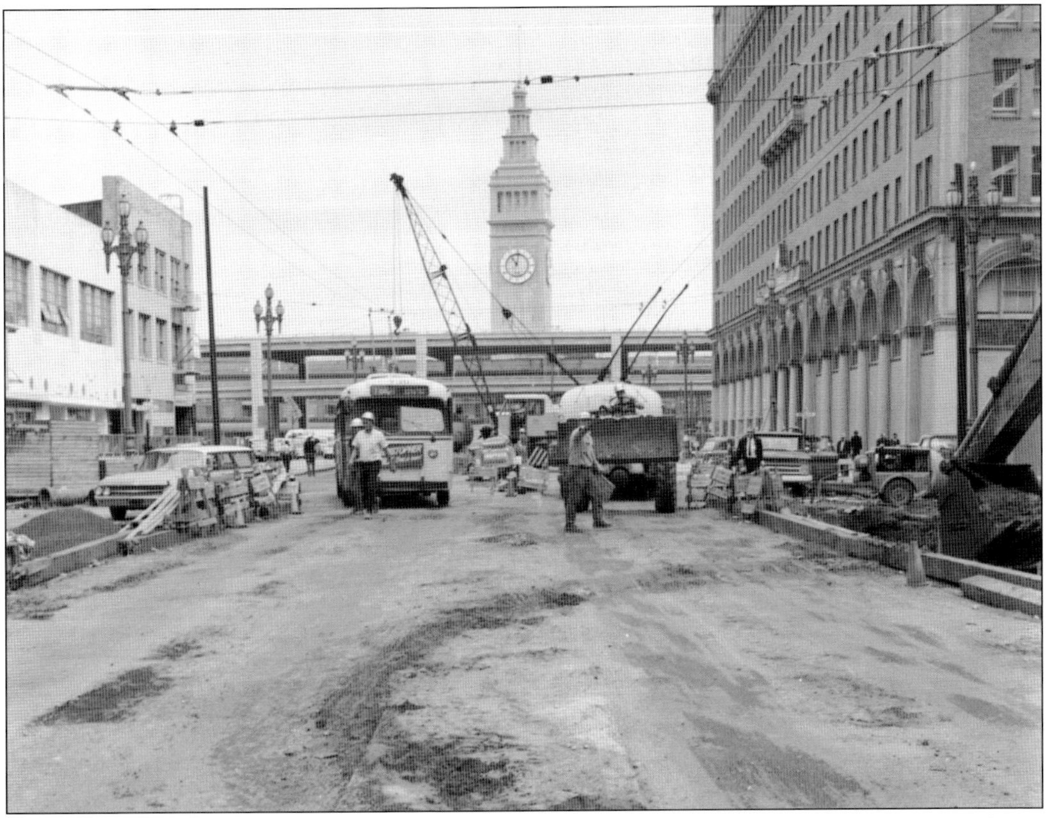

One reason that the freeway was elevated was to try to ease congestion along the waterfront. Another plan to manage Bay Area traffic was to build a rapid transit system. In this 1968 photograph, construction crews tear up Market Street during construction of the Bay Area Rapid Transit line, BART. The Ferry Building looks down on the action. (Photograph by Marshall Moxom, SFMTA Photo Archive.)

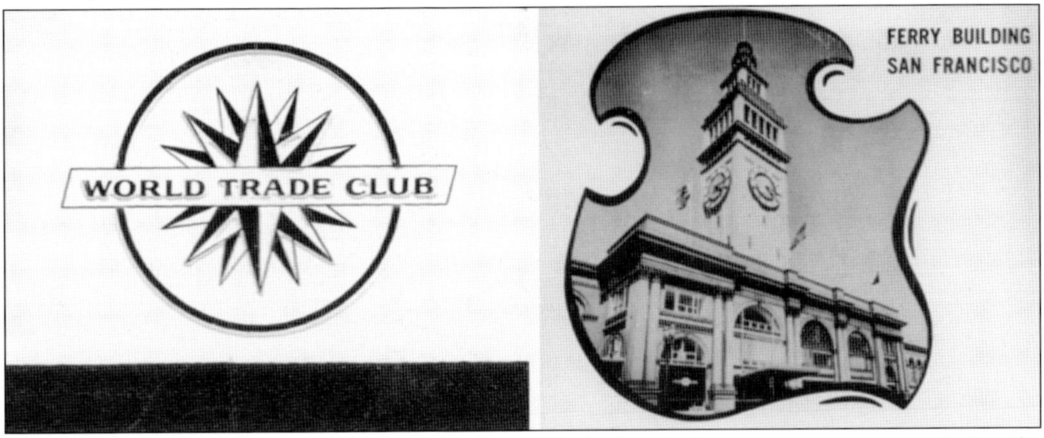

In 1957, Cyril Magnin, one of the city's leaders and the head of a prominent mercantile family, along with George Killion, chief executive of American President Lines, founded the World Trade Club, which was located in the building. This matchbook was one of its giveaways. The club described itself as "San Francisco's premier international business association." The club closed in 2006. (Author's collection.)

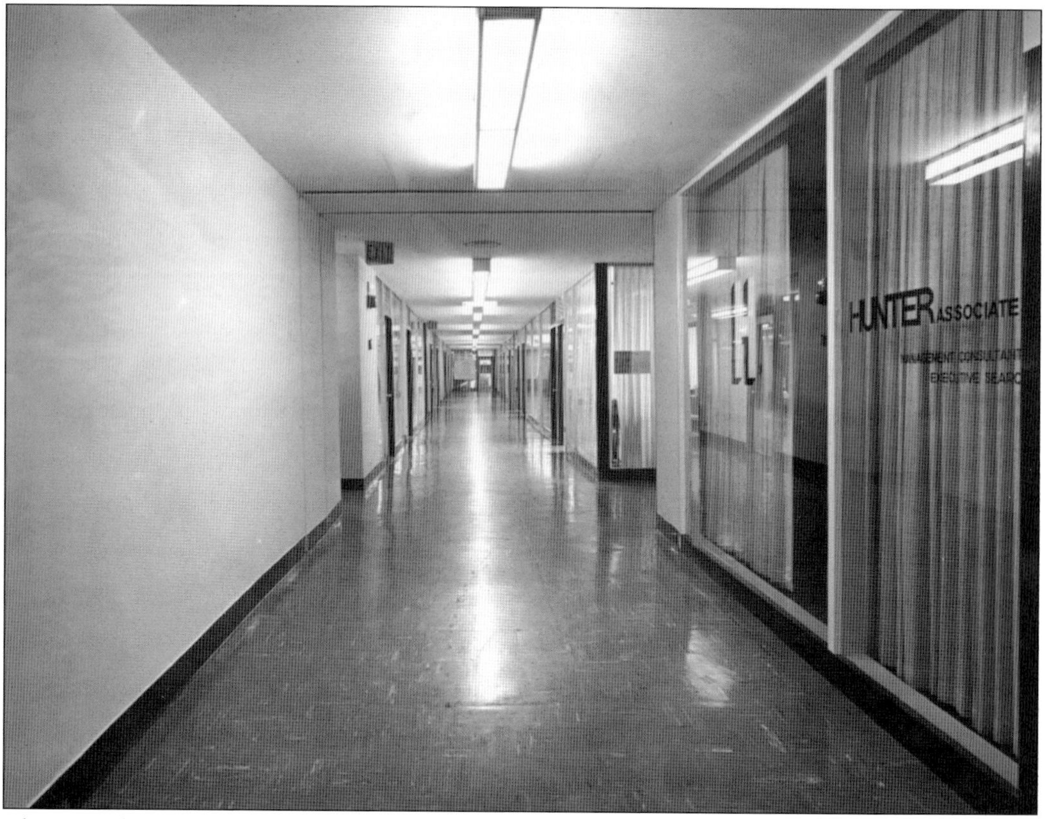

The port of San Francisco, once a mighty, vibrant place, declined in the 1940s and 1950s because of competition from other Bay Area ports—especially Oakland—that had geographical advantages and better access to rail and truck transportation routes. To help staunch the port's declining revenues, the port sought to establish a Foreign Trade Zone (FTZ). Generally, FTZs allow for customs duties to be deferred until the goods enter US commerce. The San Francisco FTZ No. 3 (still in existence) was established in 1948, the third in the United States after New York and New Orleans. In 1955, the World Trade Center (WTC) opened in the remodeled north end of the Ferry Building. The above 1977 image shows the second floor of the WTC, and below is an image of the third-floor balcony. (Both photographs by Orie Damewood, National Register of Historic Places.)

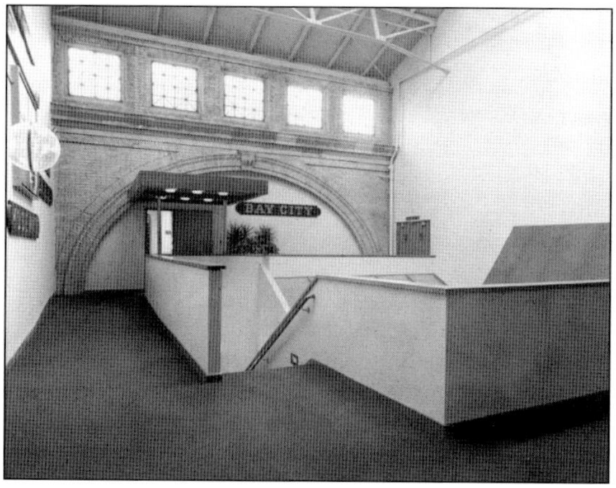

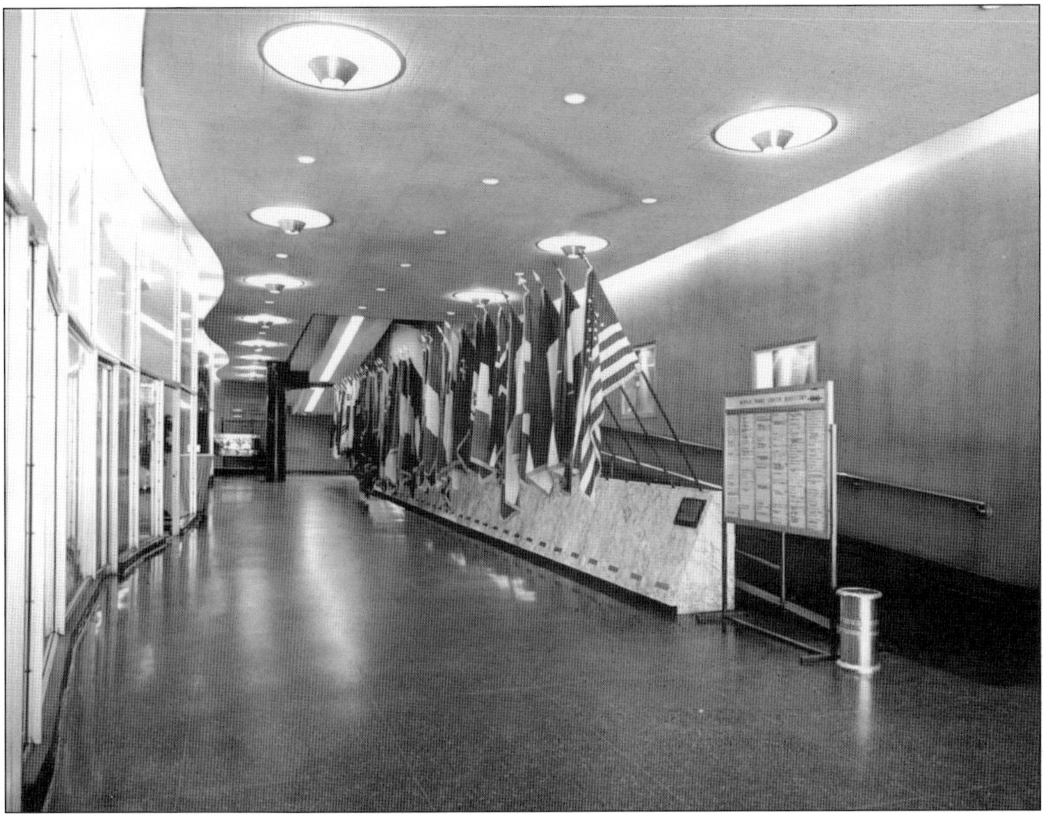

According to a Board of State Harbor Commissioners report (BSHC n.d.: date unknown), the WTC provided offices for businesses and agencies engaged in world trade, as well as conference rooms, a library, and display space. It also provided services such as "merchandising and public relations assistance, translation and interpretive service, and secretarial service." The 1977 image above, with flags decorating the walkway, is of the entrance to the WTC in the Ferry Building; the photograph below shows the second floor of the center. According to an optimistic newsletter issued by the FTZ, "The establishment of this facility is the Pacific Coast's most useful contribution toward promoting and expediting international commerce since the opening of the Panama Canal." (Both photographs by Orie Damewood, National Register of Historic Places.)

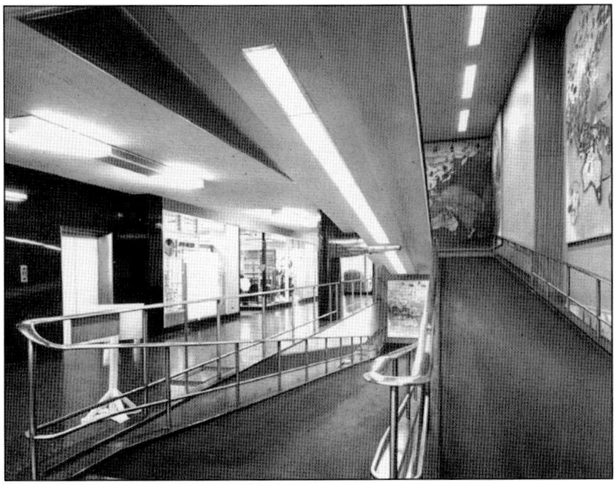

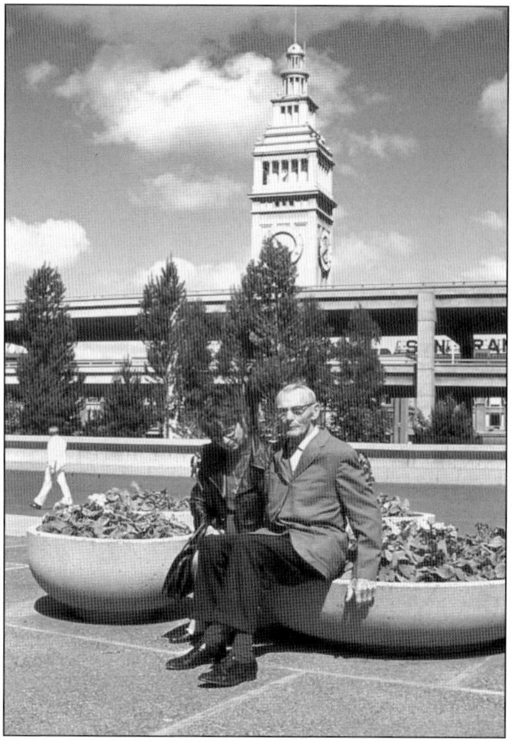

The Ferry Building looms in the background of this photograph of an unidentified father and daughter sitting on the west side of the freeway in 1974, but the building's majestic tower is blocked by the freeway and trees. (Bruce Morris.)

"Instead of helping port businesses, the freeway severed downtown from the waterfront, emphasizing the city's shift away from its historical maritime origins as it moved into its service sector future," writes Jasper Rubin in *A Negotiated Landscape*. His statement aptly captures the bleak nature of the Ferry Building's situation. (San Francisco History Center, San Francisco Public Library.)

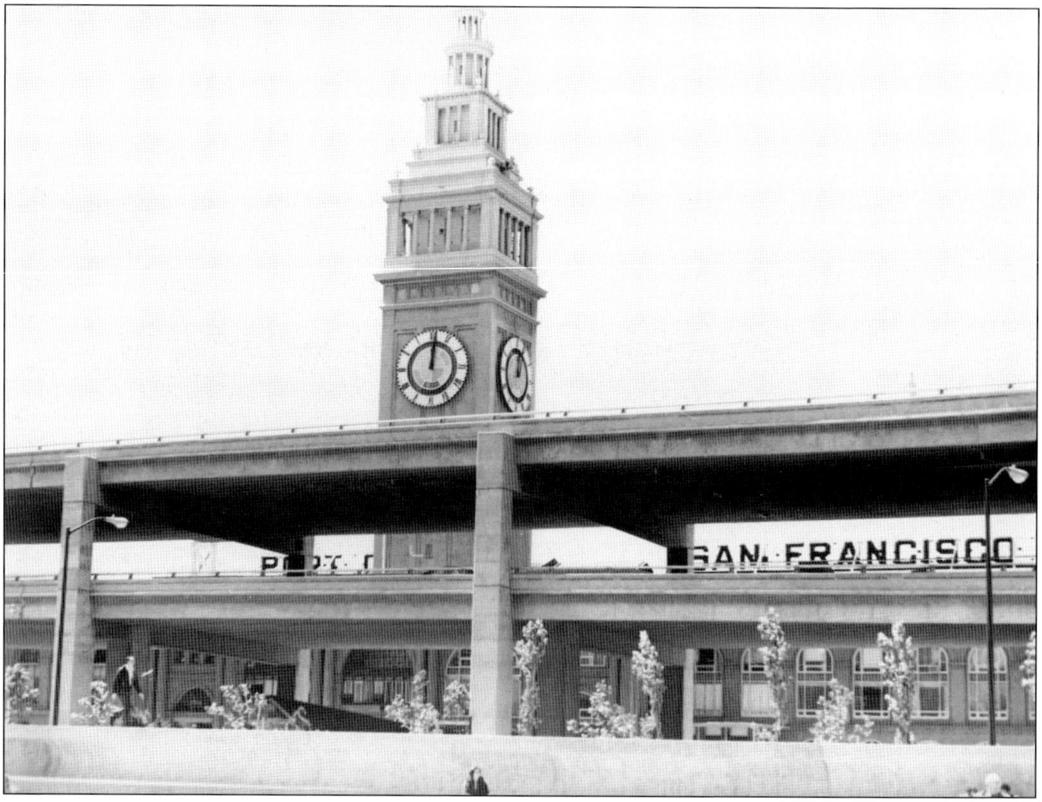

The 1989 Loma Prieta earthquake, and the damage it caused to the San Francisco–Oakland Bay Bridge, Oakland's Cypress Freeway, and Embarcadero Freeway, made water and rail transit the only options for transbay travel. The Bay Bridge was closed for a month, and other transportation services, including ferries and buses, were expanded during the closure. At right, a bus, Flyer Coast 4566, travels on the narrow roadway in front of the Ferry Building a few days after the earthquake, with the massive double-decker freeway flanking it on the right. Below, rescue personnel are lowered by crane to a collapsed section of the Cypress Freeway during recovery efforts. Its double-decker structure collapsed during the earthquake, killing 42 people. (Right, photograph by Carmen Magana, SFMTA Photo Archive; below, National Archives.)

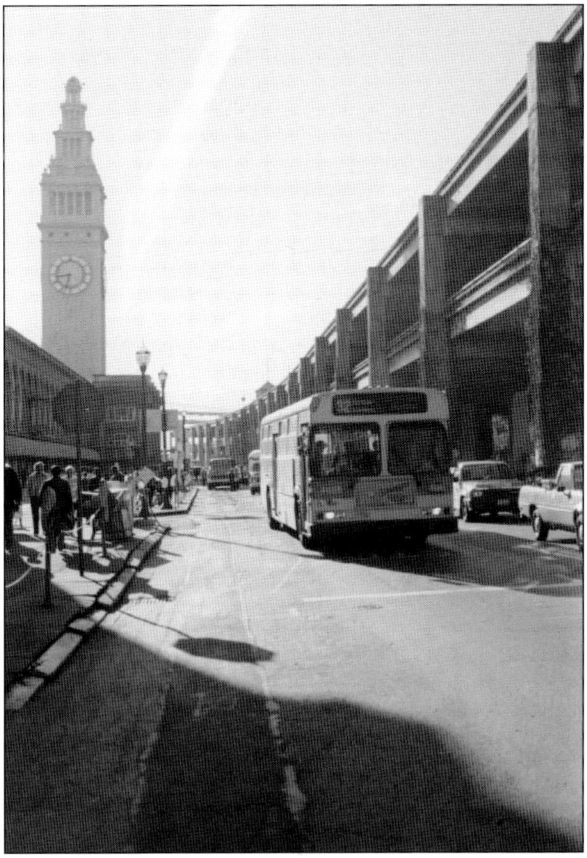

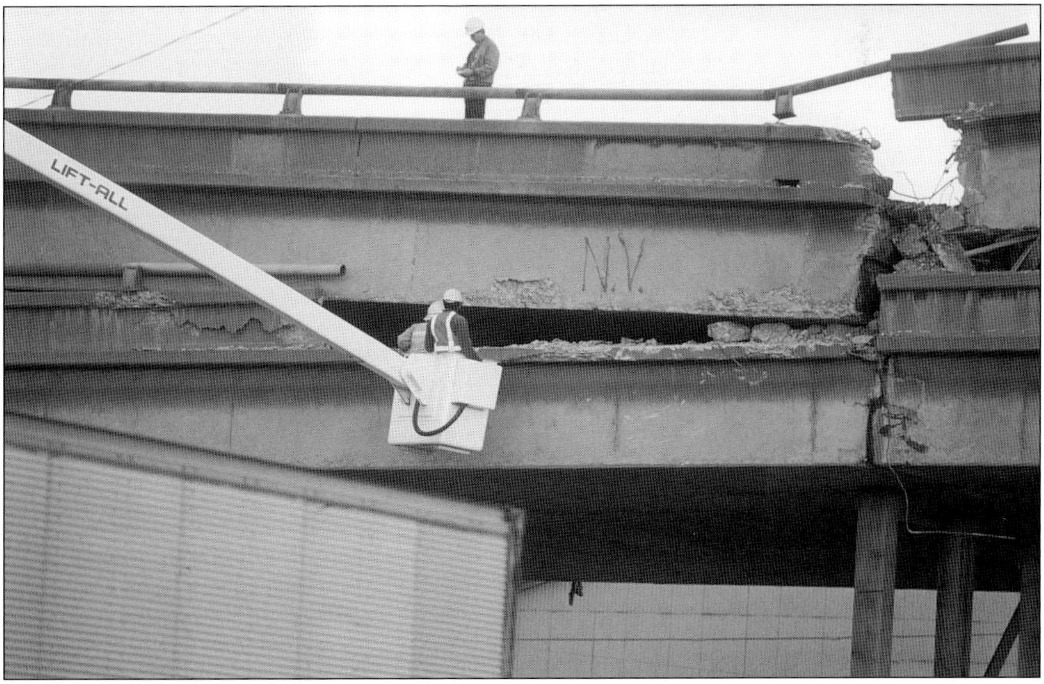

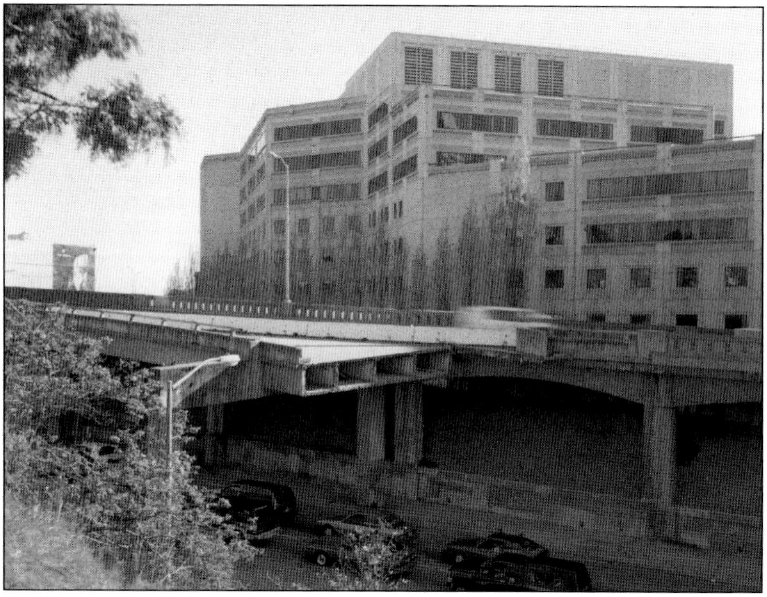

Many people thought the Embarcadero Freeway was ugly, but were wary of traffic congestion if it was removed. Although the freeway had been retrofitted for earthquake safety in the early 1980s, it was still severely damaged by the magnitude 6.9 quake. This view shows the semi-demolished upper-deck off-ramp and remnant stub. (Photograph by Dennis Hill, Library of Congress.)

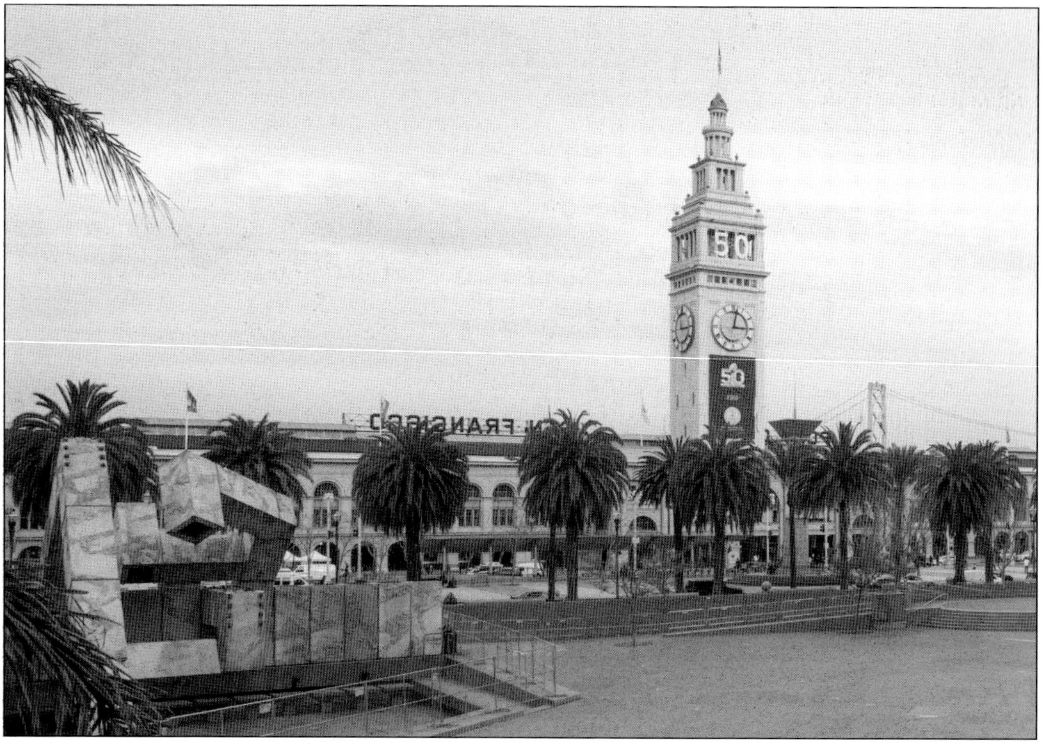

In 1971, in Justin Herman Plaza at the foot of Market Street across from the Ferry Building, the Vaillancourt Fountain (left) was unveiled. It was controversial, and supposedly designed to mock the Embarcadero Freeway. People either loved or hated the jumble of cement pipes created by Canadian artist Armand Vaillancourt. In the early 2000s, water was shut off to conserve electricity. (Photograph by Jeremy Menzies, SFMTA Photo Archive.)

Eight

A Grand Restoration

After the Loma Prieta earthquake damaged the Embarcadero Freeway in 1989, San Francisco mayor Art Agnos worked diligently to get it removed rather than repair it. In an April 16, 1990, article in the *San Francisco Chronicle* calling for the freeway's demolition, Pulitzer Prize winner Allan Temko, the newspaper's architecture critic, says the decision did not require panels of experts "to see that this excrescence should be removed from the waterfront." Building the freeway, Temko writes, "transformed one of the loveliest waterfronts in the world into one of the most obscene."

By 1992, the freeway was finally removed, over 30 years after the "Freeway Revolt" that had helped put a stop to other freeway plans in the city. A wide, palm-lined boulevard was built and, as John King, architecture critic for the *San Francisco Chronicle*, noted on October 17, 2004, "Take a walk today on the two-and-a-half mile promenade between Fisherman's Wharf on the north and China Basin on the south, and it's hard to believe that an elevated freeway ever scarred the open air."

But the question of how to revitalize the Ferry Building and the derelict downtown waterfront remained. The Port of San Francisco sought to revive the Ferry Building as "the elegant jewel of the waterfront" in the comprehensive port development plan that was eventually adopted. The plan sought to revitalize the area, provide public access, and reintroduce ferry service. It was a huge undertaking, and after some false starts and much political wrangling, the developer and other team members, including historic preservation specialists, urban designers, and architects, were in place. The vision centered on a building that not only had offices and stores but also focused on locally sourced food producers and artisans.

Many agencies had jurisdiction over the project—to name just a few, the Port of San Francisco, the Bay Conservation and Development Commission, the federal Office of Historic Preservation, the San Francisco Landmarks Preservation Advisory Board, the California State Office of Historic Preservation, and the State Land Commission.

What emerged in 2003 after the four-year, $100 million meticulous restoration was a beautifully restored grand landmark with retail marketplace space—including the popular Ferry Plaza Farmers' Market—open-air cafés, restaurants, and prime office space.

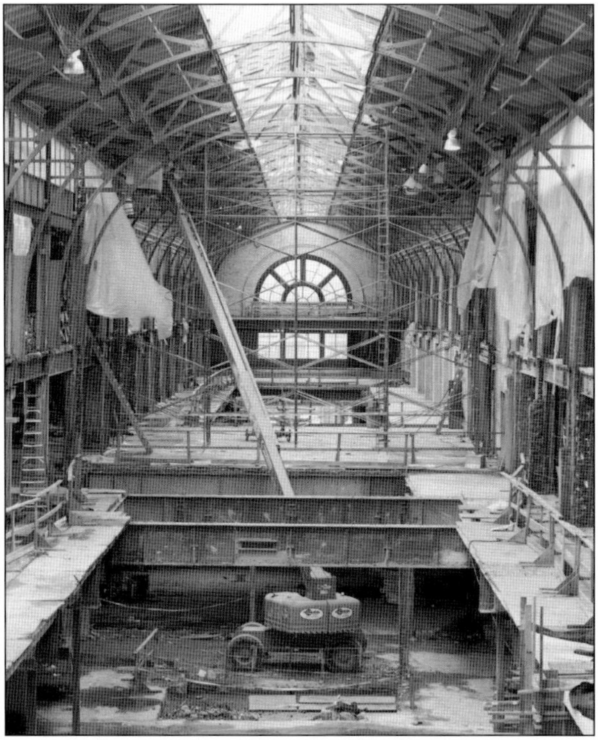

The greatest change to the building during the renovation, which was very controversial at the time, was the opening of the floor in the Grand Nave, as shown at left. As Tom Dufurrena, a principal at Page & Turnbull, the historic preservation firm involved with the restoration notes in the Page & Turnbull Oral History in 2012, "Jay [Jay Turnbull, founding principal] went to Washington and the National Park Service came here. We modeled it, just to try to show them that the character wouldn't really be degraded by opening these elements up. In fact, it would share the experience with a lot of other people." Crews removed incompatible windows (below) and replaced 19 missing or damaged arched clathri (latticed) windows and spandrels (the triangular spaces between arches). (Both, Tom Paiva Photography.)

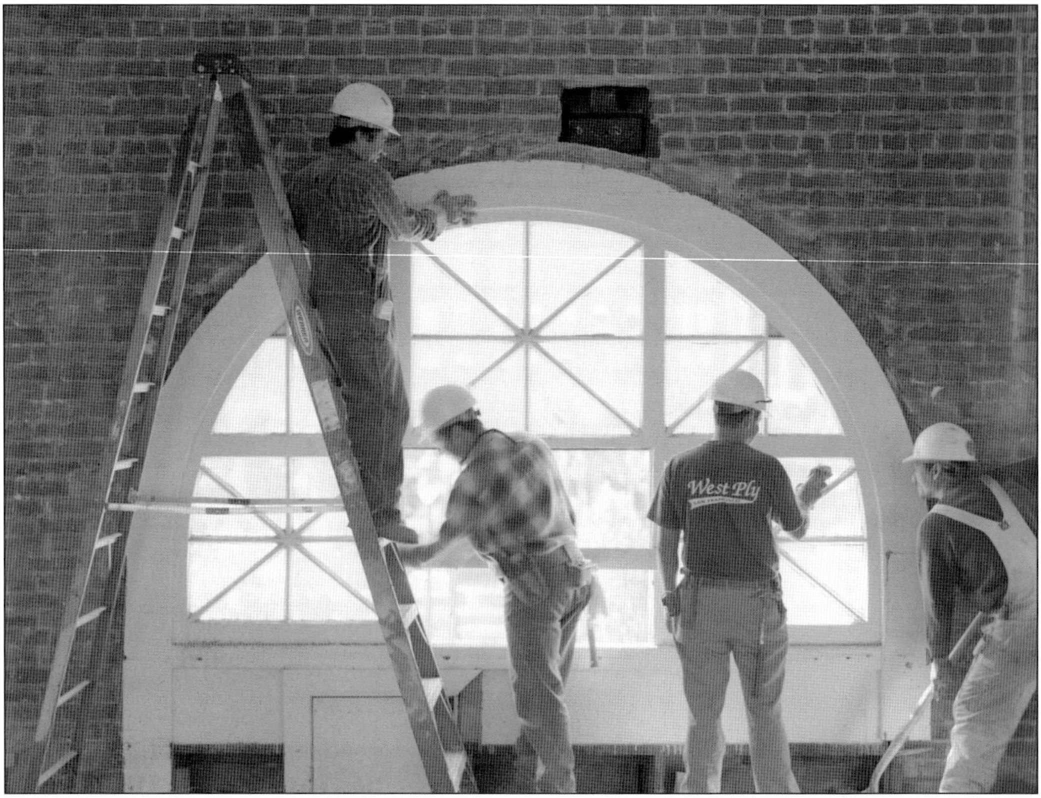

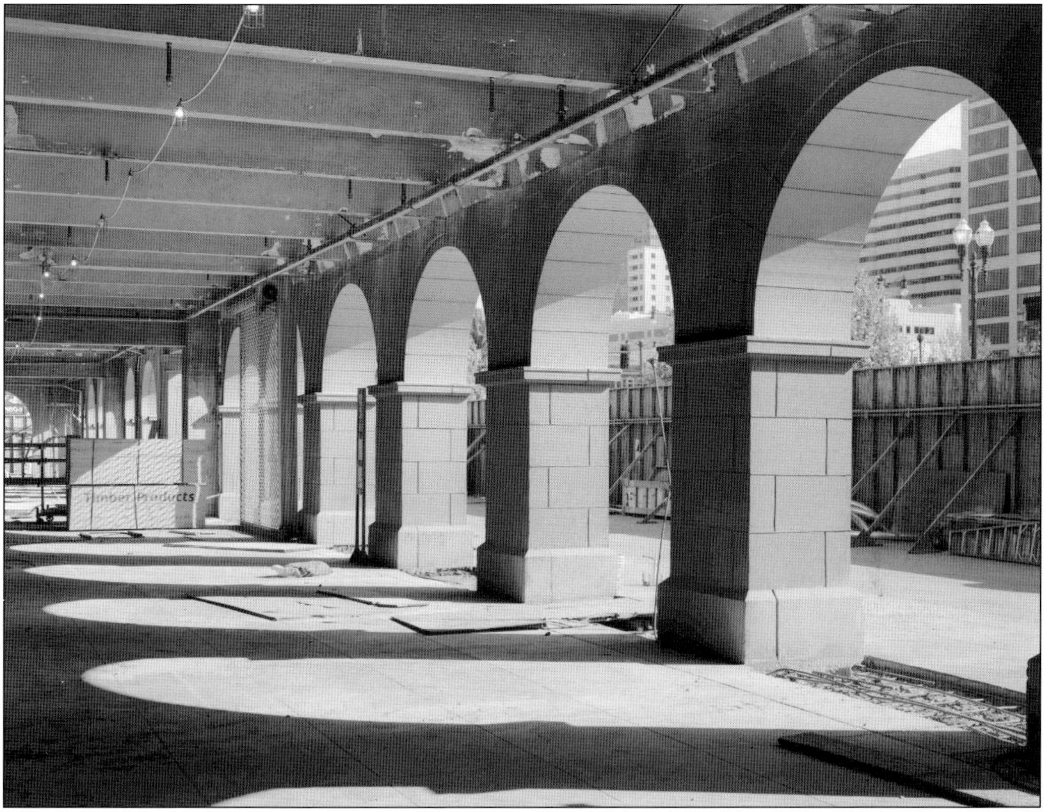

Today, outside these arches (pictured during the renovation) on the west side entry to the Ferry Building, stalls line the side of the building at the bustling, triweekly Ferry Plaza Farmers' Market where local farmers showcase their high-quality products. CUESA (Center for Urban Education about Sustainable Agriculture) operates the market. (Tom Paiva Photography.)

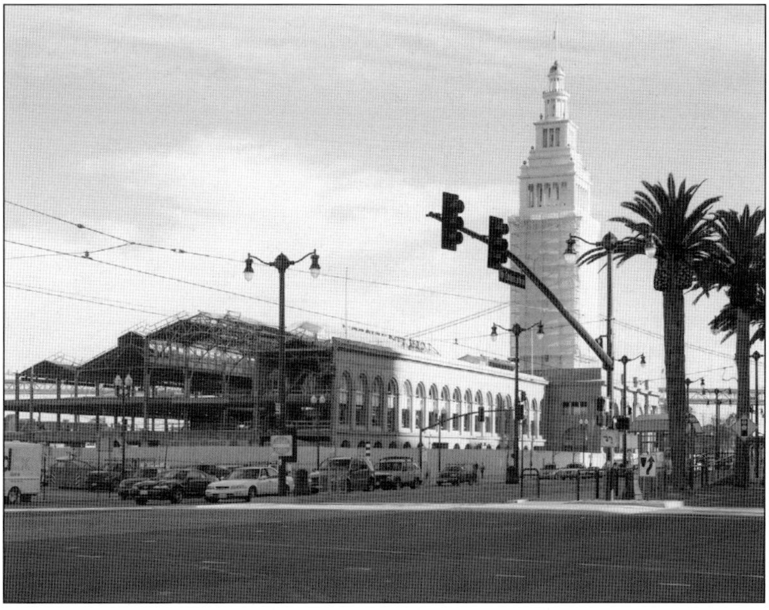

In the 1950s, an additional floor was awkwardly inserted into the Grand Nave, in an attempt to provide modern office space. The renovation created prime office space on the second and third floors and a new Hearing Room for the San Francisco Port Commission. (Tom Paiva Photography.)

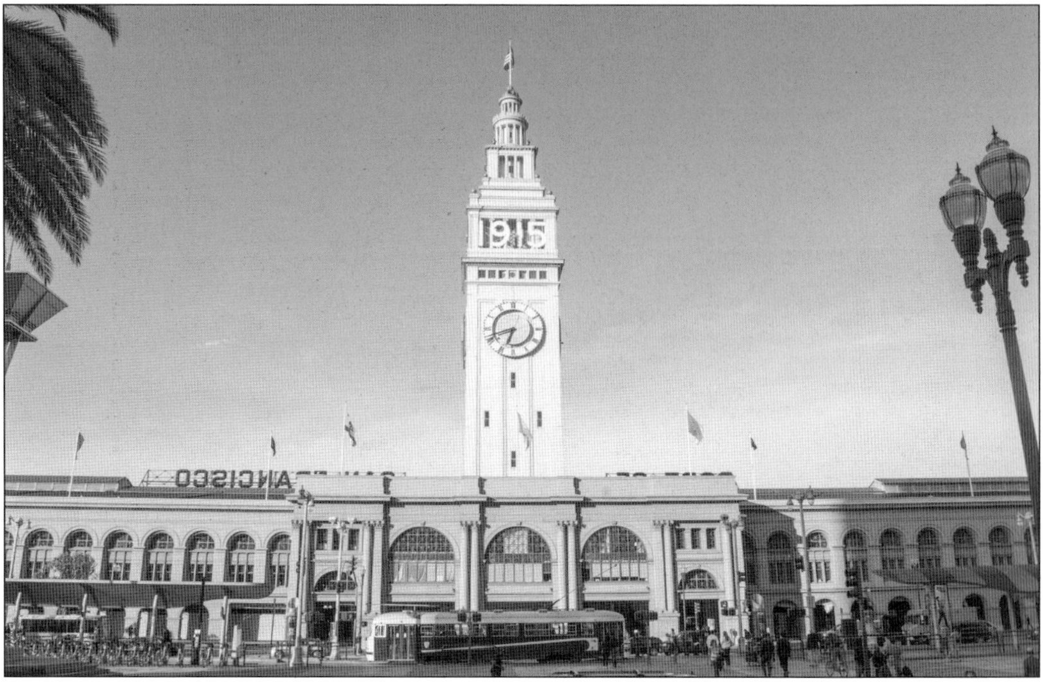

During the restoration, workers carefully refurbished the Ferry Building's clock tower. They added new steel bracing to the core, and a new lighting system made the tower even more visible at the foot of Market Street. In the above image, pedestrians cross Harry Bridges Plaza, which sits at the foot of Market Street and extends to the Ferry Building. Below, during Muni Heritage Weekend, two 1934 "boat trams"—their nautical air whistles gaily tooting—travel the Embarcadero in front of the Ferry Building. The 222 palms trees (Canary Island date palms) that line the tracks were planted after the Loma Prieta earthquake. Unfortunately, many of them need to be replaced because they have a fungal disease. (Both photographs by Jeremy Menzies, SFMTA Photo Archive.)

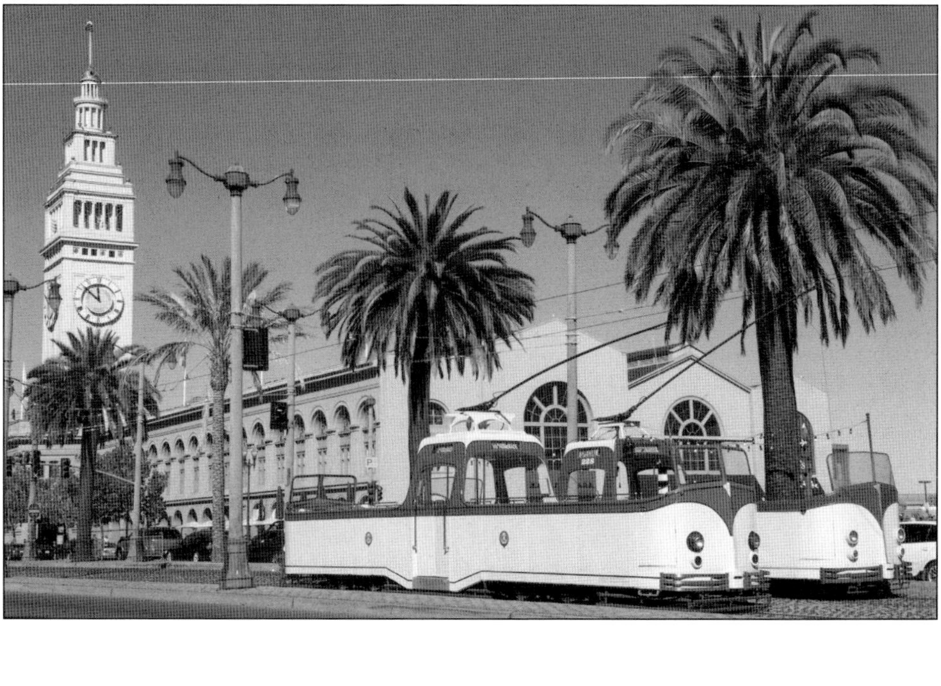

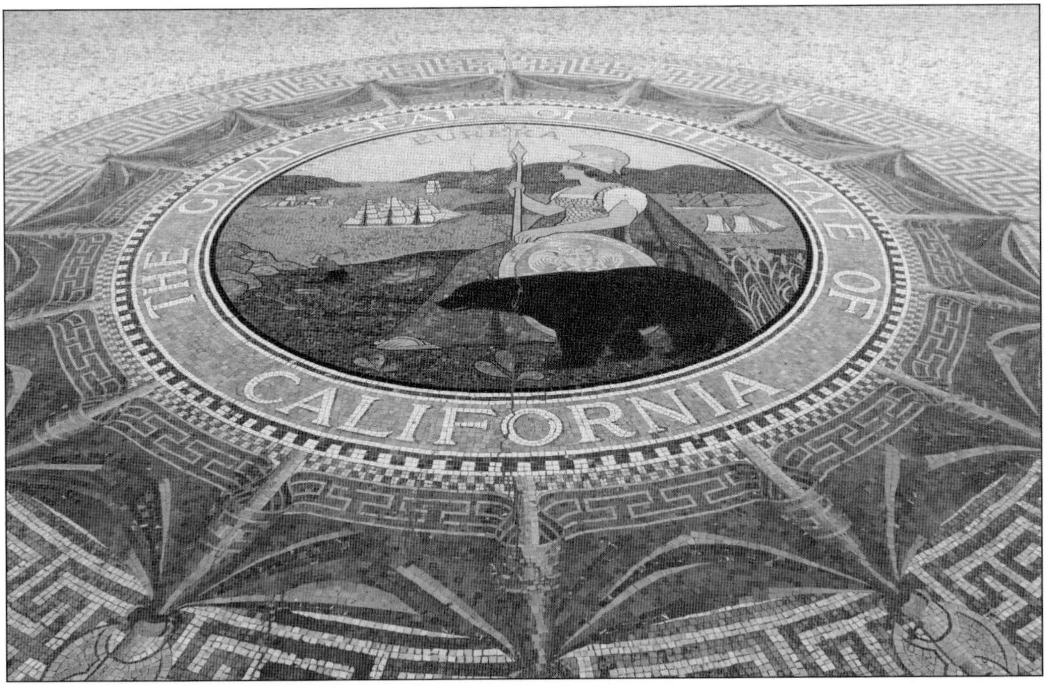

On the *Great Seal of California*, a beautiful mosaic on the second floor of the Ferry Building, Minerva, Roman goddess of wisdom (Athena in Greek mythology), stands watch, surrounded by symbols that represent California's wildlife, agriculture, natural beauty, commerce, and opportunity. Designed by Maj. R.S. Garnett, US Army, in 1849, the seal was adopted at the state constitutional convention in 1849. (Cathy Cooke.)

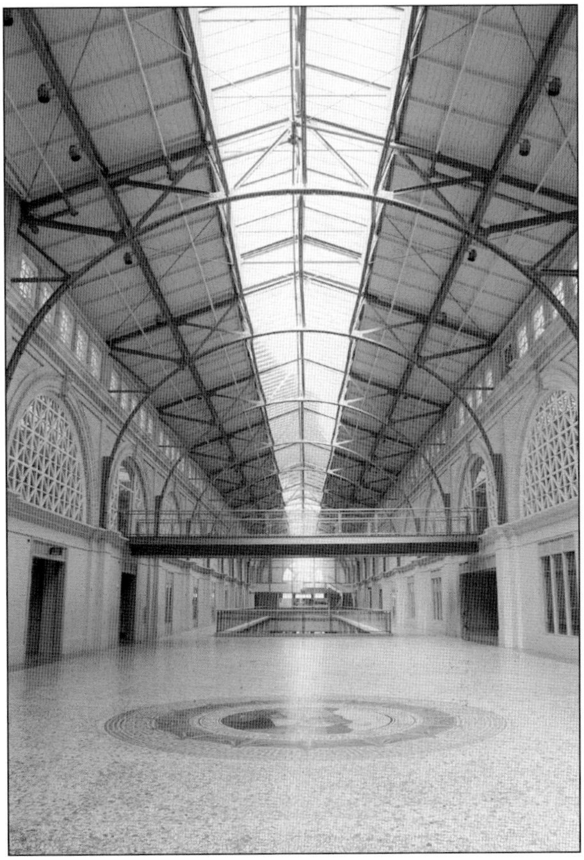

In the 1950s, the Grand Nave was filled in and partially demolished. During the renovations, following strict historic preservation guidelines, a marble mosaic floor, terra-cotta arches, and steeled arched trusses brought the nave back to its original glory. A 660-foot continuous skylight, closely matching the original, allowed light to pour through the two new 150-foot-long-by-33-foot-wide openings in the floor into the lower floor marketplace. (Cathy Cooke.)

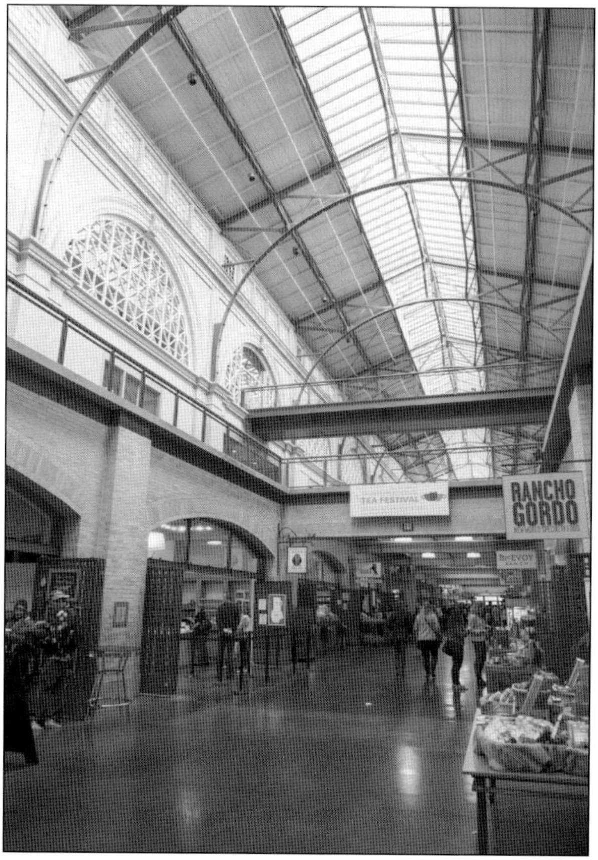

On the ground floor, which once housed the baggage area, there is a 68,000-square-foot locally sourced public food market: the Marketplace. Tourists and locals stroll the 660-foot hall, looking at some of the area's most notable food merchants' displays that showcase the Bay Area's agriculture riches and other artisanal products. (Photograph by Jeremy Menzies, SFMTA Photo Archive.)

On the east facade of the building, the side facing the bay, the renovation replaced the much-altered facade with a contemporary design that took into account the building's original features. The new 30-foot-wide public walkway includes benches for watching ferries come and go, and a large plaza at the south end provides a gathering space for outdoor vendors at the Ferry Plaza Farmers' Markets. (Photograph by Heather Moran, SFMTA Photo Archive.)

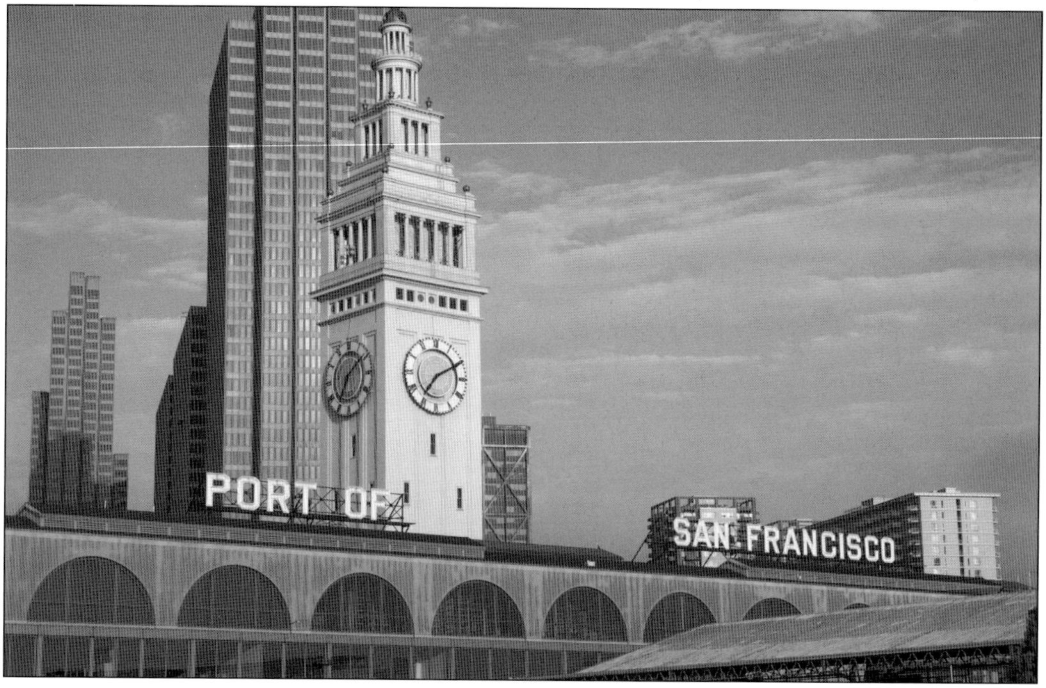

In redesigning the plaza in front of the Ferry Building, the big question was how the traffic that had been displaced by the freeway removal would be routed, considering that the roadway bisected the downtown and the waterfront. How would pedestrians access the reopened waterfront over four lanes of traffic? The eventual design of Harry Bridges Plaza, as shown at right, split the two directions of traffic around a central island, ensuring that pedestrians only had to cross two lanes of traffic at a time. This created a pedestrian-friendly space where commuters and shoppers coming from the ferry terminal could walk to the downtown safely. Below, passengers in front of the building board a heritage streetcar. (Right, Tom Paiva Photography; below, photograph by Katy Guyon, SFMTA Photo Archive.)

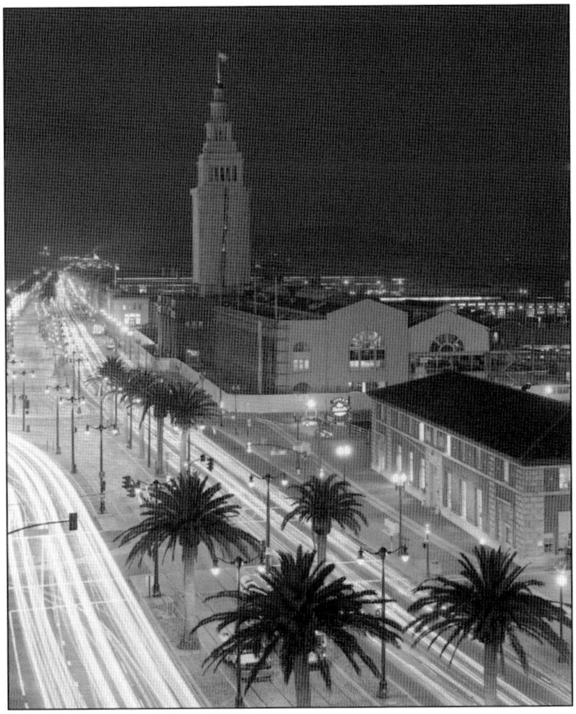

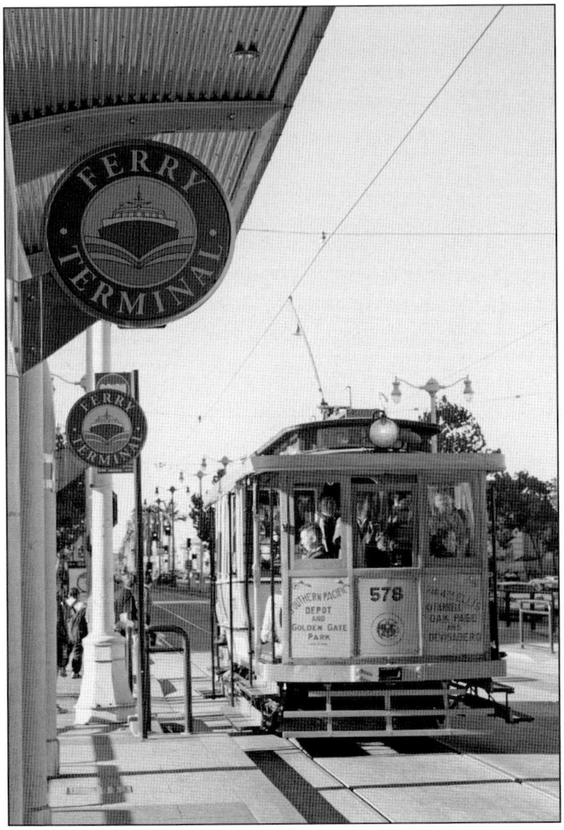

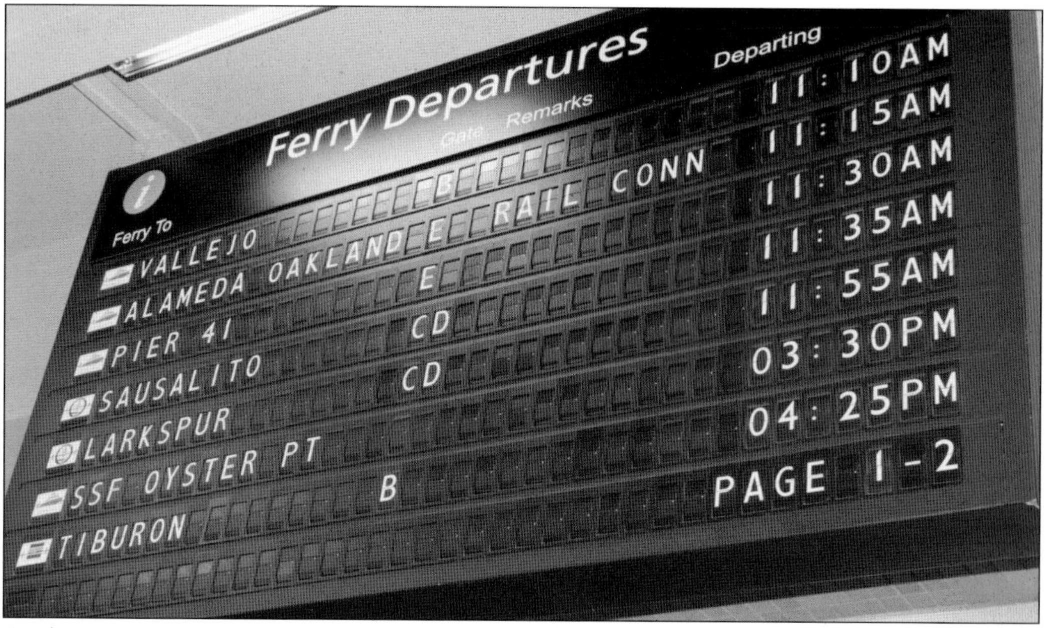

As the Bay Area's population grew and transportation by car became more difficult, demand for ferries returned. In 1970, ferry service from Marin to San Francisco started up again, almost 30 years after it was discontinued. Ferry services from Vallejo to San Francisco resumed in June 1986, and immediately after the Loma Prieta earthquake, ferry service from Alameda and Oakland began again when the Bay Bridge was damaged. Harbor Bay Isle ferry service (Alameda) began in 1992, and ferry service from South San Francisco (Oyster Point) resumed in 2012. More routes are planned as demand continues to increase. (Above, Cathy Cooke; below, photograph by Heather Moran, SFMTA Photo Archive.)

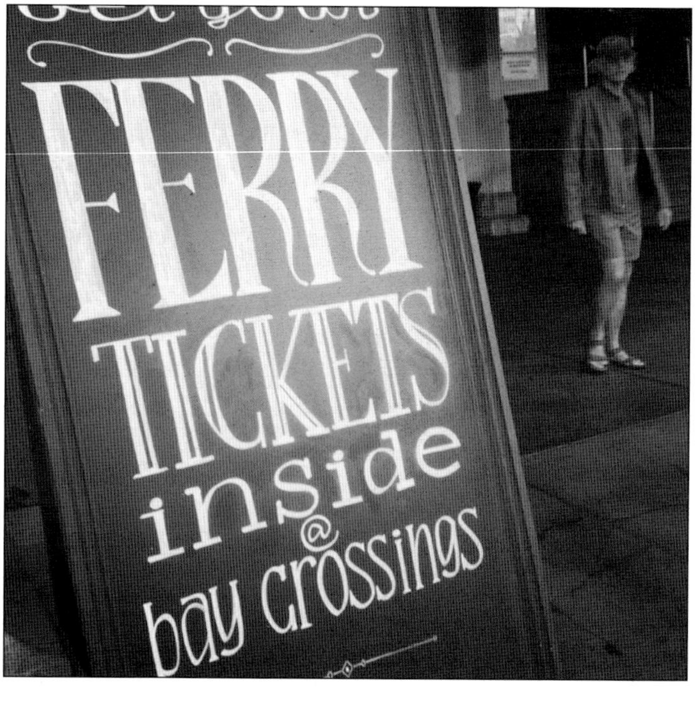

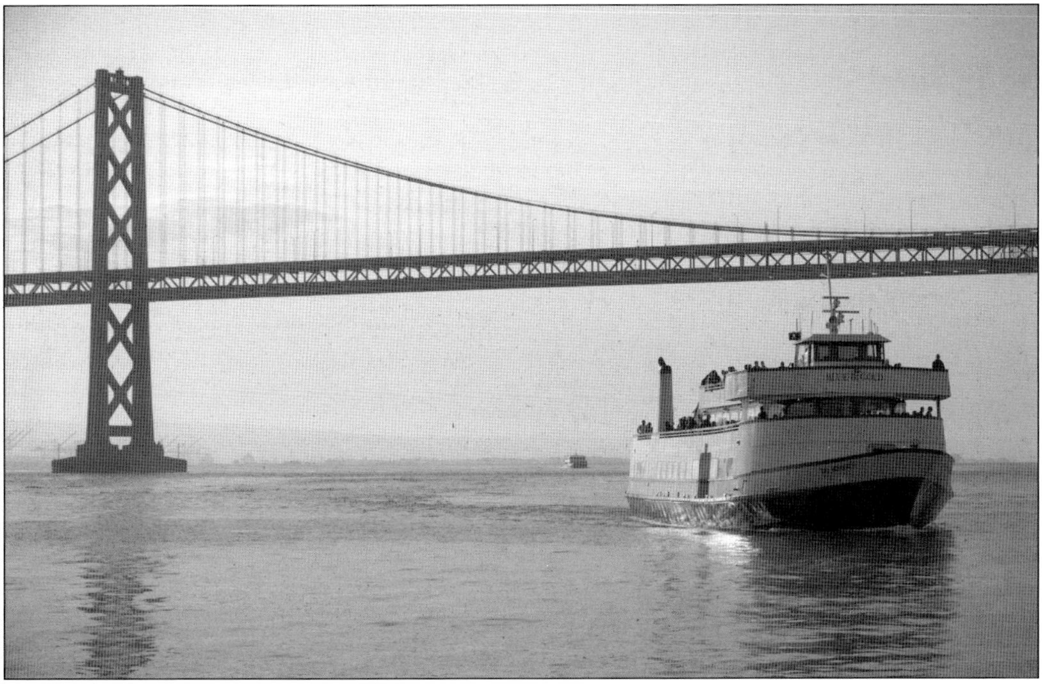

Ridership is booming on the ferries. Commuters have rediscovered what ferry riders enjoyed in the heyday of ferries: it is a pleasant way to travel. The WETA (Water Emergency Transportation Authority), the government entity that operates the San Francisco Bay Ferry, estimates that ridership has increased 72 percent since 2012. WETA plans to add seven new boats over the next four years. (Photograph by Heather Moran, SFMTA Photo Archive.)

If the pedestrians who scurry across Harry Bridges Plaza on their way to the Ferry Building would look down at the sidewalk, they would see markers like this one. A dashed line represents the former location of an Embarcadero Freeway column. Each plaque has a poem or quote about the much-maligned structure. (Cathy Cooke.)

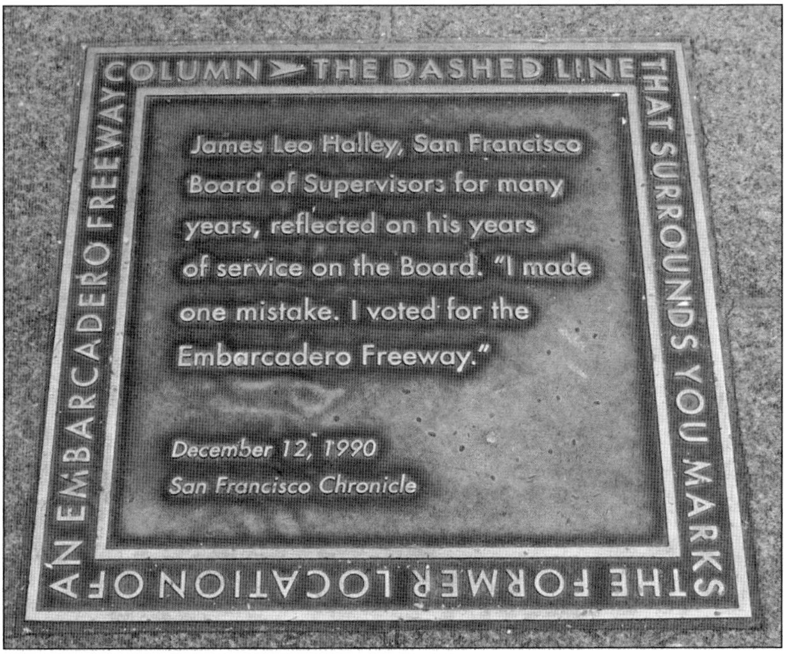

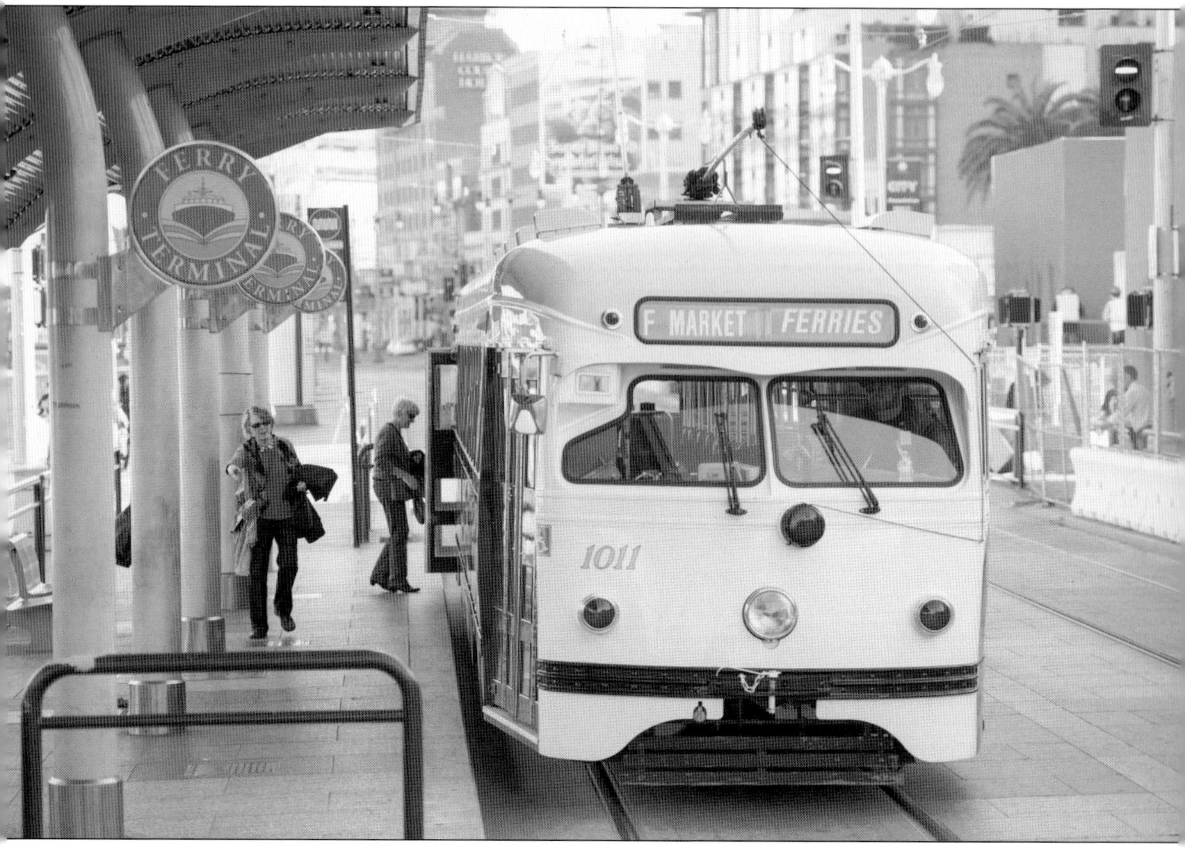

In June 1983, while San Francisco's cable cars were off the street temporarily for repair, and to stave off any decline in tourism, a group launched the first San Francisco Historic Trolley Festival, using old surface streetcar tracks. It not only drew streetcar fans and other visitors to San Francisco, but was a big hit with locals as well. The onetime festival was repeated for five summers in all, and soon, the San Francisco Board of Supervisors approved a permanent F-line to run down Market Street and along the Embarcadero. In 1995, the F-line on Market Street started, and ridership far exceeded expectations. The F-line was extended to Fisherman's Wharf in 2000 and now runs regularly from the Ferry Building. Here, car No. 1011, which has a bright yellow roof and solid white ends, picks up passengers on its way to the ferries. (Photograph by Jeremy Menzies, SFMTA Photo Archive.)

Bibliography

Corbett, Michael R., Mike Buhler, and Jay Turnbull. *Port City: The History and Transformation of the Port of San Francisco, 1848–2010*. San Francisco: San Francisco Architectural Heritage, 2013.

Harlan, George H. *San Francisco Bay Ferryboats*. Berkeley, CA: Howell-North Books, 1967.

Kaufman, William H., and Michelle S. Kaufman. *The State Belt: San Francisco's Waterfront Railroad*. Berkeley, CA: Signature Press, 2013.

Olmsted, Nancy. *The Ferry Building: Witness to a Century of Change, 1898–1998*. San Francisco: Heyday Books, 1998.

———. *Simple Pleasures Begin With Ferryboats*. San Francisco: National Maritime Museum Association, 1999.

Rice, Walter, and Emiliano Echeverria. *Key System: San Francisco and the East Shore Empire*. Images of Rail. Charleston, SC: Arcadia Publishing, 2007.

Rubin, M. Jasper. *A Negotiated Landscape: The Transformation of San Francisco's Waterfront since 1950*. Chicago: Center for American Places at Columbia College Chicago, 2011.

Scott, Mel. *The San Francisco Bay Area; a Metropolis in Perspective*. Berkeley: University of California Press, 1959.

Smallwood, Charles A. *The White Front Cars of San Francisco*. Glendale, CA: Interurbans Publications, 1978.

Starr, Kevin. *Inventing the Dream*. New York: Oxford University Press, 1985.

Ute, Grant, Philip Hoffman, and Cameron Beach. *San Francisco's Municipal Railway: MUNI*. Charleston, SC: Arcadia Publishing, 2011.

Vielbaum, Walt, Philip Hoffman, Grant Ute, and Robert Townley. *San Francisco's Market Street Railway*. Images of Rail. Charleston, SC: Arcadia Publishing, 2005.